About Island Press

Since 1984, the nonprofit Island Press has been stimulating, shaping, and communicating the ideas that are essential for solving environmental problems worldwide. With more than 800 titles in print and some 40 new releases each year, we are the nation's leading publisher on environmental issues. We identify innovative thinkers and emerging trends in the environmental field. We work with world-renowned experts and authors to develop cross-disciplinary solutions to environmental challenges.

Island Press designs and implements coordinated book publication campaigns in order to communicate our critical messages in print, in person, and online using the latest technologies, programs, and the media. Our goal: to reach targeted audiences—scientists, policymakers, environmental advocates, the media, and concerned citizens—who can and will take action to protect the plants and animals that enrich our world, the ecosystems we need to survive, the water we drink, and the air we breathe.

Island Press gratefully acknowledges the support of its work by the Agua Fund, Inc., The Margaret A. Cargill Foundation, Betsy and Jesse Fink Foundation, The William and Flora Hewlett Foundation, The Kresge Foundation, The Forrest and Frances Lattner Foundation, The Andrew W. Mellon Foundation, The Curtis and Edith Munson Foundation, The Overbrook Foundation, The David and Lucile Packard Foundation, The Summit Foundation, Trust for Architectural Easements, The Winslow Foundation, and other generous donors.

The opinions expressed in this book are those of the author(s) and do not necessarily reflect the views of our donors.

The Guide to Greening Cities

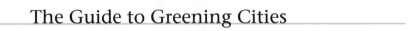

The Guide to Greening Cities

By Sadhu Aufochs Johnston,
Steven S. Nicholas, and Julia Parzen

ISLANDPRESS

Washington | Covelo | London

Island Press is a trademark of Island Press/The Center for Resource Economics.

Library of Congress Cataloging-in-Publication Data
The guide to greening cities / Sadhu Aufochs Johnston, Julia Parzen, Steven S. Nicholas, Gloria Ohland.
     pages cm

 Includes bibliographical references and index.
 ISBN 978-1-61091-376-8 (hardback) -- ISBN 1-61091-376-0 (cloth) -- ISBN 978-1-61091-379-9 (paper) 1. Sustainable urban development--North America. 2. Sustainable urban areas--North America. I. Johnston, Sadhu Aufochs.
 HT243.N7G85 2013
 307.1'416097--dc23

                         2013013812

⊕ Printed on recycled, acid-free paper

Manufactured in the United States of America
10 9 8 7 6 5 4 3 2 1

Keywords: Affordable housing, bicycle infrastructure, climate action planning, Energy Efficiency and Conservation Block Grant (EECBG), energy efficiency loan funds, green alleys, green building, green infrastructure, green jobs, green streets, greening city fleets, Leadership in Energy and Environmental Design (LEED), Living Building Challenge, Property-Assessed Clean Energy (PACE), renewable energy, STAR Community Index, stormwater infrastructure, sustainability indicators, Transit-oriented Development (TOD), Transportation Infrastructure Finance and Innovation Act (TIFIA), triple bottom line, urban sustainability, Urban Sustainability Directors Network (USDN)

Contents

Foreword

People are making their way back to cities. For the first time ever, the majority of the world's population is living in urban areas. In America, after decades of neglect and decline, cities are receiving renewed interest and are repositioning themselves as places ripe for innovation and investment. I couldn't be happier that my hometown, Philadelphia, has overcome decades of population decline and is posting census gains again. But growth brings its own set of challenges. To house, move, and employ urban dwellers now and into the future, municipalities must maintain and upgrade aging infrastructure, expand economic opportunities, and improve residents' everyday quality of life, all while adapting to the reality of climate change.

These challenges are deeply local, and local governments are taking the lead to solve them. Municipalities are flexible enough to put policies and programs into action quickly, and we can work at the ground level with community members to hear their feedback and harness their energy. In the past ten years, many mayors have realized that sustainability is a powerful framework to address these varied problems. Before I took office, during my time as mayor-elect I had an opportunity to visit Mayor Richard Daley in Chicago. He "got" sustainability and was willing to put himself out there as an early adopter. And seeing someone who had successfully managed a renaissance in his city, both downtown and in the neighborhoods, that put a new kind of emphasis on greening left a tremendous impression on me.

When I was running for mayor in 2007, a diverse community-based coalition came together to advocate for a ten-point agenda they wanted the candidates to endorse and the next mayor to prioritize. They saw what was going on in Chicago, in New York, and they wanted Philadelphia to follow suit. The Next Great City Coalition was the most vocal and organized constituency in that race, and, in retrospect, it signaled a point of change. Greenworks Philadelphia, our sustainability plan, is a direct result of their advocacy. This was their vision for where they wanted the city to go. Hearing from the coalition was a great start to the give-and-take relationship local governments and residents must maintain to succeed in greening. Advocates ask their governments to improve their homes and neighborhoods, and cities provide the leadership to show residents why sustainability measures—ranging from planting trees to reducing greenhouse gas emissions to recycling—add value to their daily lives and to their communities. Four years into implementing Greenworks, public and political support for the effort continues to grow. I consider it among the greatest accomplishments of my administration.

Our sustainability work is improving not only day-to-day life in Philadelphia but also the everyday functions of our government. We're working to involve all our departments, from the leaders, such as our Water Department staff and their groundbreaking green infrastructure approach to storm-water management, to less likely champions such as our prisons, where we harness solar power to produce hot water and compost food waste. We recognize the value not only of developing exciting, cutting-edge green initiatives but also of doing the things we already do in new, improved ways.

It helps that we're not doing this alone. Cities are coming together through organizations such as the Urban Sustainability Directors Network to share information and experiences and solve problems together. And nongovernmental organizations such as the Institute for Sustainable Communities offer training and technical assistance programs to build capacity for urban sustainability solutions and accelerate their transfer across cities. We're also working with the private sector and state and federal governments to make sure that the urban sustainability agenda is approached from multiple sectors. Partnership has been essential to the growth of this movement so far and, I imagine, will continue to drive success going forward. Capturing our collective ideas and best practices in this *Guide to Greening Cities* will help cities learn from one another's successes and avoid one another's failures. This book also captures for posterity a point in time when sustainability is becoming a focus and expertise of local government. No doubt practitioners of the future will want to revisit and understand this important transition.

Sustainability is still a relatively novel municipal responsibility, and cities will prosper by working together to harness the burgeoning energy around this work and to institutionalize these priorities over time. In Philadelphia, I'm hopeful that my administration can pass along a sustainability program that the next mayor, and the mayor after that, will be proud to build on. Efficient, equitable cities that integrate sustainability throughout the fabric of their governments will be the cities of the future.

Michael A. Nutter

Mayor, City of Philadelphia

Preface and Acknowledgments

Sadhu Aufochs Johnston

Sustainability has been part of my consciousness since I was a kid growing up in communities in India, Europe, and America, where our "school without walls" program allowed me to work in our community's construction recycling facility. There it was laid out before me, as clear to my ten-year-old self as it is to me today: materials can be reused to build our community rather than going to the dump. I went on to start the recycling program in my high school; then, as a college student, I worked for the city's recycling program.

During my first few years in city government, I found myself quite frustrated trying to figure out best practices and to learn from other places. I spent hours searching the web and then got transferred from office to office after cold-calling other municipalities to learn more about how they were greening their practices. I struggled to figure out how to structure our internal greening efforts, which initiatives to prioritize, and how to shape particular policies. It was so rewarding when I did finally connect with a peer, but often the pace of working in city government meant that there wasn't time to do a bunch of interviews and new research to learn how they put together their programs, what worked, what didn't. I was relatively new to the municipal sector, but the green city movement was new as well, and people were interested in learning more. I received many inquiries to provide advice to cities that were kicking off their efforts, programs that were struggling within cities, and groups wanting to influence and work with cities.

Largely out of frustration, in 2008 Amanda Eichel, who worked for Steve Nicholas in Seattle's Office of Sustainability and Environment, and I began working with Julia Parzen to start the Urban Sustainability Directors Network (USDN). Our intention was to develop a network of municipal staff to build relationships, share best practices, and even collaborate. I quickly realized that we weren't the only ones struggling to connect with others in the green city field, and we weren't the only ones struggling to learn about best practices from our peers. At the first USDN meeting in 2009 in Chicago, with about eighty city staff from across North America, it became clear that it was really important that the first generation of green city leaders be given opportunities to share with one another and with others entering the field. Thankfully, Sharon Alpert from the Surdna Foundation and Darryl Young from the Summit Foundation, among others, saw the opportunity and helped to fund our gathering and network-building effort. It was amazing to connect with other staff struggling with the same issues that I was and to share our lessons and stories from "in the trenches." Now, on a daily basis, dozens of municipal staff from over 120 cities share reports and experiences or connect directly over the phone to learn from one another. We're able to help people new to their position steepen their learning curve and hit the ground running, while also helping veterans of the field quickly find leading practices to keep their work moving.

So, when Island Press expressed interest in publishing a book on how cities are doing this work, it felt like a great opportunity to share my own experiences and the lessons from USDN members with others working with, or within, city government. All of the royalties from the sale of the book will be donated to USDN to support further collaboration and network development among city staff across the continent. Additional information, cases in point, and current green city news are available online at www .guidetogreeningcities.org.

I'd like to thank my wife, Manda Aufochs Gillespie, whose work on www.thegreen mama.com is an inspiring example of what can be done in the home and in our daily lives to raise our children in a conscious way. I'd also like to thank my two girls, Zella Rose and Zada Maela, for the inspiration of life and for putting up with a distracted father for the past year. I'm also thankful to the many municipal leaders involved with USDN for their work and for sharing it with us for this book. Without Darryl Young at the Summit Foundation's support of the green city movement and his encouraging us to undertake the task of writing the book, this field wouldn't be where it is today, and we wouldn't have taken this on. Finally, I'd like to thank Steve and Julia for agreeing to spend their precious time writing this book with me and to thank Gloria Ohland for her extensive work in helping us with the writing process.

Steven S. Nicholas

I first got hooked on the idea of sustainable development back in 1991, during a one-day conference in Seattle designed to gather input for the 1992 Earth Summit. "This is so clearly right," I remember thinking. "*Of course* our economic, environmental, and social health are intertwined parts of the same whole. *Of course* we should be pursuing these goals in integrated ways and thinking well beyond the next budget and election cycle." I was a senior environmental planner for the City of Seattle at the time, relatively early in my career, so this came as something of an epiphany. And since that day, I've been on the easier-said-than-done journey of putting the principles of sustainable development into action in my life and career.

A few of us who attended that conference in Seattle began scheming about what we could do to harness the blend of inspiration and urgency we were feeling and to advance "sustainable development" in the real world, starting with our own community. From those discussions emerged Sustainable Seattle, a small nonprofit organization that continues, to this day, to find creative and effective ways to increase awareness of, and action toward, sustainability in the Puget Sound region, beginning with its influential and much-emulated "Indicators of Sustainable Community" project.

Since then, I've spent most of my career in local government, including eight years as sustainability director for the City of Seattle. I quickly grew to believe in what is a central thesis of this book: that local government leadership is a critical and powerful leverage point for advancing sustainability. I came to the Institute for Sustainable Communities in 2008 to help advance its mission of building capacity for sustainable development at the community scale, with a growing focus on cities here in North America as well as in fast-growing, carbon-intensive regions such as China, India, and other parts of Asia. For me, this book is very much an extension of my "day job," which is all about helping communities actually do sustainable development by offering training and peer learning, providing efficient access to high-caliber information and expertise, and showcasing and accelerating the transfer of "promising practices" in local solutions to the global challenges of climate protection and sustainable development.

Shortly after I became Seattle's first sustainability director in 2000, coauthor Sadhu Johnston took on a similar role with the City of Chicago. At the time, we were part of a very small and largely invisible club—there were maybe a dozen or two of us across the country, and until the Blackstone Ranch Institute brought us together in 2005, we barely knew one another. The Urban Sustainability Directors Network (USDN)—which under the "servant leadership" of coauthor Julia Parzen has quickly become a high-impact learning and doing community of sustainability directors from about 120 local governments throughout North America—was not yet even a glimmer in anybody's eye.

Today, there likely are thousands of people in these positions in towns, cities, counties, and provinces throughout North America, toiling away in institutionally and politically complex—and largely uncharted—territory, armed with copious amounts of commitment and creativity but very little in the way of resources and formal authority. My mission and my hope in coauthoring this book, having done my share of toiling in similar trenches, is to share some insights, ideas, inspirations, and stories that might help this growing cadre of green city leaders toil away even more efficiently and effectively, while at the same time helping all those who work with local governments to create the healthy, strong, fair, and prosperous cities that can be—that must be—the building blocks of a sustainable future.

I deeply appreciate the support and encouragement I've received from the Institute for Sustainable Communities, in particular the inspiration, leadership, and counsel I get from our founder, Madeleine Kunin, and president, George Hamilton. In addition, a great many of the examples and insights featured in this book are drawn from the research and reflections of my team at ISC, which includes Steve Adams, Nathaly Agosto Filión, Mike Crowley, Chris Forinash, Josh Kelly, Deb Perry, and Becky Webber.

During my years with the City of Seattle, I was very fortunate to work with many outstanding leaders, mentors, and colleagues whose ideas and inspiration also undergird my work on this book. In particular, I want to thank former Seattle mayors Greg Nickels, Norm Rice, and Paul Schell; Diana Gale; Denis Hayes; Ray Hoffman; Gary Lawrence; Dennis McLerran; Diane Sugimura; Tom Tierney; and, especially, my former colleagues at the Seattle Office of Sustainability and Environment, including Jeanie Boawn, Charlie Cunniff, Amanda Eichel, Richard Gelb, Tracy Morgenstern, and Jill Simmons.

In addition, I want to thank the other colleagues and friends who contributed to this book by sharing their experiences and insights with me: Susan Anderson, Lucia Athens, Rob Bennett, Vicki Bennett, David Bragdon, Scot Case, Michelle Connor, Laurence Doxsey, Jason Edens, David Fairman, Pat Field, Katherine Gajewski, Carlos Gallinar, KC Golden, Jason Hartke, Jeremy Hays, Marty Howell, Jim Hunt, Jennifer Jurado, John Knott, Dean Kubani, Joel Makower, Anita Maltbia, Dennis McLerran, Stephanie Meyn, Aaron Miripol, Dennis Murphey, Melanie Nutter, Shannon Parry, Rob Phocas, Fred Podesta, Gayle Prest, Julian Prosser, Matt Raker, Jonathan Rose, Laura Spanjian, Gus Speth, Paula Thomas, Susy Torriente, Maggie Ullman, Andrew Watterson, Brad Weinig, Dace West, Chris Wiley, Nicole Woodman, and Larry Zinn.

Thanks to Island Press for believing in this project, to Heather Boyer for being our editor extraordinaire, and to Gloria Ohland for her work to sharpen and synthesize the three authors' respective styles and contributions.

Last but most important, thanks to my wife, Sarah McKearnan, for her sharp insights and endless encouragement, and to Sarah and our children, Dillon and Shea, for tolerating many early-morning, late-night, and weekend stints away from home to work on this project.

Julia Parzen

Four and a half years ago, Sadhu Johnston asked me to help found the Urban Sustainability Directors Network (USDN), a peer network of municipal sustainability leaders who exchange information, collaborate to enhance individual practice, and work together to advance the field of urban sustainability. Since we started USDN, its membership has tripled, the network has developed strong peer connections, and members have pursued a variety of exciting collaborations aimed at advancing urban sustainability across North America. Today USDN, a project of the Global Philanthropy Partnership, is a preeminent network of municipal sustainability leaders from 120 cities and close to 400 staff members. Sadhu has cochaired USDN's Planning Committee, and I have been the network coordinator and weaver since the network's inception. I met Steve Nicholas soon after we launched USDN. Through his leadership, the Institute for Sustainable Communities became a partner in many member initiatives.

I would like to thank all of the past and present USDN members who contributed their stories for this book, including Michael Armstrong, Roy Brooke, Cori Burbach, John Coleman, Leslie Ethen, Larry Falkin, Adam Freed, Katherine Gajewski, Marty Howell, James Hunt, Jamie Kidwell, Dean Kubani, Anna Mathewson, Doug Melnick, Nils Moe, Dennis Murphey, Matt Naud, Shannon Parry, Gayle Prest, Stephanie Smith, Laura Spanjian, Matt Stark, Beth Strommen, Paula Thomas, Maggie Ullman, Andrew Watterson, Catherine Werner, Nicole Woodman, Jo Zientek, and many others.

Contributing to this book provided me with the unique opportunity to step back and synthesize decades of work exploring the connection between environment, economic development, and equity. I believe I have been working on advancing sustainability since my first job; in 1978, with the US Environmental Protection Agency, I helped develop a plan for a venture fund for environmental solutions and a program to help small companies meet environmental requirements. I then developed renewable energy financing programs as deputy director of the Office of Policy, Planning, and Research, Department of Business and Economic Development, State of California. Then I cofounded a social venture named Working Assets, which helped thousands of people to "do good by doing well" by investing in mutual funds that embraced environmental quality and fair labor practices. When I was a program officer for the Joyce Foundation, my focus was on integrating the economic development and conservation programs. I really came to understand the way cities pursue sustainability through my two-year stint as outside advisor on the development and implementation of the Chicago Climate Action Plan (City of Chicago), and it was while working on this project that I met Sadhu.

The Guide to Greening Cities is the fourth book I have coauthored. *Credit Where It's Due: Development Banking for Communities* (Temple University Press, 1992) showed how financial intermediaries could successfully advance community development. Many of the community development financial institutions that were new at that time are now the leaders in energy efficiency lending described in chapter 5 of this book. In 1990, I coedited *Enterprising Women: Local Initiatives for Job Creation* for the Organisation for Economic Co-operation and Development, a book that explored the potential for self-employment in addressing a variety of community needs. Chapter 5 of this book also speaks to the potential to create new jobs through sustainable development. Finally, in 2004 I coauthored "Financing Transit-Oriented Development," a chapter in *The New Transit Town: Best Practices in Transit-Oriented Development*, edited by Hank Dittmar and Gloria Ohland (Island Press). Transit-oriented development remains an important framework for holistic redevelopment (described in the Denver case in point in chapter 5) that has been joined by other district-scale frameworks for sustainability, such as eco-districts.

This book demonstrates the critical importance of boundary-jumping brokers and problem solvers to the advancement of sustainable development. Writing the book reaffirmed how grateful I am to actively play these roles. Thank you to my husband, Daniel, and sons, Jonah and Simon, for believing in me as a weaver and change agent. Thank you also to Pete Plastrik and John Cleveland of the Innovation Network for Communities, who have advised me on networks and much more.

Introduction
The New Urban Imperative

Sitting in the backseat of a rickshaw at a complete standstill, eyes burning and ears pounding from the honking of gridlocked traffic in Mumbai or another of the world's megacities, is an experience that certainly begs the question "Can cities be green?" How can you not worry about the future of humanity as people continue to crowd into cities with open sewers, burning garbage piles, and sprawling slums? Yet amid this amazing chaos of urbanization *and* rapid growth there is an astonishing movement to turn cities into meccas for green living. Signs of this new form of city life can been found in the urban farms of sprawling, emptied-out Detroit; on the green roofs of Chicago, where there are beehives and prairie grasses swaying in the breeze; and in New York City's Times Square, where a plaza filled with tables, chairs, and people talking and laughing has replaced a stretch of street where cars once blasted by pedestrians packed on narrow sidewalks.

This movement is transforming how our cities are run, how residents are served, and how urban economies are growing. From New York's separated bike lanes to Austin's electric vehicle infrastructure, from Cleveland's wind industry to the dense and transit-oriented downtown of Vancouver, British Columbia, our cities are evolving, and—perhaps most surprising of all—this evolution is mostly being led from within city government. The rapid change taking place in our cities isn't without its own challenges, though, as residents and businesses try to adjust to new mandates, new programs, and new ways of building and using urban infrastructure.

The hope that our cities offer for reshaping the way we live and the impact we have on the planet offers us a new urban imperative, with cities leading the way in solving the global environmental, social, and economic challenges of our time. The new urban imperative is that cities must address the global environmental crisis. Cities are where the most people live. Cities are where the most goods are consumed and the most waste is generated, and cities are where poverty is most concentrated. Vulnerable populations living in poverty in cities are at the greatest risk as a changing climate creates havoc in fragile areas. The good news is that cities are up for the challenge. There is a new generation of city leaders who are willing to take the risks and invest the resources to create change.

While cities in the developing world are where the majority of global population growth and future environmental impact will occur, the cities of the developed world are critical at this juncture. They currently consume the majority of the world's resources and produce the majority of the world's greenhouse gas emissions, and they serve as models for cities throughout the world. The new urban imperative leaves no choice—global cities must pursue green urbanism, and cities of the developed world must lead this movement and share their experiences with their peers in the developing world. There are three main reasons why.

The first reason is the sheer number of people that our cities must accommodate. The second is the growing environmental crisis and the role that cities play—they are both the problem and the solution. The third is that cities are on the front lines dealing with the impacts of a changing climate, where the world's poorest people are affected by heat waves, storms, and flooding. Our climate is changing, and cities are bearing the brunt of this change. As life in rural areas becomes more difficult, people with few other options for survival are making their way into cities, whether to a ghetto in Los Angeles; skid row in Vancouver, British Columbia; or a favela in São Paulo, Brazil—urban areas are on the front lines of global economic inequity as the gap between rich and poor continues to grow.

The challenges that are front and center for today's municipal leaders include the growth in urban populations and increased need for services, the increase in homelessness and poverty, limited financial resources, breakdowns in public education, decaying infrastructure, massive amounts of garbage, increasing crime, food shortages, and the global environmental crisis—all problems that are exacerbated by a changing climate. And as national governments either deny that climate change exists or become less responsive to problems because of a lack of revenue or political gridlock, residents are increasingly turning to local government to take action. Increasingly diverse urban populations expect more from the only level of government they can actively and meaningfully participate in—often not understanding or caring whether it is the level of government that has the funding and the mandate to address their concerns.

Around the world, municipal governments are grappling with the local manifestations of global issues, and, thankfully, a new generation of elected officials is tackling these challenges head-on. From Mexico City to Copenhagen, from Philadelphia to San Jose, these local leaders are recognizing that by addressing issues involving climate, waste, food, water, air, and energy they can improve the lives of their residents *and* make their cities more competitive. Often pushed by their citizens and driven by opportunity—or crisis—politicians and municipal staff are leading a global transformation of urban life the likes of which have not been seen since the Industrial Revolution.

Municipal staff, sometimes working deep within departments and agencies, are using the tools at their disposal—from regulations such as building codes to municipal assets such as city land—to support this transformation, and they are unlocking value in neglected resources. This book is about their stories—how they have prioritized their work, measured their progress, and built support within their organizations and in their communities, and how this work has been paid for. On these pages, these leaders share their tips and their failures and make specific recommendations for those who want to transform their own cities.

The Century of the City

The first reason for the new urban imperative listed above is the explosion of urban populations and the need to accommodate this rapid increase in urban dwellers. In 2008, the world's urban population began outpacing the rural population. While cities in North America continued their struggle to reduce urban sprawl and out-migration, cities in the developing world continued to grow, almost exponentially. With more than 3.5 billion people now living in cities, the world's urban areas have become global engines of economic growth, and the majority of industry, commerce, innovation, and creativity is occurring within them. The world's largest cities—those with more than 1 million people—are home to just one in five of all people living on the planet, but they account for more than 50 percent of the world's economic output.[1] According to a 2012 report by the Brookings Institution, for example, in forty-seven US states, metropolitan areas generate the majority of state economic output.[2]

Currently, the global population increases by about 80 million people each year. In 1990, just 10 percent of the world's population lived in cities.[3] By 2008, the urban population had increased to more than 50 percent, and it is expected to reach 60 percent by 2030.

The rate of growth in cities is four times that in rural areas, and it is expected to result in an urban population of 5 billion people by 2030[4]—1.8 billion more urban dwellers than in 2005.[5] In the United States, 29 percent of the landmass is covered by cities, but almost 85 percent of the population lives in cities, and 93 percent of the economic output[6] is produced there.

The growth in urban populations is astonishing, and it is hard to imagine how the already taxed urban infrastructure will be able to accommodate so many more people. The growth in urban populations, however, is not expected to take place evenly around the globe. The United Nations Educational, Scientific and Cultural Organization (UNESCO) expects that 95 percent of the increase in urban populations will occur in developing countries, especially in Africa and Asia,[7] and that by 2030, 80 percent of the world's urban dwellers will be living in cities in the developing world.[8]

How can urban areas, which are already bursting at the seams, accommodate so many more people in the century ahead when housing those who have already arrived has proven to be problematic? Feeding these new residents, processing their waste, and providing them with affordable and comfortable places in which to live will truly be a challenge in coming years. Providing for this growth without further taxing an increasingly overburdened environment and exacerbating climate change will perhaps be the greatest challenge—and opportunity for change—of our generation.

While the greatest challenges in the future will likely be in the cities of the developing world, it is the cities of North America that are most critical at this point in time. There are four main reasons why: (1) Residents of North American cities consume vastly more resources per capita than do people who live in cities in the developing world, and they produce more waste and greenhouse gas emissions—which means that any improvements will be significant. (2) Cities around the world emulate North American cities, so these cities need to get it right. (3) The professionals who are working to address these challenges in North America are spending increasingly more time also working in the cities of the developing world, and they are bringing with them the lessons they have learned. (4) North American cities have more resources than most cities in the developing world, so they must do their part to solve these problems and then share the lessons learned with cities around the world through networks such as the C40 Cities Climate Leadership Group, a climate leadership group of the world's megacities.

Cities and the Global Environmental Crisis

The second reason for the new urban imperative is the growing environmental crisis, which has been exacerbated by the fact that most national governments, particularly in the United States, have been loath to take action to address climate change during global economic challenges, placing the spotlight on municipalities and the role they must play. Fortunately, municipalities around the world—the "lowest" level of government—and their mayors, councils, and departmental staff are stepping up to address challenges that many national governments are unable or unwilling to address.

Although cities cover just a small percentage of the earth's surface, their environmental impact is quite significant. The world's cities account for more than 78 percent of the planet's greenhouse gas emissions, 60 percent of residential water use, and 76 percent of industrial wood use.[9] Recent analysis shows that because urban dwellers collectively consume the most resources, they have a bigger ecological footprint than rural dwellers, who are generally less affluent.[10] But even though cities currently use most of the world's resources and produce most of the world's waste and carbon emissions, they can also provide the most environmentally friendly living opportunities in the world. Their compactness, transportation options, and living standards can enable low-carbon-intensity lifestyles.

It is because cities play such a significant role in the global environmental crisis that they can also play such a large role in addressing these challenges, though for the most part they have yet to live up to their potential in this regard. For example, in cities people often live in smaller spaces, which require less energy to heat and cool. City dwellers can walk, bike, or take public transit, and the distances they need to travel are often shorter than they would be if they lived in suburban or rural communities. Harvard University economics professor Ed Glaeser, writing for the *New York Times* about his analysis of the carbon emissions of new homes in different parts of the country, concluded:

> In almost every metropolitan area, we found the central city residents emitted less carbon than the suburban counterparts. In New York and San Francisco, the average urban family emits more than two tons less carbon annually because it drives less. In Nashville, the city-suburb carbon gap due to driving is more than three tons. After all, density is the defining characteristic of cities. All that closeness means that people need to travel shorter distances, and that shows up clearly in the data.[11]

If living in cities enables people to reduce their ecological footprint, especially when it comes to reducing greenhouse gas emissions, it is safe to say that cities are one of our most promising tools for combating the global environmental crisis. "Urbanism is the foundation for a low-carbon future and is our least-cost option," writes renowned urban designer Peter Calthorpe.[12] The national nonprofit Center for Neighborhood Technology has mapped the Chicago region's greenhouse gas emissions, showing that per capita emissions are lowest in more densely developed areas. It found that greenhouse gas emissions in Chicago are significantly higher than in suburban or rural areas outside of the city; however, on a per capita basis, people who live in denser urban environments produce fewer emissions from vehicle travel than do those who live in less dense suburban neighborhoods surrounding the urban core.

There is a growing recognition that urban living in developed nations is the greener option, but it is less well known that cities are leading this charge and delivering results in ways that national governments haven't been able to. As of September 2011, 191 countries had signed on to the Kyoto Protocol to the United Nations Framework Convention on Climate Change, but by 2012, few had reduced their 1990 levels of carbon emissions by 6 percent as called for in the Kyoto Protocol. Even fewer have been able to achieve reductions while continuing to develop their economies.

Cities, on the other hand, are demonstrating that carbon emissions can be lowered

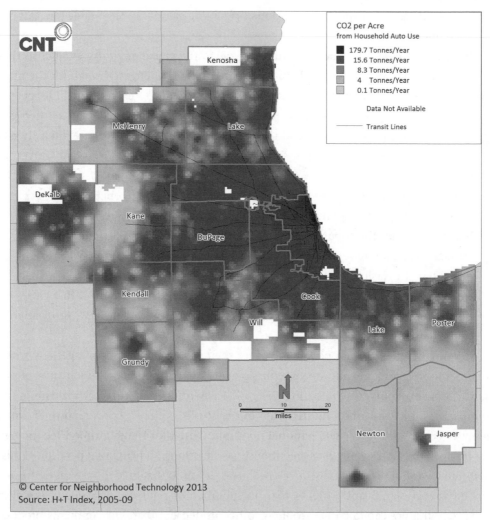

Figure I.1a. Carbon dioxide emissions per acre, Chicago metropolitan area, 2012
The traditional view of urban areas depicts cities as environmental wastelands where natural resources are turned into waste. On the basis of CO_2 emissions per acre, Chicago appears to be a scourge on the environment, whereas the suburbs emit much less carbon. Figure courtesy of the Center for Neighborhood Technology (CNT).

while economies, jobs, and populations continue to grow. In North America, more than 1,200 cities have agreed to achieve carbon reductions equivalent to those called for in the Kyoto Protocol. While most won't succeed, many have begun the work necessary to reduce carbon over the long term. Exemplars include Portland, Oregon, where emissions per person are already 10 percent below 1990 levels;[13] and Vancouver, British Columbia,

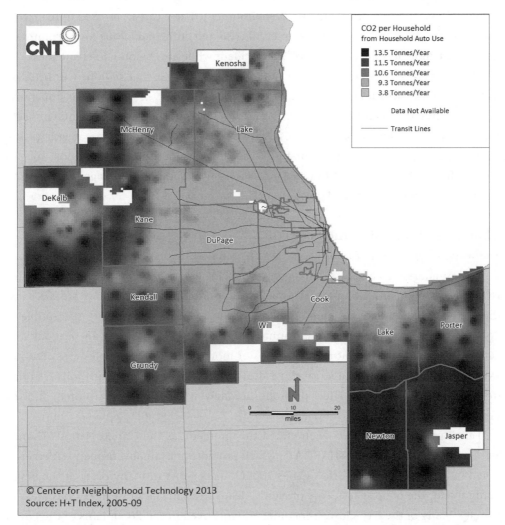

Figure I.1b. Carbon dioxide emissions per household, Chicago metropolitan area, 2012
Mapping of CO_2 emissions per household demonstrates that residents of Chicago emit much less carbon per household than do those living in the suburbs. Research shows that households near transit stations produce 43 percent less greenhouse gas emissions than the national average, and households in the central business district emit 78 percent less. Figure courtesy of the Center for Neighborhood Technology (CNT).

where emissions have fallen below 1990 levels even though the city's population has increased by 27 percent and the number of jobs has increased by 18 percent since 1990.

While most cities get very little financial support from higher levels of government—generally less then ten cents per dollar of taxes raised—municipal governments have other tools that can be used to address these challenges, including building and zoning codes, transportation infrastructure, water delivery systems, sewage treatment systems, waste disposal systems, and the form of the built environment. These can all be used to help avert climate change and the global environmental crisis and at the same time foster communities that are more livable, competitive, and resilient while also helping to create jobs.

Whether green jobs are created or not, there is no doubt that billions will be spent in the upcoming decades to protect urban areas from changes in climate. It is imperative that these investments further municipal efforts to improve their environmental impacts, including reducing greenhouse gas emissions and energy consumption and creating natural and green spaces. By utilizing many of the strategies outlined in this book, such as green infrastructure in Philadelphia or green alleys in Chicago to manage storm events, cities can be more resilient and greener.

Changing Climate and the Poor

The world's population of poor people is concentrated in cities, so urban greening solutions must address urban social and economic challenges as well as environmental ones. Heat waves, floods, and rising sea levels will disproportionately affect urban areas because there are so many urban dwellers, some of whom live in areas that are susceptible to flooding, landslides, and other environmental challenges. The European heat wave in 2003 contributed to the heat-related deaths of more than 70,000 people across Europe, with a disproportionate number of those deaths in cities. The high death tolls resulting from the urban heat island effect disproportionately affected seniors, children, and the urban poor.[14]

Hurricane Katrina in 2005 exemplified this problem, as the United Nations Human Settlements Programme (UN-HABITAT), which promotes sustainable human settlements, noted in its "State of the World's Cities 2006/7" paper: "As in many parts of the developing world, the poorest residents of New Orleans lived in the most hazardous areas of the city. Many of the city's lowest-income residents lived in the floodplains of the Lower Ninth Ward, a neighbourhood that sat below sea level and was inundated when the canals and levees failed. . . . The Lower Ninth Ward neighbourhood—where more than 98 per cent of the residents were African American and more than a third lived in poverty—was built on a reclaimed cypress swamp."[15]

But Katrina isn't the only example of this in the recent past in North America. Heavy rains throughout the southern United States in 2010 caused significant flooding, disproportionately affecting urban areas. Damage in Nashville, Tennessee, alone, where thousands of people were evacuated, was assessed at more than $1.5 billion.[16] It is clear that climate change will require significant upgrades to already taxed urban infrastructure. The United Nations Framework Convention on Climate Change estimates the cost of adaptation to be around $100 billion per year within the next several decades.[17] Despite major investments, the Intergovernmental Panel on Climate Change expects substantial population displacements within the first half of the century as a result of increased storm intensity, more drought, and higher temperatures. Again, the poor will suffer disproportionately, largely because their housing is substandard and the areas where they settle are marginal—typically in floodplains or on mountain slopes.

The estimated cost of Hurricane Sandy in 2012, the worst storm to hit the East Coast in decades, was calculated in 2013 as $71 billion. Despite the high costs to cities hit by extreme weather events, it is unlikely that the federal government will allocate increased resources to cities to help them prepare for climate change—in the months leading up to Sandy, there was even speculation that funding for FEMA, the Federal Emergency

Figure I.2. Hurricane Sandy damage, Long Beach Island
Damage from extreme storms is on the rise, and urban areas are disproportionately affected. The damages from Hurricane Sandy were estimated at $71 billion. US Air Force photo by Master Sgt. Mark C. Olsen/Released.

Management Agency, would be cut. The situation is even more extreme in the developing world, where the numbers of city dwellers and urban poor are significantly higher and there are fewer financial resources. This combination of factors could mean that billions of people will be living on the edge of survival, displaced by each major storm.

There is no doubt that cities will be spending more money in order to become more resilient to climate change. These adaptation strategies can include building dikes and rain gardens—which could create jobs for people who need them—or they can make poor people even more vulnerable if the construction of infrastructure projects results in their displacement and forces them to live in even less stable environments. Urban greening solutions must address these social and economic challenges. There are examples of policies and programs that address social inequity and poverty throughout this book: urban farms that provide jobs for homeless people, for example, and weatherization programs that make low-income homes more energy efficient while also providing jobs.

The Role of Municipal Governments in Urban Greening

During the 1990s, the term "green cities" seemed to be an oxymoron when the image that came to mind was sprawling, traffic-choked cities with hazy, polluted skies. But there were successes by early adopters such as Copenhagen, Denmark, which demonstrated that being bike friendly actually worked, and Curitiba, Brazil, which demonstrated that strategies to enhance sustainability could also lift people from poverty, improve quality of life, and reduce environmental impacts. North American cities such as Chattanooga, Tennessee, found success with green economic development strategies that addressed the toxic legacy of industrialization: Chattanooga started building electric buses in the city, providing badly needed jobs and improving air quality. In Portland, Oregon, and Boulder, Colorado, environmental policies such as green building codes and backyard composting gained traction.

For the most part, however, North American cities spent the 1970s through the 1990s cleaning up the environmental pollution and degradation that industry had left behind and trying to slow the continuing out-migration of residents and the tax base that had been encouraged by massive investments in road building and by lending policies and zoning codes that made it lucrative and easy to build large automobile-oriented tracts of suburban homes.

In 1969, when Cleveland's Cuyahoga River, then the most polluted river in the United States, was set on fire by sparks from a passing train, the incident galvanized the environmental movement and eventually resulted in the creation of the US Environmental Protection Agency, passage of federal clean air and water acts, and legislation promoting the cleanup and redevelopment of brownfields. In the 1990s, cities were creating environmental departments in order to consolidate all the regulatory and enforcement efforts necessary to meet these new federal mandates. Cities focused on figuring out how to redevelop polluted sites, how to go after polluters, and how to coordinate with other levels of government and even within municipal government to finish this work.

Cities used this new regulatory capacity to great effect, but it soon became clear that it wasn't enough to generate or sustain urban prosperity—they also had to innovate and to attract new residents by providing them with the lifestyle, housing, and transportation choices they wanted. Cities also had to attract jobs by providing businesses with well-trained and well-educated workers—especially the increasingly mobile "creative class" that author and urbanist Richard Florida, who coined the term, identifies as a driving force for economic development in postindustrial cities. Creative-class workers are scientists, engineers, artists, musicians, educators, designers, and other professionals whose economic function is, according to Florida, thinking up new approaches to problems.

High-profile mayors, including Chicago's Richard M. Daley, began realizing that in order to be competitive their cities would need to improve the quality of the urban experience and provide the lively and cultured environments where the creative class wants to live. These mayors began directing staff to pursue green agendas and to engage the private sector in the effort. Chicago was transformed from a city of pavement, concrete, and steel to a city of rooftop gardens and green streets. The city planted 150,000 trees and installed more than ninety miles of planted medians, replacing lanes of traffic with lush growth. More than one hundred miles of bike lanes were built, and there are 6 million square feet of green roofs installed throughout the city. Traffic-calming devices were deployed to slow traffic and make neighborhoods safer for pedestrians and bicyclists, and neighborhood cafés, stores, bars, and art galleries began opening up, enlivening the streets and nurturing local culture.

These mayors soon realized their greening efforts wouldn't take root without internal champions and appropriate organizational structures, and a new position within city government—that of sustainability director—began to emerge. Sadhu Johnston's official title in Chicago's Office of the Mayor was assistant to the mayor for green initiatives, and he reported directly to Mayor Daley (see chapter 1). In Seattle, Steven Nicholas became director of the office of sustainability and environment, and he too reported directly to the mayor. These staff positions were new, and they were well placed within the city structure to promote change.

In this book, we frequently refer to the people who occupy these positions as "green city leaders" or "sustainability directors," city employees who are generally empowered by their mayors and who are expected, with limited staffing and funding and mostly using the influence and power of their position, to effect change across the entire organization of the city. In many cases, these green city leaders work with staff who are dedicated to the green city agenda but work in separate departments—and these employees will be referred to as "green city champions." They work in many different city departments and typically have other responsibilities beyond green city work.

Green city leaders, who are often hired from outside of government, are charged with changing government from the inside. The number of these jobs has virtually exploded across North America since 2000. It is an organic movement that has gained momentum even though this work hasn't yet been made a part of urban planning or public administration curricula, and it is done differently in almost every city. Some green city leaders run a separate department and direct a staff of hundreds, while others work with small teams within the office of the mayor or city manager. It is a new movement pioneered by a few mayors who were willing to throw down the gauntlet and proclaim that their cities were the greenest, sparking competition with other mayors and inspiring staff to innovate. This field is young and the movement is evolving quickly, and until recently there was little coordination among cities.

Emerging Collaborations in North America

For years, these pioneering mayors and their staffs mostly figured things out as they went along, sometimes borrowing technologies and strategies from overseas to help develop new policies and programs. But sustainability staffs in different cities have started sharing their experiences, realizing it isn't necessary to continually reinvent the wheel. A private foundation named the Blackstone Ranch Institute convened one of the first meetings of municipal staff working on these issues in 2006. Green city leaders from Portland, Chicago, and other cities were able to share their experiences, eventually forming the Urban Sustainability Directors Network (USDN), which continues to meet and collaborate.

The 120-member USDN represents more than 53 million residents in cities across the United States and Canada and has become a central information-sharing network. There is more information about USDN in chapter 4, and members and their work are discussed throughout the book. In partnership with USDN, the Institute for Sustainable Communities (ISC) in Vermont soon began offering educational programs for municipal staff; discussions that have taken place at ISC leadership academies have also informed this book.

Urban Greening and Sustainability

It was the United Nations' World Commission on Environment and Development (known as the Brundtland Commission) that in 1987 first defined sustainable development as development that "meets the needs of the present without compromising the ability of future generations to meet their own needs."[18] This concept of sustainability and the "triple bottom line" approach to growth that it incorporated—with a focus on social, environmental, and financial results—resonated with a broader public, and the term "sustainability" gained hold. Companies around the globe created chief sustainability officers to pursue the social and environmental components of their work, and cities framed their work around the concept.

But the term "sustainability" and its association with the triple bottom line is confusing because staff tend to focus on achieving one bottom line—typically the environmental one—to the exclusion of the others. The environmental component of sustainability work has come to be known as "green urbanism," "green cities," "green development," "urban livability," and myriad other terms, and it is usually the focus of the green city leader. Walker Wells and Ted Bardacke of the national nonprofit organization Global Green USA define green urbanism as "the practice of creating communities mutually beneficial to humans and the environment."[19] Urban planners and architects such as Patrick Condon and Douglas Farr have documented the ways their profession can design greener cities. Academics and authors such as Timothy Beatley have documented work happening in Europe, Australia, and elsewhere. According to Beatley, green cities can be defined as follows:

- Cities that strive to live within their ecological limits, fundamentally reduce their ecological footprints, and acknowledge their connections with and impacts on other cities and communities and the larger planet. . . .
- Cities that are green and that are designed for and function in ways analogous to nature. . . .
- Cities that strive to achieve a circular rather than a linear metabolism, which nurtures and develops positive symbiotic relationships with and between its hinterland (whether that be regional, national, or international). . . .
- Cities that strive toward local and regional self-sufficiency and take full advantage of and nurture local/regional food production, economy, power production, and many other activities that sustain and support their populations. . . .
- Cities that facilitate (and encourage) more sustainable, healthful lifestyles. . . .
- Cities that emphasize a high quality of life and the creation of highly livable neighborhoods and communities.[20]

The definition of green urbanism that Beatley articulates is the primary focus of this book. But it is important to note that throughout North America there are many pioneering collaborations that involve sustainability staff, other city departments, and nonprofit organizations in order to pursue all three components of the triple bottom line—the environmental, the social, and the economic. While it might be ideal if all these functions were brought together in one sustainability department, that is not the norm, certainly not in larger cities, but these looser collaborations are proving effective as well. This book will discuss examples of green urbanism that achieve the triple bottom line, a plus in myriad ways, but the primary focus is on the greening component.

The Goals of This Book and Its Audience

This book is different from other books on urban greening in that it is written from the perspective of green city leaders and champions who are working inside city governments in North America and who have succeeded in pushing forward innovative green projects. The book is designed to inspire and, more important, to assist all who want to green their cities, their neighborhoods, or even their own nonprofit organizations or companies, either from inside or outside government—including city leaders and their staffs as well as academics, students, urban design professionals, and business and community leaders.

The book was written by three authors in one voice, with the exception of chapter 1, which draws lessons from Sadhu Johnston's adventures and misadventures in working to green Chicago and Vancouver. Chapter 2 explores how cities are leading by example and greening their own operations—from green fleets, green city buildings, and green municipal procurement to recycling and zero waste. Chapter 3 is about how municipal governments are extending their reach out into the community, using their leverage and power to engage the broader public in initiatives such as the development of policies that encourage or require the private sector to build green.

Chapter 4 discusses how leadership is encouraged, how staff can be positioned for success, and the structures that are needed to drive these initiatives within government. Chapter 5 is all about the money: how cities are paying for this work, green economic development, and innovative finance. Chapter 6 explores how cities are measuring their progress and holding themselves accountable and how they are reporting on their challenges and successes.

Throughout the book, cases in point provide behind-the-scenes perspectives on programs and policies that are having the most impact. Additional cases in point appear on the website for the book. These cases in point explain how cities are implementing green initiatives—the challenges, partnerships, and key tips for achieving success—all told from the perspective of staff.

Top Ten Lessons Learned from Green City Leaders

While the green cities movement is still evolving, municipal staff collectively have a great deal of experience, and many lessons have been learned. Because the politics, resources, and organization are unique in each city, staff must develop their own approach. But we offer the following ten key tips for green city leaders, distilled from our research for the book:

1. *Work to achieve the triple bottom line.* Cities no longer have the financial resources to spend time or money addressing one problem with one solution. Greening strategies address multiple challenges across multiple city functions and offer multiple benefits. A program to reduce computer waste can also provide training in electronics repair to people who need jobs. And it can supply community centers and low-income households with repaired computers to help close the digital divide.

2. *Focus and align.* You can't do everything and do it well. Focus on key areas in which you can make progress toward targets that are aligned with priorities of the mayor, city council, city manager, or other key stakeholders. If you align your priorities with the priorities of elected officials and staff, you can keep the sustainability program from existing in a parallel universe as a satellite effort, disconnected from the mother ship.

3. *Lead by example.* If the city can't do something, don't expect the private sector to do it. For example, complete energy retrofits of city buildings before requiring that privately owned buildings become energy efficient. Engage with facilities staff and use their experience to shape programs and policies.

4. *Build relationships.* One person, one department, or even an entire city government can't do this alone. Build relationships internally and externally to help address challenges, provide support, and develop programs and policies. If you want more green buildings, develop a relationship with a construction association. If the contractors are concerned about how long it takes to get a building permit, work with them to develop a faster green permit process. They will be happy, and they will support your program.

5. *Be an enabler.* Use the city's resources to help your partners succeed. Use land, buildings, regulatory powers, and other resources to enable community and business initiatives. A vacant city site awaiting development can become an urban farm in the interim and help you win more partners, resources, recognition, and support.

6. *Cultivate leadership.* Engage the mayor, senior leaders, and other champions, and ask them to make presentations about the city's greening initiatives at conferences and press events so that your partners take ownership and share the credit.

7. *Measure and report.* Measure progress and report challenges as well as success. Governments don't like bad news—who does?—so it is hard to go public when the scores aren't good. But the public and your partners will trust you more if you develop real metrics and report them.

8. *Share stories and credit.* Cultivate media interest—including social media—in your

stories in order to get recognition and praise, but make sure the spotlight is shared by all partners.

9. *Tap into competitive instincts.* Mayors, department heads, or even your partners may be competitive, and you can take advantage of this to get more work done. Mention to the city council that a neighboring city has launched a program that might be appropriate in your city, or be overt and stage a competition between departments to determine, for example, whose employees bike to work the most.

10. *Do not let perfect be the enemy of the good.* You will need to compromise to get things done. Embrace this fact, even if the results aren't exactly what you'd intended, and enjoy the victory of a task completed.

1.

Greening from the Inside
Stories from Working within City Government

This book was a true collaboration between the three authors. This first chapter, however, is solely from the perspective of one author, Sadhu Aufochs Johnston. It tells his story of working within the city governments of Chicago, Illinois, and Vancouver, British Columbia, and serves to illustrate the lessons given throughout the book. It was written at the urging of the other two authors because while greening initiatives need to be discussed in terms of political agendas and dollars and cents, it is the people living and working within these cities who have the power to lead real change.

Like many green city champions, I never intended to work in government. I transitioned from trying to influence government from the outside to working on the inside because of a chance encounter with Chicago's Mayor Richard M. Daley in 2003.

I began urban greening work when I started a nonprofit organization in 1999 that was focused on greening Cleveland, Ohio. Members of our newly formed organization wanted Cleveland to consider greening its building codes and creating policies to promote green building, but city officials hadn't been exposed to green building strategies, so we decided to create a demonstration green building. We bought a historic five-story bank building in the inner city that had been vacant for over ten years and created the Cleveland Environmental Center. We made the building a living demonstration of innovative green and historic restoration with many innovative approaches—including on-site storm-water infiltration, solar power, and geothermal heating and cooling—in order to prove that green building strategies worked in the urban context, even in a historic building.

In addition to demonstrating innovative green building techniques, we brought leading green experts, practitioners, and thinkers to Cleveland from around the world to help us explore ways that environmental thinking and approaches could help a struggling Rust Belt city reinvent itself. These speakers often addressed large audiences in packed auditoriums and conducted workshops, tours, and interviews with local media. We would always take them to city hall to meet and share their work with city staff. We did see change in the city, but it was mostly because the business, nonprofit, and philanthropic communities became engaged and embraced the ideas and opportunities. In contrast, the city and its institutions, including organized labor, seemed uninterested or incapable of changing. This only confirmed the negative view that I, like so many other members of the younger generation, had of government. Now, fifteen years later, it's great to see that Cleveland has become a real leader in the urban food movement and has dedicated staff focused on greening the city.

Nonetheless, at the time it never occurred to me that I could try to change government from the inside; that is, until I was asked to give Mayor Daley, who was visiting Cleveland, a tour of the nearly finished Cleveland Environmental Center. As we walked around the center, I was inspired by this mayor, who was so passionate about green approaches to urban issues. He asked good questions and talked about how he was integrating the same ideas we were using in our small building into his efforts to green a large city.

A few weeks later, a member of his staff called to ask if I'd be interested in coming to work for him in his quest to green the city of Chicago. I initially said "No, thanks," without giving it much thought, but I was encouraged by my future wife, Manda, to reconsider. I toured some of the city's green projects and met many city staff who were knowledgeable and passionate. The trip changed my mind, helping me realize that perhaps I could contribute to making a better world from within city government.

I learned valuable lessons from my work in Chicago and later in Vancouver, British Columbia, that built on my foundational work in Cleveland.

Don't Ask Others to Do Something Until You've Done It Yourself: Lead by Example

During my interview, Mayor Daley said something, with a soggy, unlit cigar sticking out of his mouth, that I would hear him repeat again and again over the years I worked with him: "We can't ask our residents or our businesses to do something that we haven't already done ourselves." The city had to lead by example, and while good work had been done, most of it, he said, had been on demonstration projects. The city still hadn't institutionalized green policies and practices, and he wanted me to work with his senior staff to make sure that the city was a leader in greening its own operations. When I was offered and accepted the job, this was my directive, and over the next seven years I found that making green practices a routine part of city operations was in fact more difficult than formulating regulations to bring about change. But the mayor—to his credit—was insistent that the city practice before preaching.

When I went to work for Mayor Daley in 2003, he had already been in office for fifteen years, during which time he'd won several elections by more than 70 percent of the vote. He was one of the first mayors—and at the time the only one from a large American city—who espoused the greening of the city. He saw that greening the city could improve the planet, improve quality of life for residents, and give the city a competitive economic advantage. I was amazed by the resources he had allocated to achieving this goal. He'd spent millions of dollars replanting urban trees and demonstrating green building strategies. He was the first mayor in the United States to install a green roof on a city-owned building.

He had even created a Leadership in Energy and Environmental Design (LEED) Platinum–certified green building resource center to teach the local building industry about green building practices, on a site that had been used as an illegal dump near downtown. The facility, called the Chicago Center for Green Technology, served as a test bed for new approaches to green construction practices, included a teaching center, and provided tours to thousands of building industry professionals so they could see green building practices in action.

Without much in the way of resources or information about best practices—which, given the relative newness of this field, hadn't yet been established—I set about creating a process to build understanding and buy-in within the city organization. The vision was to use the power of the mayor's office to create a plan for key city departments and their leaders to guide their investments in greening their operations. These departments oversaw airports, housing, city facilities, fleet, streets and sanitation, buildings, and water; each was led by a city commissioner appointed by the mayor. These commissioners already had a great deal on their plates, however, and developing this plan would require a significant investment of their time. So I began meeting with the commissioners individually, quickly realizing that while they all understood that the mayor expected them to "go green," they didn't understand what this meant for their departments. They weren't resisting his directive; they just didn't know what to do.

We began by establishing the Green Initiatives Steering Committee, which included the commissioners as well as representatives from the city's "sister agencies"—the Chicago Park Board, the Chicago Transit Authority, and the Public Building Commission of Chicago—whose boards were chaired by the mayor. Members were invited to the first steering committee meeting by the mayor's chief of staff, who also attended the meeting in order to send the signal that the mayor took this effort seriously. The steering committee was to meet monthly, and I asked each member also to chair a small working group of internal and external topic experts with the goal of completing three tasks over the next nine months: to inventory their current green activities, to compare their work with work being done in other cities, and to develop action plans for the next five and ten years.

I didn't have any staff, and most of the commissioners didn't have staff with this expertise, so I worked closely with the first deputy at the city's Department of Environment, who assigned a department employee to staff each committee, to take notes and support the work with background research. It soon became clear, however, that each department and agency needed to hire an internal green champion or assign someone the job. Once this was under way, we created a Green Team of these staff members, which also met monthly so members could apprise one another of their progress and get advice from the group or from me to help them address emerging issues. Green Team members were challenged by the fact that they were charged with helping entire departments go green, yet they had little power, little or no budget, and no outside help to assist them in getting this job done.

I faced similar challenges. Chicago city government is hierarchical, and, as with many large organizations, this made internal communication difficult. I began to understand that just as the mayor and his chief of staff had helped me communicate the importance of this effort to the commissioners, I had to help these internal green champions communicate the importance of their intradepartmental efforts to the commissioners and also help them talk about the barriers they faced.

In the meantime, their green plans began taking shape, and it was time to get the mayor's feedback. Each commissioner and his or her key staff had a private meeting with the mayor, and when they presented their draft plans, Mayor Daley pushed them to do more, sometimes asking them to pursue particular initiatives. These meetings really helped promote leadership among the commissioners because they heard from Mayor Daley personally about what he wanted them to do.

After a year the plans were finally done, compiled into a document called the Environmental Action Agenda, and ready to be shared more broadly. We scheduled a meeting of the mayor's entire cabinet, with its eighty-plus members, to be held off-site at a visiting "Big and Green" exhibition of innovative green practices from around the world. It was the first cabinet meeting ever to focus exclusively on the city's green agenda. All the commissioners involved with the Greenest City Steering Committee made presentations about their current activities and gave recommendations from their plans. Then Mayor Daley, who was in attendance to reinforce the importance of these initiatives, told his cabinet members bluntly that he was intent on greening every city department, and if they weren't on board with this agenda, they could find another job. It was a brief speech, but the impact was such that you could have heard a pin drop.

When the mayor later pulled me aside to ask if he'd been too forceful, I assured him that if he wanted the city to meet his objectives, he would have to be very clear about the importance of this work. But I was positively giddy. The mayor had not only paved the way for another six years of progress; he had also greatly enhanced our chances of success. Although I'd been in city government only a short time, I had learned that having the mayor on board and pushing his staff was perhaps the most important ingredient in moving things forward. A big part of my job was to keep him informed and engaged and to let him know if our progress was at risk, as well as to help the commissioners succeed in greening their operations.

Despite the mayor's commitment, significant implementation challenges remained, even to initiatives as basic as recycling. Change is hard, and leading by example (the topic of the next chapter) requires endless innovation. And while I tried to avoid using the influence of the mayor's office to get things done, I often had no choice. But slowly, over the next few years, using the Environmental Action Agenda that the Green Initiatives Steering Committee had developed as our guiding document, we made significant progress.

While it was a little chaotic, staff in virtually all parts of city government explored ways to improve the city's environmental performance. We used our experience gained from some high-profile pilot green building projects to develop and adopt a policy to build all new city facilities to a minimum of LEED Silver certification. We saved millions of dollars annually in energy costs through lighting and energy retrofits of existing buildings. We used city hall's green roof as a model to install green roofs on other city facilities. We learned that we could divert over 80 percent of the waste from our construction sites and then adopted the most aggressive construction site recycling policy in the country for all larger buildings being built in the city. We introduced recycling into city facilities and schools and reduced the city's use of hazardous chemicals by using healthier paints, carpets, and pest management strategies. We piloted the use of waterless urinals in city hall and at the airport and then battled to change building codes to allow them to be used more broadly. We integrated these green and healthy construction strategies into the low-income housing we built.

We used warm-mix asphalt in our street paving, which saved energy, improved working conditions, and resulted in lower greenhouse gas emissions. We further greened our public works operations by using permeable pavement in alleys (see "Case in Point: Permeable Pavement and the Green Alley Program in Chicago" in chapter 4). We began testing ice and snow removal systems that didn't use salt. We implemented an anti-idling policy for city vehicles, purchased greener vehicles, started powering the city's fleet with alternative fuels, and installed alternative fueling infrastructure.

These changes weren't easy, and there were many battles along the way. I went head-to-head with senior managers who worried about implementing unproven practices and with powerful unions that didn't like some of the changes, such as waterless urinals. Sometimes I succeeded—as with the school recycling program, which took a long time but was well worth it—and sometimes I had to compromise, as in our efforts to allow waterless urinals in all buildings. Perhaps most important, we discovered that while we reduced the city's environmental impact we also saved money, about $6 million a year on utility costs and $2 million because of the anti-idling policy, for example.

In retrospect, I realized our greening effort could have been more focused. The Environmental Action Agenda should probably have been shorter and more concise so that the priorities were clearer and the departments more easily held accountable. In spite of these challenges, the city benefited from the mayor's focus on leading by example, which provided a platform for engaging the public and members of the business community and asking them to take similar steps. While demonstrating leadership in city operations was critical, even in a large city such as Chicago, the environmental impact of city operations was small compared with that of the larger community; thus, getting the community involved is critical.

Get the Community Involved

We had been testing green practices before asking the public to follow suit, but now that we'd found some things that worked, it was time to engage the broader public. Early in my time with the mayor's office, I met with members of the Home Builders Association of Greater Chicago to talk to them about following the city's lead in constructing green buildings. While the city had committed to achieving LEED Silver certification for every new building and every major renovation project, relatively speaking we constructed a small number of new buildings compared with the number built by the private sector.

As with so many of my visits to industry associations, however, this discussion didn't go as intended. Instead of convincing the builders to go green, I had to listen as they vented their frustrations with the city. They mostly complained about the length of time it took to get a permit and how the lack of transparency made it difficult to track where a permit was in the process. It was clear that these problems had to be addressed before we could even begin a conversation about green building, but that meeting planted a seed for what eventually became one of the first green permit programs in North America.

We evaluated our options for engaging the private sector in green building. While some cities required that all public buildings meet LEED certification standards, the mayor wanted to use an incentive, not a mandate. We agreed that we needed to address the industry's frustrations with our building permit process by improving service, so we developed a program that would deliver permits for green buildings in thirty days instead of one hundred, the average processing time for a regular building permit. Some city departments were concerned, however, that while it was good to use an expedited process to incentivize green building practices, the process should also incentivize buildings that met the priorities of other departments, including construction of affordable housing, rehabilitation and reuse of existing buildings, high-quality design, and investment in disadvantaged neighborhoods.

We came up with a program that required projects to meet minimum green requirements as well as affordable housing and transit-oriented development goals. The program was intended to promote innovative technologies including green roofs, rainwater harvesting, and renewable energy systems such as solar panels, wind turbines, and geothermal systems. A LEED-certified housing development would get permitted in thirty days instead of about one hundred, and if developers added other features, such as additional affordable housing units, or increased the accessibility of the units, they could get even faster permitting and a waiver of up to $25,000 in permit fees. By broadening the options beyond green strategies, we won support within city government from the affordable housing and accessibility departments, as well as in the advocacy community. While it was initially a compromise to include non-green building strategies in the Green Permit Program, without adding these components we probably wouldn't have gotten enough support and resources from the city to make the program a success.

The Green Permit Program differed from approaches taken by many other cities in that it offered incentives instead of issuing mandates. Because the permits were reviewed by multiple employees in each department and several departments had to sign off, it took us a while to communicate to staff that they were to prioritize the green permit projects. And because we were the first city to create this kind of program, many questions emerged that had to be answered. For example, should the city allow construction of wind turbines in residential neighborhoods? What color should be used for pipes carrying potable water and what color for gray water?

The building industry appreciated the fee waivers and faster permitting as well as the additional staff to help builders navigate the new process. They were particularly pleased with the addition of a Green Permit Program manager who had a deep understanding of green building technologies and could answer their questions. Within a few months, the new program was working well and any problems that arose could be raised with the program manager, who would convene a meeting of relevant staff to resolve the issue quickly. By 2008, when the program had been in operation for a couple of years, Chicago had more projects seeking LEED certification than did any other North American city (including those that mandated LEED certification), and the city's signature Green Permit Program signs, which were displayed on buildings all over town, were understood to indicate a project that was both green and of high-quality design and construction.

My other attempts to convince the private sector to go green were more of a mixed bag. Cities across the United States have tried many different approaches to engage residents and businesses, offering incentives such as rebate programs for people who install water-efficient toilets and curbside recycling to make participation easy. Generally speaking, though, municipalities are more inclined to mandate and regulate, and while this sometimes works, making it attractive for residents or businesses also works. If cities make it easy, convenient, and "cool" to participate, they can increase public participation.

Keep Sustainability Leaders Out of Silos

Across North America, green leaders generally work in the mayor's office, lead a sustainability office, or are embedded in a department. During my time in Chicago, I worked in the mayor's office first as assistant for green initiatives, next as commissioner for the Department of Environment, and finally as deputy chief of staff. For people not familiar with city government, it can be quite surprising to see how each department is like its own silo, in which staff don't coordinate, or even communicate, with staff in other departments. The most significant benefit of being in the mayor's office is that it allows green city leaders to break out of the silos of individual departments and work across departments, thereby having a broader influence. Being a silo-buster can be extremely satisfying because you can cajole people into working together. The challenge is that in this role you do not have direct oversight over staff or budgets.

During my tenure as commissioner, we focused on creating the Chicago Climate Action Plan (CCAP), one of the first climate plans to address and integrate both adaptation and mitigation (see the CCAP case in point at www.guidetogreeningcities.org). Up to this point, cities in the United States had mostly focused on mitigation strategies to reduce carbon emissions, while only a few had worked on adaptation strategies to prepare for a changing climate. Chicago's plan prioritized actions that would address mitigation and adaptation concurrently. A green roof, which has plants and soil, for example, addresses an adaptation issue—the urban heat island effect—because it keeps the roof cooler than would a traditional roof, which is typically black and absorbs heat. The plants on the green roof help to keep the roof surface cooler and the soil provides additional insulation; together this reduces temperatures in the building, reduces energy consumption, and results in a more comfortable building with lower greenhouse gas emissions.

With a strong team and the resources of my department, I was able to take the time to develop partnerships in the business and nonprofit sectors, and we leveraged our relationships with civic, philanthropic, and nonprofit leaders to raise more than $2 million for research that supported the plan's concepts and goals. We hired leading scientists to downscale global climate projections and predict what Chicago could expect from climate change.

It would have been more difficult to be this ambitious if I were still working in the mayor's office, where I wouldn't have been in control of the staff and financial resources required to do the job. But, as we struggled to break out of our departmental silos and get the commissioners and their staffs to prioritize CCAP implementation, I realized that the plan was so ambitious that it was going to be difficult to implement unless the mayor owned it and championed it. So, after several years at the department, I moved back into the mayor's office as chief environmental officer, mostly to ensure that we adopted and implemented the CCAP. From this seat of power, I could more readily get sign-offs from the departments and the support of the mayor. Having operated from these various vantage points within Chicago's municipal government, I concluded that while running my own department definitely provided benefits, I could get more done from a centralized position of leadership in the mayor's office.

When I started working in Vancouver, British Columbia, as the deputy city manager, I realized that there is a "magic middle ground." In Vancouver, I was in a senior position within the city and had the committed leadership of the mayor, the city council, and a talented city staff. In the City of Vancouver it isn't just the city leadership pushing the idea of going green; residents are demanding it.

Although my father is Canadian and I had spent time in the country during my teens, moving there to work still required some adjustments. I'd come from a city with a strong mayoral system and a mayor who'd been in office for years, whereas Vancouver's system is structured to give more power to the city council than to the mayor. In Vancouver the mayor has to work with the city council to shape policy and the city manager takes direction from the council to oversee policy implementation and city operations. There's a distinct separation between politics and the city bureaucracy. Having worked with two such different cities made it clear to me that the lessons of greening can be pertinent regardless of the municipal structure and that ultimately success depends on citizen participation, which drastically increases when participation is easy and appealing.

Make Green Living Easy and Appealing

By 2012, Vancouver had reduced its overall carbon emissions below 1990 levels, even though the city's population had grown by 27 percent during that period and the number of jobs had increased by 18 percent. The city could never have achieved these emissions

Figure 1.1. Yaletown neighborhood, Vancouver, British Columbia
Vancouver has the fastest-growing residential downtown in North America. Nearly 40,000 people have moved downtown in the past decade, many of them to transit-oriented neighborhoods such as Yaletown, where residents can easily live without cars. Photo courtesy of the City of Vancouver.

reductions had residents not changed the way they lived and supported planning and policy changes that made it possible for new residents to live low-carbon lifestyles in Vancouver's dense and transit-oriented downtown.

Unlike many cities in North America, which were built or retrofitted to accommodate travel by car, Vancouver has managed to avoid the same level of car orientation. Residents successfully fought efforts to build a highway through the downtown in the 1960s (which would have required demolition of the house in which I now live), and as a result Vancouver has one of the only downtowns in North America that can't be accessed by highway. This 1960s resident uprising helped shape the urban form of the city over several decades, including development of a transportation plan in 1997 that prioritized walking, followed by cycling, public transit, goods movement, and, last, the car. During the following decade, the city significantly reduced car trips and increased walking, biking, and transit use. This progressive transportation plan provided the people of Vancouver with greater and greener transportation options, such as a citywide cycling network.

The city could never have achieved such impressive emissions reductions if land use and transportation planners hadn't aligned their plans and policies so that people could live in "complete communities" close to shops, services, and jobs, so they didn't have to drive. Land use planners promoted development near transit and complete communities where people can walk or bike between shops, work, and home. Zoning and other regulations encouraged the development of large multifamily residential buildings near transit and focused most of this development and infrastructure investment downtown. By the middle of the first decade of the 2000s, downtown was truly the heart of the city, proving that downtown living in a small city such as Vancouver could be as attractive as living in Manhattan or San Francisco.

The success of downtown Vancouver also demonstrated that thoughtful city plans and policies—especially those that create appealing, convenient, and compact housing choices and multimodal transportation choices—can result in low-carbon lifestyle choices. From 1996 to 2011, while the number of people living downtown increased by 75 percent and the number of jobs downtown increased by 26 percent, the number of cars entering downtown decreased by 20 percent. Vancouver had demonstrated what many thought wasn't possible in North American cities: there was population and job growth at the same time that carbon emissions were reduced and the city provided its residents with a very high quality of life.

These results were impressive, and city leaders wanted to do more. Because buildings accounted for 55 percent of the city's carbon emissions, the city turned its attention to advancing renewable energy. Nearly all of the city's electrical power was hydroelectric, but natural gas was used for both space and water heating. One way that cities have reduced natural gas consumption is to build district energy systems that use renewable sources of energy. Vancouver decided to try this, building a district energy system that supplied heat for the 2010 Olympic Village and the surrounding neighborhood.

District energy systems distribute heat that is generated in a central location for residential and commercial heating—and sometimes cooling—within a "district" or neighborhood. Energy is distributed to the buildings through a system of insulated underground pipes, eliminating the need for boilers or furnaces in individual buildings. The City of Vancouver's Southeast False Creek (SEFC) Neighbourhood Energy Utility is the first district energy system in North America to recover heat from the sewer system. A large sewer pipe transports sewer water from downtown to a treatment facility, and because residents and businesses send a lot of hot water down the drain from showers, dishwashers, and other uses, the sewer water is hot. When the city needed to upgrade one of its pump stations, instead of the typical pump station, it built an energy center. The heat from the sewer water is transferred to hot water pipes and used to fulfill the heating

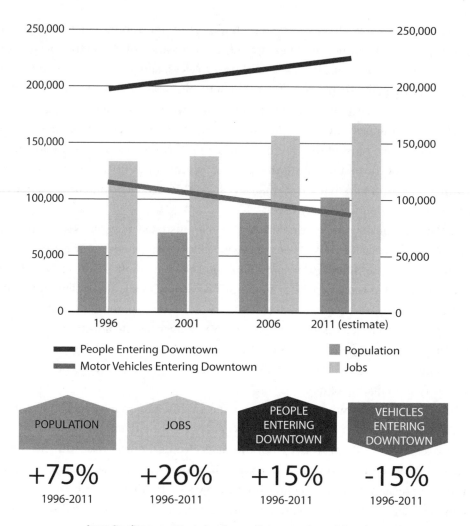

Source: City of Vancouver estimates based on screenline counts and census information.
Change in population & job numbers have been rounded to the nearest 1%, and screenline counts to the nearest 5%.

Figure 1.2. Downtown Vancouver vehicle and person trips, 1996–2011
Vancouver has demonstrated population and job growth with reduced greenhouse gas emissions: from 1996 to 2011, the number of people living, working, and shopping downtown more than doubled while the number of vehicles fell by 15 percent. The Vancouver community's carbon emissions are below 1990 emissions despite over 25 percent growth in population. Figure courtesy of the City of Vancouver.

needs, such as domestic hot water and space heating, of buildings in the neighborhood. Producing heat for these buildings, which currently amounts to about 2.7 million square feet of space, in this way reduces greenhouse gas emissions by 70 percent and costs less than 3 percent more than if the heat were provided by furnaces powered by natural gas.

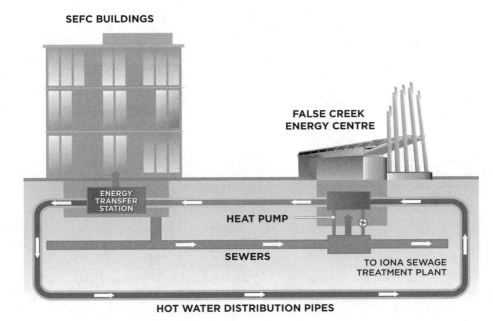

SEFC BUILDINGS

FALSE CREEK ENERGY CENTRE

ENERGY TRANSFER STATION

HEAT PUMP

SEWERS

TO IONA SEWAGE TREATMENT PLANT

HOT WATER DISTRIBUTION PIPES

FALSE CREEK ENERGY CENTRE - How it works

Figure 1.3. Vancouver district energy facility diagram
The City of Vancouver's Southeast False Creek (SEFC) Neighbourhood Energy Utility was the first district energy system in North America to recover heat from the sewer system and distribute it via insulated underground pipes throughout the neighborhood—allowing residents to live with 70 percent lower greenhouse gas emissions from space heating and domestic hot water heating. Figure courtesy of the City of Vancouver.

The energy center was given a prominent location in the city, and an artist designed innovative smokestacks in the shape of a hand coming out from under a nearby bridge, with light-emitting diode (LED) lights in the "fingernails" that change color depending on how much energy the neighborhood is using. By this approach, the city has made it simple, affordable, and convenient for Vancouver residents to have significantly lower carbon emissions.

Municipal leaders are often frustrated because they feel they have few tools to reduce greenhouse gas emissions from energy consumption. But district energy systems that utilize renewable energy demonstrate that cities can employ land use planning and infrastructure investments to reduce greenhouse gas emissions. On the basis of the success of this approach, the city adopted policies requiring new developments to either build a district energy system or connect to an existing system. In October 2012, the city council unanimously adopted a comprehensive district energy strategy to ensure the expansion of systems across the city.

Figure 1.4. Vancouver district energy stack
In an attempt to educate residents about energy consumption, the City of Vancouver installed an artist-designed stack for the SEFC Neighbourhood Energy Utility in the shape of a hand; LED lights in the "fingernails" change color according to the amount of neighborhood energy in use. Photo courtesy of the City of Vancouver.

In short, Vancouver's integrated land use, transportation, and energy planning enables residents and businesses to reduce their carbon emissions. Despite significant strides, achieving Vancouver's green ambitions require even fuller participation from the public. Shortly after I arrived in Vancouver, Mayor Gregor Robertson and the city council directed staff to develop a plan that would make Vancouver the greenest city in the world, requesting that we engage the community in its development.

Consult with the Community

The first step toward making Vancouver the greenest city in the world by 2020 involved the mayor seeking advice from a group of experts called the Greenest City Action Team. These experts compiled ten goals with specific targets, a series of "quick starts" to be pursued immediately, and longer-term actions that needed to be developed further. The plan was ambitious but achievable, as long as residents and businesses were willing to work with the city in its implementation.

In Chicago, I struggled to engage residents and businesses in greening the city. When we introduced the Chicago Climate Action Plan in 2008, we asked residents to take a

Figure 1.5. Carrall Street Greenway, Vancouver
Separated bike facilities such as Vancouver's Carrall Street Greenway make walking and bicycling more safe, comfortable, convenient, and appealing—which makes children, seniors, and others more willing to bike. Photo courtesy of the City of Vancouver.

pledge to reduce their carbon emissions. On our website was a list of fourteen actions that people could take, ranging from reducing the indoor temperature to turning off the faucet while brushing their teeth to installing a motion detector for outdoor lights, and they could calculate their greenhouse gas reductions and also the annual household savings that would be a corollary benefit. To publicize this effort and encourage people to take the pledge, we got a grant to distribute millions of dollars' worth of compact fluorescent lightbulbs at energy fairs and community centers. The giveaway was a huge success, except that very few people actually bothered to take the pledge. We didn't even come close to our goal of 50,000 residents.

Despite similar challenges faced by many cities when it comes to engaging the public in urban greening, Vancouver's Mayor Robertson was determined to succeed. We launched the Talk Green to Us program, a multifaceted campaign to get residents' input and support for the Greenest City 2020 Action Plan (GCAP), in partnership with the University of British Columbia and notable thinkers, using the popular PechaKucha presentation format, in which speakers deliver insight and inspiration accompanied by twenty images, each shown for just twenty seconds. This partnership allowed us to tap into an existing audience rather than create our own, and we sold out the event at the city's largest theater. There were 2,000 people in the audience and 13 speakers, each with six minutes to present his or her ideas about how to make Vancouver the greenest city. At the event we also launched our website, www.talkgreentous.ca, and asked residents to submit their ideas and vote on their favorites.

Residents and businesses submitted more than 750 ideas, and thousands of people voted for their favorites. The top 5 ideas were presented at a public forum, where the mayor, staff, and several sustainability experts responded to their ideas. We continued to reach out to the public by staging potlucks in parks and an "unconference" at which the audience created the agenda for the day's discussions. We offered residents a DIY (do-it-yourself) tool kit so they could host their own parties to provoke discussions and gather ideas. We used several innovative online platforms and partnered with so many residents and community organizations that we ultimately involved more than 35,000 people. One of the strengths of the campaign was the partnership approach: instead of asking people to come to our events, we went to their events to solicit their ideas.

After the GCAP was adopted by the city council in 2011, it was recognized that real community participation would require ongoing focus and resources, so we developed the Greenest City Fund in partnership with the Vancouver Foundation. The city and the foundation each contributed $1 million to create a $2 million fund to help community groups implement the GCAP in their own neighborhoods.

In addition to involving our residents, we knew we also needed our students to be involved, so we pursued one of the top ideas from our online engagement, which called for a collaboration between Vancouver's six postsecondary academic institutions to create a "semester in the city." Twenty students from a variety of disciplines worked collaboratively out of an office donated by the city to help implement the GCAP and support it with research, while another 300 students in "partner" courses at the six schools studied the same issues. Over the first two years of the program, more than 40,000 hours of student time has been contributed to implementing projects and conducting research to further the GCAP. One of my favorite projects involves what are called "orphaned sites": students map forgotten or underutilized neighborhood spaces, pick one or more locations, and build something that contributes to the GCAP. Now, in these formerly abandoned little spaces, a bicycler might find a bike repair station or a bench and a frame highlighting the majestic backdrop of mountains.

CityStudio is the most successful program for engaging university students and faculty in a municipal greening program that I've ever come across. It's clear that it works best if a city can find a way to get residents and businesses to share their own ideas and then help implement these ideas through policy or by providing resources.

Enable the Business and Nonprofit Community

While involving businesses and residents in sustainability work has the potential to magnify the efforts of the city and drastically increase its effectiveness, it can be contrary to the way cities normally operate and therefore often requires additional work. On the basis of my work in Chicago and Vancouver, it's my observation that city government can have a real impact through partnerships with business that leverage underutilized city assets such as land or buildings. For example, one of the goals of Vancouver's GCAP is to double local food assets: community gardens, urban farms, farm markets, and neighborhood food networks. Many of these efforts are managed by nonprofits, but the city can play a supportive role and help them to succeed.

A nonprofit named Sole Food Street Farms, which provides jobs for the homeless growing food on raised beds in Vancouver's low-income neighborhoods, approached the city for help in finding sites to develop. We found a site and worked with the city council to lease it to the organization for $1 per year. The site was a brownfield, but Sole Food's founders believed that because the food would be grown in containers, it could work. It didn't, and the organization came back to the city to ask for a different site.

It was a frustrating situation because it meant we had to go back to the city council, but Sole Food had a donor willing to contribute several million dollars if the organization could get four acres of urban land into production before the summer growing season. Cities often struggle to move quickly on initiatives like this, but we geared up and found three sites that weren't going to be developed in the near term, and the city council agreed to lease the sites on a year-to-year basis. Sole Food had developed an innovative raised bed built on a shipping pallet, so the beds could be picked up with a forklift and transported to other sites should the land be developed. This arrangement made it possible for Sole Food to employ an additional twenty people to get the sites up and running by the summer, and the city supported this valuable initiative, thereby helping to create twenty green jobs and to double the acreage of urban farms in the city.

However significant these efforts are, they can be extremely difficult to implement, given municipal intolerance for risk and purchasing policies that are designed for the purchase of services or commodities, not for development of innovative partnerships. In Chicago, for example, I was responsible for our brownfield cleanup program. One of the most difficult properties in our portfolio was a forty-acre site on Chicago's South Side where a low-income African American community had for more than thirty years lived alongside a highly contaminated site still used for illegal dumping. The buildings had been demolished over the years, but large basements remained, some of them filled with water. The city had taken possession of the land before understanding the extent of the soil contamination. We partnered with the National Brownfield Association to find in-novative ways to clean it up.

We were told that a simple cleanup would cost $2 million, whereas a thorough clean-up could cost over $10 million, and that the site, when cleaned up, would be worth about $2 million. The cheaper strategy required that part of the site be paved for roads and parking so as to "cap" some of the worst areas, but until we found someone who was interested in the site, we were stuck with a blighted property that had a negative impact on the entire neighborhood.

Then representatives of the region's largest electric utility expressed an interest in building a solar power plant in Chicago. They needed a large swath of cheap land, and they were interested in the brownfield site. Over a period of months, we put together a deal that got them the entire forty acres for twenty-five years at reduced rent if they would clear the land, fill the basements, cover the entire site with gravel, and install 36,000 solar panels, thereby temporarily capping the brownfield. Moreover, this project would create local jobs, support local businesses whose equipment would be used in the project, and generate positive media coverage for what would be the world's largest municipal solar power system, able to power 1,200 homes with renewable energy.

The mayor was on board with the idea, and I was enthusiastic enough about the project that I overlooked several reasons why the site had been vacant for so long. As we neared the time for closing the deal, I was struggling to get the legal department and the budget office to sign off. Together they started pushing back on the terms of the deal, arguing that the utility wasn't paying enough rent. I couldn't believe that a few hundred thousand dollars over a twenty-year lease stood in the way of a project that would net the city so many benefits. But these departments were convinced we were "giving up" the site for twenty years, during which time we might need it or might have an opportunity to make more money from it. The utility, however, couldn't justify investing nearly $80 million in a site with a shorter-term lease.

Following a few sleepless weeks, we finally convinced the utility to pay a slightly higher rent. I convinced city staff to sign off, and we did get the project built. The solar panels now track the sun, creating clean energy, attracting other companies to the neigh-borhood, and garnering the attention of visiting delegations from other cities interested in green work. The experience taught me an important lesson: I realized that while I thought of this as a win-win partnership, to some of my coworkers it was simply a real estate transaction. I was so committed to the concept of leveraging an underutilized asset to achieve green goals that I had moved too fast for other city departments and had put an important project at risk.

That experience convinced me, however, that cities can and should leverage their physical assets to help reach green goals, even if the green goals are driven by someone else's agenda. When cities use their physical assets and resources to help others succeed, while furthering municipal goals, it can save the city time and money in the long run. In Vancouver in 2012, for example, many downtown parking garages, including city-owned lots, were only half full; driving had been declining because of the increasing popularity of other modes of transportation. This meant that city revenues were down because physical assets were underutilized.

When representatives of a local clean technology company named Alterrus Systems, which had developed vertical farming technologies, approached the City of Vancouver, we were enthusiastic about working with them. The company signed a long-term lease with the city and built one of the first vertical farms in North America on the top floor of one of these underutilized parking garages. It now grows 150,000 pounds of produce in just 6,000 square feet of space. Leafy greens are grown in trays suspended on racks on a moving conveyor system that provides maximum exposure to water and light. The produce is sold to customers within a radius of a few miles of the farm, reducing their need to drive, and the proceeds pay the rent on space that had been mostly vacant for several years.

In addition to physical assets, cities are starting to leverage their financial assets. A number of innovative funds and financing programs have started up across North America, and I have spent a good deal of time trying to launch them in Chicago and Vancouver. In Chicago, I spent several years trying to launch a fund with local banks to help get buildings retrofitted and I also tried to launch a local carbon offsets fund to invest in projects that reduce greenhouse gas emissions. Despite considerable time and effort, these efforts didn't get off the ground.

In Vancouver we have had somewhat more success. Vancouver's Greenest City 2020 Action Plan calls for achieving carbon reductions through greening existing buildings, which requires significant building retrofits. The plan calls for a 20 percent reduction in energy used in existing buildings in the city by 2020. While some mandates, such as greening the building code, are necessary, we felt it was important to complement mandates with financial incentives, so we established a pilot program for energy retrofits with low-interest loans for single-family homes and another for condominiums.

To develop a fund for these green retrofits, we issued a request for expressions of interest (RFEOI) from financial institutions, which allowed us to choose a financial partner committed to innovation. We selected Vancity, Canada's largest community credit union. With funding from the city and from a community foundation associated with Vancity, we established a loan loss reserve fund to be used to cover losses from bad loans, thereby enabling the bank to make loans that might be riskier.

After several years of working on this fund, we were ready to go with two pilot projects. The first was for energy retrofits of single-family homes and offered loans of up to $10,000 for a ten-year fixed rate of 4.5 percent, with payments added to the homeowner's property tax bill. It was a partnership involving the city's two energy utilities, both of which offered grants to complement the loans. Natural Resources Canada, a federal agency charged with improving energy efficiency, signed a memorandum of understanding with the city allowing its approved energy auditors to offer audits. The program was modeled on the property-assessed clean energy (PACE) approach taken in the United States (see chapter 5)—an innovative financing mechanism that allows consumers to take out loans that are repaid via an annual assessment on their property tax bills—and it was a first for Canada. But despite considerable efforts to reach out to homeowners through social media, workshops, and other means, the program had very low participation. There was capacity for 500 homeowners, but far fewer applied.

The second pilot, to help condominium owners complete detailed energy audits and energy retrofits, was also a first for Canada, and it met with more enthusiasm. Fifteen buildings, totaling thousands of units, were signed up. Completing the energy retrofit for each building, however, required getting the support of every condo owner, which was quite time-consuming. Cities across the continent are rethinking their traditional roles and finding ways to partner with financial institutions in order to reduce energy use. Chapter 5 discusses many efforts that have been successful. After investing considerable time and resources on efforts in Chicago and Vancouver, I am not convinced that these types of programs leverage the strength of the city or are worth the level of effort required to implement them.

Measure and Report on This Work

Politicians don't like bad news. This may seem obvious, but I learned it the hard way in Chicago after working for months on an environmental scorecard to track key sustainability indicators such as "number of ozone action days" and "gallons of water used per capita." The scorecard was linked to a municipal performance measurement program that we were developing, and I thought it was a good balance of metrics that would hold us accountable but wouldn't bury us with data gathering. The city had control over many of the outcomes that were being measured, but there were just as many over which we had no direct control, though we had some influence. I was commissioner at the Department of Environment at the time, but I couldn't get it past the mayor's press office because staff members were concerned that if trends went the wrong way we'd be obligated to report bad news.

They said one thing that stuck in my head. Why, they asked, should we take a hit for negative outcomes over which we have no direct control? And while initially I disagreed, I came to see merit in their argument. When selecting what to measure, it's important to balance long-term trends over which the city has some influence—such as community-wide greenhouse gas emissions—with trends over which the city has more direct control, such as waste diversion from city facilities. So we decided to track and report on the measures over which we had direct control, and the city's nonprofit environmental organizations could report on other factors such as air quality, over which the city had little control.

We got better and better at measuring the performance of city operations, such as the cost per pothole fixed and the time it took to follow up on an inspection request. We developed metrics that virtually every department could track and shared metrics that each department would report on monthly, such as the amount of fuel and paper used. We also created specific measures for each department, including the amount of water used by the fleet department for cleaning vehicles and the length of time it took to issue a permit through the Green Permit Program. Each department was expected to review these metrics with the city's chief of staff, who would report the results directly to the mayor. My attendance at these meetings allowed me to raise questions and thus better understand where the city had the most potential to reduce its environmental impact.

Cities are becoming increasingly sophisticated about using data to measure performance. In many cities, the green city leader is becoming the "smart city leader" by integrating innovations in the digital sector that enable a city to better track and improve its efficiency. For example, following a major heat wave in the 1990s, Chicago focused on reducing the urban heat island effect by planting trees and installing green roofs. But our mapping showed that the city wasn't strategic about planting trees where they were most needed. We were planting trees where residents requested them, but we should have been planting them in lower-income neighborhoods, where the heat island effect was most severe and people could least afford air-conditioning. Once we had the urban heat island map, we focused our tree-planting efforts in the hottest parts of the city and also approached property owners in these neighborhoods to ask them to plant trees.

Achieve the Triple Bottom Line

Throughout this book, there are stories about cities leveraging their resources and investments to reduce environmental impacts in their own communities and on the planet while improving the lives of their citizens. This integration of environmental, social, and economic objectives is some of the most inspiring work happening in cities. In Vancouver, for example, we helped launch a home weatherization program that also provided jobs for hard-to-employ workers. It was jointly funded by the city and the two energy utilities, each of which matched the city's contribution to start up the program. Within two years, the nonprofit that ran the program had established a weatherization company, which quickly expanded into a green renovation company that employed even more people.

In Vancouver, we did a pilot project that involved the "deconstruction" of two homes, which involved taking them apart piece by piece and selling the materials directly off the site so they could be reused and not sent to a landfill. The city hired a dozen at-risk youths to take them apart, with the result that 93 percent of the materials were diverted. Following this success, the city developed an expedited permit program for projects that would be deconstructed instead of demolished.

In Chicago, we opened an electronics collection center where residents could drop off old computers. We then expanded our Greencorps Chicago program, which had been training ex-offenders to build community gardens in the city, to train them in inventory and refurbishment of dropped-off electronics. The computers were then donated or sold to low-income households, schools, and community organizations. This win-win-win project enabled the city to reduce the waste stream of computers picked up by garbage crews, provided jobs for hard-to-employ residents, and provided computers to low-income residents.

There are many other examples of triple bottom line approaches throughout this book and on the accompanying website (www.guidetogreeningcities.org). I consider this some of the most inspiring work being done in the greening of our cities. Triple bottom line projects and approaches illustrate how we can reduce our environmental impact, help businesses become more competitive, and provide benefits for our residents all at the same time, with the result that all parts of the urban ecosystem work synergistically. Everybody needs to step up—nonprofits, academic institutions, city leaders, the private sector, residents—with the goal of using resources creatively to achieve multiple objectives. The future of people on this planet depends on all of us working together in this way to leverage our passion and assets.

Having worked to improve Cleveland from outside city government and having worked in various positions in Chicago and Vancouver to improve performance from the inside, I am more convinced than ever that cities are positioned to lead the transition to a new economy, with the goal of protecting people and our planet and making our communities even better places to live. This book is full of stories about the amazing work being done in cities. Not all the efforts will succeed, but the lessons learned will be shared through emerging networks that will enable cities to leapfrog over one another in their quest to be better places. Vancouver and Chicago are very different cities, but both are part of a global movement that we can all take part in.

2.

Leading from the Inside Out

Greening City Buildings and Operations

*"The first step to drive urban
sustainability is city leadership.
It is very hard for us to ask someone
else to do something if we haven't
done it first. Businesses and
residents are listening because
the city has done it first."*

—Laura Spanjian,
sustainability director,
Office of the Mayor,
City of Houston

It was the late 1990s when Lucia Athens and other green city leaders in Seattle saw a big opportunity to transform the design and construction industry throughout the Puget Sound region. The Emerald City was on the cusp of its biggest surge in civic infrastructure investment since the rebuilding that followed the Great Seattle Fire of 1889, which destroyed the entire central business district. Athens and her colleagues believed that the best way to catalyze change was to lead by example and to start by greening city buildings.

City buildings slated for construction or major renovation included a city hall, a justice center, and a central library in the heart of downtown, plus dozens of community centers, libraries, and police and fire stations sprinkled throughout nearly every neighborhood of the city. "If we weren't doing it ourselves, how could we ask others to?" observed Athens, then manager of Seattle's new green building program and now chief sustainability officer for the City of Austin. "Government must lead by example. Green building program development should first focus on an organization's own building assets, whether in new construction or in upgrades to existing buildings. Adoption by government for its own building projects sends a clear signal of commitment."[1]

So Athens and her team led a streamlined effort to convene key public, private, and nonprofit stakeholders and develop a sustainable building action plan, and in 2000 they shepherded the nation's first municipal green building policy through the city council. The policy mandated that all municipal projects of 5,000 square feet or more—including both new construction and major remodels—must "strive to meet or exceed" the Silver certification level established in the US Green Building Council's (USGBC's) Leadership in Energy and Environmental Design (LEED) program, which was brand-new at the time.[2]

"We were looking at the kind of substantial public infrastructure outlay that hadn't happened in a long, long time," recalls Ray Hoffman, then the mayor's special assistant for environmental initiatives and now director of Seattle Public Utilities. "By putting that policy in place, all of a sudden hundreds of millions of dollars' worth of public investment were going through a green screen. It was nothing short of revolutionary. There were struggles—hard questions from the budget director, interdepartmental squabbles, that sort of thing—but you have to be ready to strike when an opportunity presents itself. And we did."

This public green building activity spurred private investment in green building, and five years later Seattle was the top-ranked US city in terms of both the number of LEED-certified buildings (there were fifteen, including a new LEED Gold–certified city hall with a 13,000-square-foot green roof) and the number of LEED-accredited professionals (about 800). Moreover, there were clear signs of change in the private sector. Nearly 20 percent of new homes constructed in the Seattle area that year were certified as "Built Green," using a LEED-like program developed by the Master Builders Association of King and Snohomish Counties in partnership with the City of Seattle and others. By 2009, there were more than 150 LEED-certified buildings in Seattle, and only about 10 percent of them were city owned; nearly 100 were commercial or multifamily residential buildings, and about 50 were single-family homes.

Within a decade, green building was approaching standard practice in the Seattle region and beyond. "Pretty much any new development of significance will go for LEED

Silver or Gold certification," says Diane Sugimura, director of the Seattle Department of Planning and Development. "Developers realize they need to build green to be competitive." Sugimura cites as examples the LEED Gold–certified three-building complex at the base of the iconic Space Needle, which houses the Bill & Melinda Gates Foundation, and Amazon's soon-to-be-built new headquarters, which will include eleven new LEED Gold–certified buildings in the recently revitalized South Lake Union neighborhood, just north of the downtown core. Nationally, the green building market grew from 28 percent to 35 percent of nonresidential construction starts in 2010, up dramatically from just 2 percent in 2005 and 12 percent in 2008, according to a report by McGraw-Hill Construction.[3]

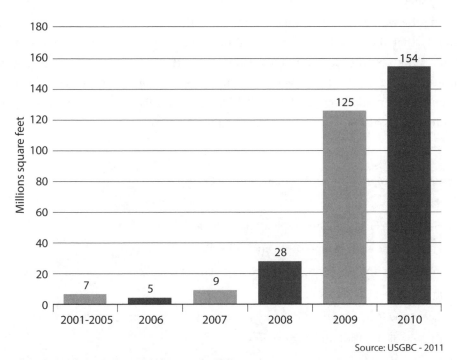

Source: USGBC - 2011

Figure 2.1. Growth in commercial green building
US Green Building Council vice president Jason Hartke says that city policies are the most powerful accelerant for green building and that "those initial leadership-by-example actions that cities and counties take are invaluable." Figure courtesy of the USGBC.

"City policies are *the* most powerful accelerant for green building," says Jason Hartke, vice president of national policy and advocacy for the USGBC. "Those initial leadership-by-example actions that cities and counties take are invaluable. They start the shift and trigger the transformation. These cities are putting a stake in the ground that says, 'This is what we stand for. This is where we're going.' And the market responds to that."

Leading by example—greening the city's own facilities and operations—is the essential first step toward greening the whole city. When green city leaders start with what they know the best and have the most control over—their own buildings and real estate, vehicle fleets, power supplies, and purchasing practices—they have the nearest and clearest opportunities to deliver tangible, visible, relatively near-term results. The benefits range from lower bills for homeowners and business owners to healthier and safer public buildings, parks, and streets. Very often, these benefits extend well beyond the city's boundaries because they inspire other local governments and institutions to take similar actions, thereby transforming markets and whole industries and influencing state and federal policy.

Along the way, green city leaders demonstrate their value and build the capacity and credibility that they need to be successful on a bigger scale and over the longer haul. "I don't think you can do a very effective job of getting others to change their behavior unless you've demonstrated you're willing to do it yourself," says Dennis Murphey, chief environmental officer for the City of Kansas City, Missouri. "It provides the moral grounding necessary for advocating this on a broader scale."

Box 2.1. The Myriad Benefits of Leading by Example

- Save taxpayers money.
- Help create local business and job opportunities.
- Protect the health of employees and residents.
- Improve air and water quality and reduce climate pollution.
- Improve employee morale.
- Gain experience and build capacity for future policy and program development.
- Earn credibility for future endeavors.
- Inspire others to act.

Loads of Leverage and the Will to Use It

Simply put, cities should lead by example because they *can*. They have more than ample influence—and the ability and willingness to wield it. They design, build, and manage large numbers of buildings, from high-rise office buildings downtown to small neighborhood libraries, community centers, and police and fire stations. They own and operate relatively large and visible fleets of cars and trucks. They own and manage streets, alleys, bridges, and other critical assets that are the backbone of the local and regional economy.

They directly manage a lot of the land in the city—from parks to streets—and regulate most of the rest. And they buy large quantities of goods and services. This adds up to loads of leverage and a vantage point from which to catalyze positive change.

And city governments have proven to be more willing and better able to use that leverage than their state and federal counterparts. "Cities are the best incubators," says Dennis McLerran, who ran several local and regional government agencies before taking the helm at the US Environmental Protection Agency's Region 10. "They are able to be more entrepreneurial, they're able to move faster, and they're able to engage with citizens on the ground much more directly than either state or federal government."

Joel Makower, the creator of GreenBiz.com and a leading thinker, writer, and strategist on corporate sustainability practices, adds: "We've reached a point in the sustainability movement where we need to be thinking more about systems and less about components. And there's no better system in which to effect change than cities. They have the right critical mass, the right geography, and in many cases city government and city leaders are more enlightened, perhaps because they are 'closer to the ground'—they're closer to the people they govern, and they drive the potholed streets, experience the electricity outages, breathe the air, and suffer through the traffic congestion. So it's harder for them to get gridlocked politically or to simply ignore the problems and hope somebody else deals with them."

Which isn't to say it's easy—leadership never is. Municipal governments are very complex institutions, composed of a mishmash of agencies with different missions, mandates, and cultures, embedded in a fast-paced operating environment with limited resources and thorny politics. Overcoming inertia and active resistance to change—the "but we've always done it this way" syndrome—can be the biggest hurdle. Green city leaders are asking everyone to think differently about their roles and their jobs and to take a risk and try something that, unlike business as usual, hasn't been tested by time.

Working across historically disconnected departments that are accustomed to doing their own thing in their own way can be enormously challenging. It is, however, absolutely necessary, since most initiatives for green city operations require coordinated action by multiple agencies. Securing and sustaining the necessary support and funding is another big challenge. Even in the best of economic times there is usually intense competition for discretionary resources, and green city programs can be a hard sell, especially if they require up-front investments that won't be repaid in the city's one- or two-year budget cycle.

Despite these and other challenges, green city leaders and the local governments for which they work are taking Mahatma Gandhi's advice—they are "being the change they wish to see in the world"—and along the way they are creating models and examples that shine a light for others to follow. "Seeing is believing," says Gus Speth, noted environmental lawyer, author, and activist. "That may be the best way to change behavior. There's nothing quite like showing people that, yes, this is possible. Here it is, and it works!"

Greening City Buildings, Blocks, and Districts

In many cities, greening begins with buildings, and with good reason. The design, construction, renovation, and management of city-owned buildings offers green city leaders an enormous opportunity for impact and influence, for three simple reasons: (1) Cities build, own, and operate a lot of buildings that many people see or visit every day. (2) These buildings tend to constitute a large percentage of the city's overall energy demand. And (3) new, improved, and more cost-effective ways of doing business—from healthier building materials to more resource-efficient heating, cooling, and lighting technologies—have been emerging at a steady rate over the past fifteen years.

According to the US Energy Information Administration, buildings account for 73 percent of electricity use in the United States, 41 percent of overall energy use, and 38 percent of carbon emissions.[4] These percentages can be higher at the local scale, especially in hotter cities and in cities where fossil fuels are the predominant source of electricity. Green buildings, though, typically use 26 percent less energy, produce 33 percent fewer carbon emissions, have 13 percent lower maintenance costs, and have 27 percent higher occupant satisfaction rates.[5] As for economic benefits, a 2008 analysis by McGraw-Hill Construction found that green buildings show a 6.6 percent improvement in return on investment compared with conventional buildings, 8–9 percent lower operating costs, 7.5 percent higher property values, and 3.5 percent higher average occupancy rates.

By systematically and aggressively greening their own portfolios of new and existing buildings, cities can save money—if not right away, over time—and create healthier environments for those who visit or work in the buildings, which often leads to increased productivity and morale. Greener buildings also produce less waste and conserve more energy and water, and they can help jump-start the local green building industry. A 2008 study by Booz Allen Hamilton and the US Green Building Council estimated that the green building industry would support nearly 8 million jobs and contribute $554 billion to gross domestic product in the United States between 2009 and 2012, despite the economic downturn.[6]

With these data and trends in mind, dozens of North American municipalities have put programs in place to green new and existing city buildings. Many cities, following Seattle's lead, have made commitments to design and construct new buildings in accordance with strong green building standards. Many now are going well beyond the USGBC's LEED Silver rating—and indeed beyond the LEED program entirely. Some are experimenting with the concept of net zero buildings, as well as with the Living Building Challenge, widely considered to be the most strenuous green building standard in the world. Created and managed by the International Living Future Institute, the Living Building Challenge lays out performance-based standards in seven areas: site, water, energy, health, materials, equity, and beauty.[7]

Seattle, one community that is trying out this approach, launched its Living Building Pilot Program in 2009 to facilitate and expedite permitting and design review for "highly sustainable projects." The first pilot project under this new program was not a city-owned building but rather the Bullitt Center, the new headquarters for the Bullitt Foundation, which opened for business in late 2012. The six-story, 50,000-square-foot Bullitt Center could be the first commercial building in the world to be certified as a Living Building. It features a rooftop solar array that will generate as much energy as the building uses and a rainwater-harvesting system that will collect, store, and reuse all of the rainwater that falls on the building. In addition, it has composting toilets and inviting, accessible stairways that promote walking between floors. And it will serve as the anchor for an eco-district that

Figure 2.2. Bullitt Center rendition
Seattle's Bullitt Center aims to be the first large commercial building certified as a Living Building. Bullitt Foundation president Denis Hayes says it will function "like a forest of Douglas fir trees, getting its energy from the sun, soaking up the rainwater, and serving as an incredible public amenity."

is being planned for the surrounding neighborhood, which is just a ten- to fifteen-minute walk from downtown Seattle. "It was an old parking lot that spewed polluted storm water into Puget Sound," says Bullitt Foundation president and Earth Day cofounder Denis Hayes. "Now it will function like a forest of Douglas fir trees, getting its energy from the sun, soaking up the rainwater, and serving as an incredible public amenity."

At the same time that the green bar is being raised for the design and construction of new buildings, there is a big push under way to increase the energy efficiency of existing buildings in cities, which constitute the vast majority of buildings and tend to be relatively old and inefficient. Some cities have hired resource conservation managers to lead systematic efforts to drive down energy use in city government buildings, while others have initiated large-scale, multimillion-dollar initiatives to install more energy-efficient technologies in public buildings and facilities. The City of Houston, for example, is in the middle of one of the largest municipal building energy retrofitting programs in North America as part of a broader strategy to transform the city from an energy production capital to an energy conservation capital. With help from utility company rebates that incentivize large energy users to choose more energy-efficient appliances and technologies, the city changed out 17,000 lighting fixtures in 62 municipal buildings, saving an estimated $465,000 annually. Now the city is busy retrofitting all of its buildings, more than 270 in all, totaling 8 million square feet and including city hall, the municipal court, 100 fire stations, 81 police stations, 40 libraries, and 34 health care facilities.

With support from the Clinton Climate Initiative and the C40 Cities Climate Leadership Group, a network of megacities committed to addressing climate change, Houston hired two large energy service companies under multiyear contracts to provide a full range of services, from investment-grade audits to the design, construction, and monitoring of specific energy efficiency improvements—including upgrades to heating, ventilation, and air-conditioning systems and lighting systems, installation of energy management systems, and water conservation measures. By 2012, the city had retrofitted 80 buildings, about one-third of the total goal. This project is expected to generate millions of dollars in annual cost savings while shaving about 68,000 tons of greenhouse gas emissions per year off the city's own carbon footprint.[8]

Houston is a hot city with a lot of buildings that require air-conditioning, so the business case for energy retrofitting is strong and clear. "The city buys 140 megawatts of energy a year, and all of it on the open market," says Laura Spanjian, Houston's sustainability director. "So for us doing this project makes huge sense." Spanjian and her team have branched out to encourage energy efficiency improvements in commercial buildings throughout the city through their Houston Green Office Challenge and Energy Efficiency Incentive Program, as well as their participation in the US Department

Figure 2.3. Houston wind power turbine
Houston's new one-stop permitting center, an old warehouse transformed into the LEED Gold–certified Green Building Resource Center, is the nation's largest. It will showcase innovative green city solutions, including four urban wind turbine technologies.

of Energy's Better Buildings Challenge, which provides technical assistance for energy efficiency initiatives.

Two other large public sector energy users in Houston—the school district and the regional transit agency—have also launched large-scale building energy efficiency programs, in large part inspired by and modeled on the city's program. Both have received lots of encouragement, support, and direct assistance from the city. "These are large government agencies, with a lot of square footage and a lot of older, inefficient buildings, that have seen our success and are doing something similar—providing a lot of low-hanging fruit," says Spanjian.

Cities from Portland, Oregon, to Kansas City, Missouri, to North Charleston, South Carolina, are also looking beyond single buildings and working to green entire blocks, neighborhoods, and districts. In Denver, Colorado, a nonprofit organization called Living City Block is partnering with the city, local and national businesses, and other nonprofits on a demonstration project to turn two blocks in the historic Lower Downtown district into "a working model of how one block within an existing city can be transformed into a paradigm for the new urban landscape."[9] The focus is on forging a collaboration among all owners of the seventeen buildings in the district (sixteen of which are historic buildings), including a mix of affordable and high-end market-rate rental housing, condominiums, commercial offices, and retail shops. The goal is to reduce their collective energy use by 50 percent in the first two years of the project and by 75 percent by the summer of 2015. By 2016, at least two of the historic buildings in the demonstration area are expected to reach the net zero energy goal.

In Fort Collins, a public-private-nonprofit partnership including the city, Fort Collins Utilities, Colorado State University, and a number of local employers and clean energy companies is working to turn a section of the city, dubbed FortZED, into a zero-energy district that over time produces at least as much energy as it consumes. They are well on their way. In the summer of 2011, five participating employers, including the New Belgium Brewing Company, managed to reduce their consumption of peak-load energy from the grid by more than 20 percent during a four-week trial run, thanks to a combination of on-site generation of solar power and energy conservation measures informed by real-time energy use data provided by newly installed smart meters.

Austin, Texas, is also focused on more holistic, integrated, district-scale development. Block 21 is a large LEED-rated redevelopment project across the street from Austin's city hall, including a W Hotel and condominium tower and a new home for *Austin City Limits*, the iconic live music program. The Mueller neighborhood is a green redevelopment of a twenty-acre site that was an airport and that will feature, among other things, mixed-use housing, plentiful open space and trails, and a LEED Platinum–rated children's hospital. The Pecan Street Project features large-scale rooftop solar installations, charging infrastructure for one hundred electric vehicles, and state-of-the-art smart grid technologies.

"This is the next wave," Austin's Chief Sustainability Officer Lucia Athens says of these large, complex redevelopment projects. "There are huge opportunities for district-scale work, but it's just so overwhelming. As soon as you start talking about crossing property lines, you end up with challenges. By and large, we're really not very good at doing large-scale infrastructure planning that's truly integrated—that looks at all the infrastructure systems in an integrated fashion. Instead, we're still trying to solve problems building by building."

New tools are available to guide efforts to green whole neighborhoods or districts. The USGBC's LEED for Neighborhood Development rating system, for example, integrates the principles of smart growth, urbanism, and green building into a national system for neighborhood design, and the EcoDistricts Framework, developed by the Portland Sustainability Institute, focuses on the district as an important scale for building green communities. These initiatives go well beyond the greening of city facilities, involving privately owned land and partnerships between public, private, and nonprofit sector stakeholders; they are described in more detail in chapter 3.

Greening Streets, Alleys, and Infrastructure

Many people are surprised to learn that streets, alleys, and public rights-of-way constitute a significant percentage of the landmass in cities—20 percent or more in many large and midsize cities—making the design, construction, and management of these facilities another huge leverage point for green city leaders. The percentage of land devoted to streets is 30 percent in New York City; 26 percent in San Francisco; 25 percent in St. Louis, Missouri; 24 percent in Miami and Chicago; and 20 percent in Milwaukee.[10] So decisions about how wide and straight streets are, what materials are used for paving, and how the streets are used, cleaned, and lit make a big difference. City governments have a great deal of influence and control over these decisions, both through the direct investments they make in designing, building, and maintaining city-owned streets and alleys and through policies that guide and regulate the design, construction, and use of city streets by private developers and property owners.

Conventional approaches to designing, building, and managing streets and public rights-of-way have proved problematic because they have focused mostly on moving motor vehicles quickly and efficiently, which can create unsafe and unpleasant conditions for people walking, biking, or taking the train or bus—the greenest modes of travel.

As a result, many cities across North America are rethinking, reimagining, and reinventing their streets to save money, protect water quality and aquatic habitat, reduce carbon emissions, and create healthier and more beautiful public places and spaces. The proliferation of "complete streets" policies and programs is one indicator of the transformation that is under way. In recent years, more than 350 cities, counties, regions, and states have adopted complete streets policies, which "formalize a community's intent to plan, design, operate and maintain streets so they are safe for all users of all ages and abilities" and "direct decision makers to consistently fund, plan for, design and construct community streets to accommodate all anticipated users, including pedestrians, bicyclists, public transportation users, motorists and freight vehicles."[11] New York City's Sustainable Streets plan, one of the most comprehensive efforts in rethinking and retrofitting urban streets, is discussed in chapter 3.

In addition, many cities are experimenting with greener paving materials such as permeable pavement, which allows rain to filter into the ground, providing for a more natural water cycle. (See, for example, "Case in Point: Permeable Pavement and the Green Alley Program in Chicago" in chapter 4.) Other cities are increasing the frequency of street cleaning to reduce the runoff of polluted rainwater into urban waterways and converting their street sweeper fleets to use cleaner fuels, such as compressed natural gas.

Street lighting can consume a lot of energy and be a public safety concern and maintenance headache. Greening of streetlights presents a big opportunity for reducing energy consumption and saving money while improving public safety and neighborhood quality of life. In Los Angeles, green city leaders are implementing the most extensive green streetlight retrofit initiative in North America, with a goal of replacing all 140,000 of the city's streetlights with more energy-efficient and otherwise superior light-emitting diode (LED) bulbs.

Launched in 2008 and dubbed Bright Lights, Safe Nights, the LED Energy Efficiency Program of the City of Los Angeles is a collaboration between the city's Department of Public Works and Department of Water and Power and the C40. As of July 2012, nearly 92,000 streetlights had been converted to LED lights, saving the city more than $3.8 million a year, reducing energy use by 61 percent, and avoiding more than 25,000 tons a year of greenhouse gas emissions.[12]

But perhaps the most significant transformation occurring on the streets of many North American cities has to do not with the streets' role in managing traffic but with their role in managing rain. The fact that streets, roads, alleys, and sidewalks have been paved with asphalt and concrete has wreaked havoc on the natural hydrologic cycle in cities. These hard, impervious surfaces prevent the replenishment of groundwater aquifers and send large volumes of storm water rushing into the nearest creek, lake, or estuary, where it can wipe out habitats for fish and degrade water quality. Moreover, conventional approaches—including the paving and repaving of streets and initiatives to manage flooding, erosion, and the pollution of creeks, streams, rivers, lakes, and estuaries—are expensive to build and maintain.

Many cities are working to convert their streets—historically the prime purveyors of urban water pollution—into critical components of a new green storm-water infrastructure. Cities are moving away from the traditional "pipe to pond" approach that has proven so costly to urban environments and municipal budgets. Instead, cities are capturing and treating rain where it falls by means of green roofs, green walls, and green streets, which are made with permeable pavement and flanked by engineered wetlands called bioswales that capture and filter most of the water on-site. Programs are under way in many cities, including Chicago, Philadelphia (see "Case in Point: Sewer Overflows and Sustainable Infrastructure in Philadelphia" in chapter 3), Milwaukee, and Seattle.

Through its Natural Drainage Systems strategy, Seattle was one of the first US cities to begin experimenting, in the late 1900s and early 2000s, with what was then considered a radical redesign of urban streets. Some streets were narrowed and curved slightly, using less paving material, leaving more room for drainage, and making them safer for walking and biking by calming car traffic. These streets were flanked on both sides not by conventional curb-and-gutter drainage systems but by wide swaths of greenery—heavily vegetated swales that soak up rainwater as well as greening and beautifying neighborhoods.

Seattle Public Utilities, a municipal water and waste utility with responsibility for protecting urban water quality, led the effort, beginning with a pilot project dubbed the Street Edge Alternatives Project (SEA Streets), along a single block in Northwest Seattle. This neighborhood is in a relatively new part of the city that, much to the chagrin of residents, lacked a formal drainage system with sidewalks, curbs, and storm drains. As a result, runoff was dumped directly into nearby Piper's Creek, one of five remaining urban creeks. Initially, opposition to the natural drainage pilot project was intense, both inside and outside city government. Stakeholders worried that it wouldn't work and that roads and property would continue to flood, and there was concern that fire trucks couldn't navigate the narrower, more curvaceous streets.

"People were also nervous about the cost and effectiveness of this new technology and about sidewalks that looked like they were paved with Rice Krispies," says Ray Hoffman, then special assistant to the mayor for environmental initiatives and now director of Seattle Public Utilities. But Hoffman and other green city leaders worked intensively with stakeholders, establishing an interdepartmental team that worked with residents throughout the design and construction process. And in the end, SEA Streets was beloved by the neighbors, who report that the street design has lured them into spending more time outdoors walking and getting to know one another. There are indications that property values have increased, and a study is under way.

An independent analysis of SEA Streets by water quality experts at the University of Washington found that the street design reduced runoff by 99 percent and at a lower cost to ratepayers—$325,000 per block, compared with $425,000 for a traditional street.[13] On the basis of this success, the city scaled up the initiative, using the natural drainage approach with larger projects, including the fifteen-block Broadview Green Grid Project and a huge 120-acre redevelopment in the High Point neighborhood on a site owned by the Seattle Housing Authority. Natural drainage was also used in denser neighborhoods, including the Swale on Yale project in the Capitol Hill neighborhood, just north of the downtown core.

Today, green storm-water infrastructure has become a central component of Seattle's overall strategy for managing rainwater and combined sewer overflows. In addition, the city has developed a number of programs to encourage residents and businesses to implement green infrastructure solutions on their own properties, including reduced drainage rates for property owners who install permeable pavement and rainwater capture-and-reuse systems. In addition, a program called RainWise provides technical assistance and financial incentives to residents who plant rain gardens and trees and install cisterns and porous pavement. "Ten years ago green infrastructure was an experiment—now it is a standard part of what we do," says Hoffman.

Figure 2.4. Seattle green infrastructure
Green infrastructure is a central component of Seattle's strategy for managing rainwater and combined sewer overflows. The city offers reduced drainage rates and other incentives for property owners who install permeable pavement and rainwater capture-and-reuse systems.

Greening City Fleets

City governments historically have owned and operated relatively large fleets of cars and trucks to provide convenient transportation for employees conducting city business. Greening these fleets—from the smaller vehicles that employees use to attend meetings, read water meters, and conduct building inspections to the larger vehicles that troll city neighborhoods picking up trash and recyclable materials—is one of the best opportunities that city governments have to improve air quality while saving taxpayers money, bolstering local markets for greener vehicles and fuels, and reducing greenhouse gas emissions. Transportation-related carbon emissions account for nearly 30 percent of the US total, according to the US Environmental Protection Agency (EPA), and about 80 percent of those emissions are from cars and trucks. In most cities, on-road vehicles are one of the top sources of air and climate pollution, and they are a major contributor to water and noise pollution as well.

Because municipal fleets are relatively large (1,000 to 4,000 vehicles in midsize and large cities) and visible in the community, green city fleets can inspire residents, business owners, and managers of other large government or corporate fleets to follow suit. "For fleet managers, the world has changed drastically over the past decade," Elisa Durand wrote on *Government Fleet* magazine's website in October 2011. "Whether you are managing a municipal, city, state, or non-governmental fleet, the demand for increased sustainability and cost reduction is a looming new social and corporate mandate that's here to stay."[14]

The City of Houston has been systematically greening its fleet as part of a broader effort to brand itself as a green city. About half of its 1,600 cars, for example, are now hybrid gas-electric or all-electric vehicles. Most recently, the city entered into a partnership with the national membership-based car-sharing company Zipcar to launch the innovative Houston Fleet Share program, which has outfitted fifty city vehicles, including twenty-five all-electric Nissan Leaf vehicles, with Zipcar's fleet-sharing technology, allowing city employees to go online and reserve a car for immediate or later use. By allowing a smaller number of vehicles to be shared more efficiently and broadly by city employees, the program saves fuel, energy, and money; reduces air and climate pollution; and bolsters the local electric vehicle (EV) industry. More than 200 EV charging stations have been installed throughout the city, thanks in large part to partnerships with several local companies, the US Department of Energy, and ECOtality.[15]

The range of strategies cities are employing to green their vehicle fleets includes using these kinds of management efficiencies to reduce emissions and costs as well as downsizing and rightsizing fleets and transitioning to greener vehicles and fuels.

Downsizing. Many cities are reducing the number of vehicles in their fleets by retiring old, underutilized vehicles; encouraging employees to walk, bike, or take public transportation; and shifting to car-sharing services. Philadelphia, Pennsylvania, was the first city in North America to try car sharing when it entered into a partnership in 2004 with a local nonprofit organization called PhillyCarShare. The move allowed the city to reduce its fleet by 330 vehicles, saving more than $1 million annually in fuel, maintenance, insurance, and parking costs. In 2009, Washington, DC, became the first city to partner with Zipcar and use its technology to manage the city's fleet more efficiently. Many cities, including New York, Chicago, Boston, and Houston, followed suit.

Rightsizing. Many cities also are working to rightsize their fleets and vehicles by purchasing "the right vehicle for the right job" and encouraging employees to use the most fuel-efficient and lowest-impact mode of transportation possible for the task at hand. For example, city employees in Seattle, Chicago, and other cities use personal mobility devices—such as Segways—when reading meters and collecting parking fees. And many cities, including Vancouver, British Columbia, now have bikes available for employees who need to travel relatively short distances.

Purchasing greener vehicles and fuels. Many cities are purchasing greener vehicles for their fleets and requiring cleaner vehicles and fuels when negotiating large city contracts for garbage-hauling and construction projects. For example, by 2012, half of Seattle's fleet of more than 3,000 cars and trucks consisted of advanced technology vehicles, including more than 200 hybrid gas-electric cars such as the Toyota Prius, more than 40 all-electric vehicles such as the Nissan Leaf, and a number of diesel-electric trucks. Denver was one of the first US cities to purchase hybrid hydraulic trash trucks, which are 25–50 percent more efficient than conventional trucks. Half of the 3,500 vehicles in Denver's fleet are alternatively powered—hybrid gas-electric, compressed natural gas, biodiesel, or electric—including the hybrid gas-electric FREE MallRide shuttles that whisk residents and tourists around the 16th Street Mall, which is otherwise closed to vehicle traffic.

Improving operational efficiencies. Using city vehicles sparingly and efficiently is fundamental to green fleet management. Sacramento, California, and Columbus, Ohio, are installing advanced global positioning system (GPS) technology in city vehicles to make driving more efficient. Many cities have established policies and employee education campaigns to raise awareness about vehicle choices, the increased air pollution and fuel consumption that result from unnecessary vehicle idling, and other ways to "drive smart." Chris Wiley, the City of Seattle's green fleet coordinator, says, "A lot of our fuel reductions have come from operational efficiencies—better route-planning and getting departments to share vehicles and facilities. We've seen a real sea-change in employees' attitudes and behavior."

Vehicle and fuel technologies are advancing rapidly, making it tricky to decide which types of vehicles and fuels to buy. In the 1980s, Seattle and many other cities invested heavily in compressed natural gas—purchasing cars and building fueling infrastructure—only to find that these cars were hard to come by when manufacturers chose other technologies. Similarly, many cities that were early adopters of first-generation biodiesel ran into a series of setbacks ranging from engine problems to spiking prices to serious questions about the emissions benefits of the fuel.

Seattle moved away from soy-based biodiesel altogether in 2010 because of rising prices, concerns about the impact on food supplies, and an EPA report concluding that

carbon reductions were much lower than previously believed. Instead, the city began testing biodiesel made from used cooking oil and became an anchor customer for General
Biodiesel, a local startup company that partners with local restaurants and other food
service establishments. The company collects used cooking oil and converts it into one
of the lowest-carbon fuels available—with an 85 percent reduction in life-cycle carbon
dioxide emissions compared with conventional petroleum diesel.

Greening City Purchasing

In the early 1990s, a number of cities grew increasingly worried about the potential adverse health and environmental effects of the cleaning products they were buying and
using in schools, parks, and other public buildings, so they began looking for alternatives.
They didn't find much. A handful of cities—including Santa Monica, San Francisco, Seattle, and Portland—started developing their own definitions and standards for green cleaning products, "causing chaos and confusion among manufacturers and suppliers," recalls
Scot Case, a national expert on green purchasing and director of market development at
UL Environment, a company that supports the development and use of environmentally
safe products and services.

Case was working for the nonprofit Center for a New American Dream at the time,
and he brought together a number of cities and counties, formed the Responsible Purchasing Network, and facilitated the development and use of a common set of criteria for
green cleaning products. "Once that happened, the industry had a consistent definition
to work with and was able to reformulate products to meet that definition," Case says.
"Government purchasing drastically changed the entire cleaning products industry. I am
convinced that it's possible now for me to go to my local grocery store and buy a greener
cleaning product because ten or twelve years ago city and county governments started
demanding those products."

Government purchasing is a large part of the economy—about 20 percent is directly
tied to government purchases, according to Case. By harnessing that formidable "power of
the purse," cities—working individually and together with other cities, counties, and state
governments—can save money, create healthier and safer environments for their workers
and for the community, and bolster the supply of cleaner, healthier, and safer products
and services for everybody. Green purchasing means buying products that have less impact on health and the environment but that perform as well as or better than conventional products and cost about the same. Green products may be recyclable or made with
a high percentage of recycled-content material, they may be made using renewable energy
sources, and they may be made locally and responsibly. Green products are designed to be
durable and so that they can be managed safely and responsibly at the end of their useful

life. Potential benefits include saving money; reducing waste, energy consumption, and greenhouse gas emissions; and keeping money circulating in the local economy.

The best green purchasing initiatives are often stand-alone programs that are well integrated into related efforts, such as greening city buildings by buying Forest Stewardship Council–certified wood, energy-efficient windows, and low- or no-emission paints; greening fleets by purchasing cleaner vehicles and fuels; and greening city power supplies by buying less fossil fuels and renewable energy. The goal of San Francisco's green purchasing initiative, one of the most comprehensive and effective in North America, is to lead by example, protect the health of employees and customers, and drive the marketplace by promoting innovative green products.[16] Unhappy with the lack of information about the chemical content of many products used by the city, San Francisco's green city leaders created SF Approved, a preapproved list of more than 1,000 products that met strict health, environmental, energy, and cost performance criteria laid out in the city's groundbreaking 2005 Precautionary Purchasing Ordinance. SF Approved was originally intended only as a guide for city department purchasers, but in 2010 the San Francisco Department of the Environment took the unprecedented step of launching a website, www.SFApproved.org, where the information could be shared with other communities and the general public. "There are 80,000 chemicals in the marketplace today for which we have inadequate data sets on toxicity," Chris Geiger, San Francisco's green purchasing program manager, said at the time of the launch. "As a city, we believe that if there's a safer alternative we should know what it is, and we should use it."

The city has engaged staff in the selection of product categories and the development of product specifications and has created an online Buy Green Scorecard to track the participation of departments and promote a friendly cross-departmental competition to bolster participation and accountability. "That has been really critical to getting adoption of the program and buy-in from city staff," says Melanie Nutter, director of the San Francisco Department of the Environment (SF Environment). "We've got the support of the ordinance and the mandate, but we also invest in ensuring that city staff understand the program, and we offer incentives for participation. That's key to compliance."

The amount of green products the city purchases increased from 80 percent in 2009 to 91 percent in 2010, Nutter says, adding that 99 percent of the office paper purchased by the city in 2010 was green (the paper was chlorine free and made of 100 percent recycled materials)—as were 80 percent of the janitorial products and 79 percent of the lighting fixtures. In addition, 81 percent of computers purchased were certified as being more energy efficient and easier to recycle.

When Apple, one of the world's most profitable and powerful companies, announced in July 2012 that it was withdrawing its products from the leading green electronics registry EPEAT (Electronic Product Environmental Assessment Tool), the City of San Francisco announced it could no longer purchase Apple's popular iPhones, iPads, and Macintosh computers. The city's green purchasing policy mandates that the city buy only products that have achieved a Gold rating—the highest—from EPEAT, unless staff go through a cumbersome process to get a waiver. Other major customers also expressed disappointment with Apple, and several days later the company announced it would reregister its products. "That was a really clear demonstration of the impact municipal purchasing policies can have at the national and even international level," Nutter says.

Transforming the way cities buy goods and services is no easy task. "Getting the buy-in of our custodial staff was a huge hurdle," says Dean Kubani, director of Santa Monica's Office of Sustainability and the Environment. "The janitors worried that if it didn't smell like a powerful chemical, it probably wouldn't work and would make their jobs harder." Kubani and his team were successful in convincing the custodial staff that green products were safer to use, and he worked with them to test alternatives and develop new specifications for products that would be both safe and effective.

But if skepticism is one hurdle to negotiate, another is concern about costs. It is especially hard for cities to justify paying more for green products when budgets are tight, an increasingly common state of affairs. Many cities, following San Francisco's example, are trying to better understand the life-cycle costs of products—the total cost of ownership—and to factor that into purchasing decisions. But this type of analysis isn't yet common.

Another challenge is the fact that city purchasing tends to be decentralized, making coordination, enforcement, and accountability difficult. Few cities have the staff expertise, time, or money to determine what's green and what's not. A range of helpful third-party labeling and certification programs have emerged in recent years, including LEED for buildings, EPEAT for computers and other electronic devices, the Forest Stewardship Council for lumber and other building products, Energy Star for appliances and buildings, and Green Seal for a range of common products such as janitorial cleaners and paints. But the proliferation of these programs can be downright dizzying for purchasing staffs, and there's conflicting and confusing information as well as significant gaps.

A number of networks and resource organizations have emerged to help cities meet the challenges. The Responsible Purchasing Network, a large network of buyers who promote socially and environmentally friendly products and services, provides a range of resources, including calculators that measure the environmental benefits and cost savings of green products and a model responsible-purchasing reporting template. The British Columbia–based BuySmart Network supports Canadian organizations seeking to green their procurement practices through training workshops, technical assistance, and other services. The National Association of Counties, in conjunction with other partners—the

Responsible Purchasing Network, the U.S. Communities Government Purchasing Alliance, and the nonprofit Green Seal—created and maintains a green purchasing tool kit, an interactive web-based resource that, among other things, shares innovative practices in local government green purchasing.

Thanks in part to programs such as these, green purchasing initiatives have progressed a great deal, from a relatively narrow focus on recycled paper by a few cities in the 1980s and 1990s to much more sophisticated and comprehensive approaches, including products ranging from graffiti removers to street-cleaning detergents; take-back provisions that require manufacturers to collect and dispose of their products at the end of their life cycle; and purchase power agreements such as solar rooftop leases that allow cities to buy solar power but not the panels that produce it.

Greening City Power

With the not-so-simple stroke of a pen on Earth Day 2000, the City of Seattle made a green power pledge that in the coming decade would trigger a series of decisions and investments that saved homeowners and businesses millions of dollars, significantly shrank the community's carbon footprint, helped close the largest coal plant in Washington State, and jump-started the clean energy industry in the Puget Sound region and beyond. On that day, the Seattle City Council unanimously passed a resolution directing Seattle City Light, the utility serving 370,000 residential, commercial, and industrial customers in the central Puget Sound region, to achieve net zero emissions of greenhouse gases within five years.

To be sure, Seattle had a head start because nearly 90 percent of the city's electricity was already produced by clean hydropower rather than from fossil fuels. Still, getting to zero required a concerted effort and an innovative mix of strategies, including ending the purchase of coal-powered electricity, significantly increasing its investment in wind power and energy efficiency, and purchasing carbon offsets for the small percentage of emissions it was unable to eliminate. In November 2005, a little more than five years after the Earth Day resolution, Mayor Greg Nickels announced that Seattle City Light had reached the net zero emissions target, saying, "We have a fundamental belief that we can power the city without toasting the planet."

In 2010, about ten years after the net zero emissions pledge, the State of Washington and the owners of TransAlta's coal-fired power plant in Centralia, Washington—the largest in the state—reached an agreement to shut the plant down. "It all started with the city's commitment," says KC Golden, policy director at the nonprofit Climate Solutions and a leading advocate for clean energy in the Pacific Northwest and nationally. "People started seeing renewable energy coming on line, and they started seeing other ways we could meet our energy needs and grow our economy. At the end of the day, everybody from the shop steward at the plant to the chamber of commerce to the governor was ready to say, 'We can do better than that.'"

Cities use about three-quarters of the world's energy. The burning of fossil fuels for electricity alone accounts for 40 percent of the carbon dioxide emitted in the United States, and it's the single largest source of industrial air pollution, contributing to everything from smog to acid rain. In addition, fossil fuel prices are volatile, and the lingering uncertainty about future emission regulations creates additional financial risk. So greening municipal energy supplies—transitioning toward renewable sources such as wind, solar, biomass, biogas, geothermal, and low-impact hydropower—represents a big opportunity for green city leaders to reduce health, environmental, and financial risks and help promote sustainable economic development, including local green businesses and jobs. Converting to green power also supports national goals to increase energy independence and security.

Cities throughout North America are seizing this opportunity by setting ambitious renewable energy goals for their governments and their communities and increasing their own commitment to green power, either by purchasing green power directly from the utilities that service them or by buying renewable energy credits (RECs) that promote the development of green energy elsewhere. Some cities are producing renewable energy themselves by installing solar panels on city buildings or facilities such as wastewater treatment plants, for example, and encouraging residents and businesses to do the same.

Some cities, including Seattle and Austin, own the utilities that produce and distribute electricity to their residents and businesses, but most cities purchase electricity from privately owned utilities. A growing number of those cities are pushing their electricity providers to transition to cleaner and greener energy sources, such as wind power, by adopting ambitious green power goals. For example, Ann Arbor, Michigan, set a goal of meeting 30 percent of its energy needs from renewable sources by 2010; Philadelphia wants to purchase and generate 20 percent of the city's electricity from alternative energy sources; and Boston set a goal of meeting 15 percent of its needs with renewable energy by 2012.

Calgary, Alberta, has perhaps the most ambitious municipal green power program in North America. The city set and then met a goal to transition from heavy reliance on fossil fuels to 100 percent renewable energy by 2012, through a long-term fixed-price contract with its electricity provider. In 2002, the city developed the continent's first 100 percent wind-powered public transit system, a light-rail train service dubbed "Ride the Wind." In 2004, the city council adopted the City of Calgary Corporate Climate Change Program Action Plan, which included the 100 percent renewable energy goal. At the time, the city's purchase of 350 million kilowatt-hours of mostly coal-based electricity per year accounted for about 60 percent of Calgary's overall carbon footprint.

In 2009, the city struck a twenty-year, $250 million deal with ENMAX Corporation, the local natural gas and electricity company, requiring that at least 75 percent of the city's electricity come from green power by 2010, increasing to 100 percent by 2012. To meet the agreement, ENMAX built a $140 million, 80-megawatt wind power facility in Taber, Alberta, about 120 miles southeast of Calgary. "The Taber Wind Farm is . . . a great example of our government and industry working together," Canadian parliamentarian Bob Mills said when the facility opened in October 2007. "These collaborations are important if we want to achieve our goal, which is supplying clean, renewable energy to all Canadians."[17]

Many other cities, following Calgary's lead, are increasing the pressure on privately owned electricity providers to green their supplies, and in some cases they are turning to alternatives when those demands aren't met. The City of Boulder, Colorado, for example, is in the process of creating a new municipal utility, partly because the city wants to move more quickly toward its green power goals than the current electricity provider is willing to do.[18]

Cities are also greening their power supplies by purchasing certified RECs, especially in places where green power is not locally available. An REC represents proof that 1 megawatt-hour of electricity was generated from an eligible renewable energy resource. It can be sold, traded, or bartered so that the owner can claim to have purchased renewable energy. Houston is the largest municipal buyer of green power, according to the EPA. The city is purchasing 438 million megawatt-hours of electricity—about 35 percent of its total energy use—from wind power generated in the state of Texas. Green city leaders in Houston had two main motivations: an interest in greening their energy supply and an interest in supporting their state's fast-growing wind industry, the largest in the United States. "We thought, here's this rich, renewable resource right here in our state, and it's cost-competitive. So why not take advantage of that?" says Houston's sustainability director, Laura Spanjian, noting that wind power has become only slightly more costly than the conventional power the city was buying from its investor-owned energy provider. Now Austin and Dallas have followed Houston's lead, and these three Texas cities are the top three municipal green power purchasers in the United States.[19]

Smaller communities are getting into the act as well, pooling their purchasing power to get green power and drive down costs. In New York State, for example, fifty-six municipalities have come together to aggregate their demand and buy wind power at reduced rates. In 2007, the New York State Municipal Wind Buyers Group was purchasing 32 million kilowatt-hours' worth of RECs annually, about 20 percent of the group's total energy demand.

A growing number of cities are producing renewable energy for themselves at city facilities, by either buying a system outright or installing a system owned by a third party and then buying the electricity that system generates. On-site generation enhances the reliability and often the quality of the power supply, protects the city from price volatility, and provides a visible demonstration of leadership. The City of Milwaukee installed a 31.5-kilowatt solar system on top of the 30,000-square-foot roof of the Milwaukee Public Library, which generates about 40,000 kilowatt-hours annually—about 10 percent of the overall electricity needs for that building. The project is one component of Milwaukee Shines, a comprehensive program to increase the adoption of solar power citywide, which includes an educational program for residential and commercial consumers, access to low-interest financing, and streamlined permitting. It is part of a broader, multifaceted initiative to reduce the city government's energy use by 15 percent.[20] Similarly, as part of Greenworks Philadelphia, the Philadelphia Water Department installed a 250-kilowatt solar array at its Southeast Wastewater Treatment Plant. The system produces enough electricity each month to power thirty-two typical Pennsylvania homes.[21]

A number of cities that are greening their own power supplies are actively encouraging their residents and businesses to do the same. Boston Buying Power, for example, is a city program designed to help small local businesses such as restaurants, dry cleaners, nightclubs, colleges, and health-care facilities reduce their energy consumption and costs by aggregating their demand.[22] Philadelphia and other cities have similar programs, and more than thirty US cities and towns are participating in the EPA's Green Power Communities program, which helps organize community-wide green power campaigns to encourage local businesses and residents to buy or produce green power, with technical assistance and recognition from the EPA. Collectively, these communities are buying more than 4 billion kilowatt-hours of green power annually, enough to produce electricity for 367,000 average American homes.[23]

More and more cities are exploring Community Choice Aggregation, a tool that allows cities and counties to aggregate the buying power of individual customers to secure alternative energy supply contracts. The City of Cincinnati, for example, pooled the buying power of 53,000 households and small businesses and put out a request for proposals from electricity providers to serve that demand. The contract was awarded not to the city's existing electricity provider, Duke Energy, but to FirstEnergy Solutions, which committed to providing participating households and businesses with 100 percent green power at an average annual cost savings of $133.

A number of cities are systematically trying to green power supplies with economic development strategies. San Antonio's Mission Verde plan, for example, is an energy and economic development strategy that combines the city's green power purchases with policy incentives to attract renewable energy manufacturers and related companies to the city. (See "Case in Point: Growing Green Businesses and Jobs in San Antonio" in chapter 5.) The City of Knoxville, with help from the US Department of Energy's Solar America Cities program, is investing heavily in solar power and, in partnership with the Oak Ridge National Laboratory, the University of Tennessee, and the Knoxville Chamber, is actively recruiting green energy companies to the Knoxville–Oak Ridge Innovation Valley of East Tennessee. In 2011, the Brookings Institution rated Knoxville second in the nation for growth in green jobs.[24]

Ann Arbor, Michigan, has set a goal of meeting 30 percent of the city government's electricity demand with wind power generated by turbines manufactured in the state. Austin, Texas, buys green power from in-state producers, including solar power produced in San Antonio. "It really comes down to leadership, to mayors and city councils and departments of environment that see an opportunity to send a signal, to align the city's goals with those of the business sector," says Joel Makower, founder of GreenBiz.com. "We're seeing this in renewable energy, where government procurement by cities and states is helping to catalyze green energy markets, which in turn catalyze smaller businesses that help service those markets for the design, production, installation, repair, and maintenance of renewable energy systems."

Reducing City Waste

Municipal governments across North America are spending a lot of time, energy, and money on reducing the amount of garbage produced in their communities. Many are having significant success at increasing the recycling and composting of food and yard waste by providing convenient curbside collection; setting up drop-off centers for computers and other electronic devices that can be recycled rather than sent to landfills; and reducing construction debris by requiring that it be recycled. But reducing, recycling, and reusing waste produced by the city government itself has received less attention and has been less successful. There are, however, great opportunities for municipalities to lead by example, and while efforts to manage this waste may not yield significant reductions in tonnages, it sends a very important message to city employees, visitors to city facilities, and residents and businesses.

Construction and Maintenance Materials

Cities can produce significant financial and environmental benefits by reducing and recycling the debris left over from construction and maintenance projects rather than carting it off to landfills. Building and maintaining roads, bridges, sewers, and other urban infrastructure produces a large amount of waste, including concrete, asphalt, brick, sand, and soil—much of it clean and potentially reusable. Diverting these products from landfills makes good economic sense because landfill fees for construction and demolition debris tend to be high, and purchasing virgin materials such as concrete, which cities use in large quantities, is increasingly expensive.

Many cities are changing their ways—and getting good results. In Vancouver, British Columbia, for example, City Engineer Peter Judd understood the magnitude of this opportunity to reduce waste and save money, and he worked with the city's Streets Division to come up with a plan. "Instead of hauling concrete waste from work sites over thirty kilometers to the landfill, we started to take it to one of our work yards, which was much closer, where we ran it through a grinder to get it to the right size. We ended up creating a material that could replace new material." Judd says that the city reused 143,000 tons of concrete in the first year and 177,000 tons in the second year, reducing the amount of new material that the city needed to buy by 47 percent.

Vancouver saved $800,000 in the first year. "I was amazed at the innovative approach that our own crews took in order to save money and reduce the waste going into the landfill," Judd says, adding that the city also reduced carbon emissions by 1,100 tons in the second year of the project, an amount equal to taking 220 cars off the road. He says this approach also worked well for asphalt, and the city was able to reuse an additional 10,000 tons of recycled road grindings.

Landscaping Materials

Tree trimming and landscaping is another area that can produce significant cost savings and waste reductions. Each year, cities across North America send thousands of crews to trim the trees in parks and along streets, replant ornamental garden beds, and mow millions of acres of grass—activities that use a lot of gas and produce a lot of waste that ends up in landfills. To address this problem, some cities are creating "prairies" that don't require mowing, watering, weeding, or fertilizing, and they are switching from planting annuals that need to be replanted every year to perennials that come back every year without replanting. They are also using mulching mowers, which cut and broadcast the clippings or mulch them back into the grass. Cutting grass a little shorter can allow for less frequent mowing, which saves gas.

Tree trimming produces a very high volume of materials, and many cities are looking for ways to put this to good use rather than filling up landfills. The City of Vancouver's Greenest City Scholars Program is an innovative example. The city signed a memorandum of understanding with the University of British Columbia to send the tree trimmings collected by the city to the university free of charge for five years, for use in a new biomass gasification facility that heats campus buildings. This reduces the city's waste stream and the university's carbon footprint while producing electricity to offset energy purchases. In exchange, the university provides ten doctoral students to the city each summer to do research and analysis supporting the city's Greenest City 2020 Action Plan.

Office Paper

While not yielding as much savings or waste reduction as construction and tree trimming, reducing the city's consumption of paper is one of the easiest strategies to pursue at the start. There are a few simple ways to do this, such as setting all copiers and printers to print double-sided by default—passing a policy to require double-sided printing for all municipal operations can go a long way toward saving paper and money. Simply *not* printing documents in the first place can produce instant savings. For example, the Vancouver City Clerk's Office switched from automatically printing council reports for every meeting to providing copies only on request.

There also are easy strategies for reuse that can drastically reduce waste. These can be as simple as using recyclable batteries and using glasses and mugs instead of paper or plastic in city offices. More complex strategies can involve city suppliers. The City of Vancouver, for example, worked with its office supplies vendor so it could get deliveries in a reusable, instead of disposable, cardboard box.

Developing an effective and easy-to-use recycling program for city offices is one of the most important and visible actions to demonstrate a city's commitment to the environment. In September 2012, Vancouver began a new office recycling program with separate containers for organics, paper, plastic, and cans. By May 2013, city hall's waste diversion rate exceeded 88 percent, up from less than 20 percent in September. Yet recycling isn't as common as it should be, and most municipal office recycling programs in North America are woefully inadequate. Some cities are working to expand their programs, and a few even are developing programs to collect kitchen scraps.

The City of San Jose, California, learned that it's not enough to set up a recycling program—the program needs to be monitored. For example, when the city transitioned from having city employees do custodial work to contracting the work out, a waste audit found that the vendor was putting materials in the wrong containers. The city then had to work closely with the vendor to get the program back on track, educating the vendor's employees and changing to color-coded bags that made it clear which bags went into which dumpsters. The city also works hard to promote the program. They include a presentation about it during new employee orientations, they have created posters as well as a page on the city's intranet site, and the city's green team engages employees in the recycling program.

Conclusion

The common characteristics of successful green city programs, including leadership-by-example initiatives such as those described in this chapter, are discussed in more detail in chapter 4. But four tips to keep in mind are the following:

1. Focus, focus, focus.
2. Build shared ownership and responsibility.
3. Make bets—but hedge them.
4. Use the city budget process to advance the green city agenda.

Focus, Focus, Focus

Failure to focus is one of the easiest and most potentially debilitating mistakes that green city leaders can make. With typically broad mandates and a wide range of stakeholders to engage, it's easy for green city leaders to fall into the trap of trying to do too much, spreading themselves and their teams too thin, dissipating their energy and resources, and slowing their progress. Trying to do too much is a recipe for failure, especially in the context of intense competition for resources that tends to exist in city governments.

Getting a handle on the city's carbon footprint is an essential first step in understanding the challenges and opportunities and an important part of the priority-setting process. For many cities, the carbon footprint, or greenhouse gas emissions inventory, serves as a useful indicator of the city's overall environmental impact. In most cities,

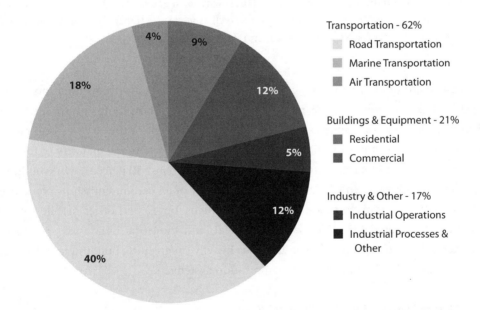

Figure 2.5a. Seattle's carbon emissions
For many cities, the carbon footprint, or greenhouse gas emissions inventory, is a useful indicator of the city's overall impact—and provides opportunities for leadership. In Seattle, transportation contributes about 60 percent of the city's carbon profile and buildings contribute 20 percent. Figure courtesy of the City of Seattle Office of Sustainability and Environment.

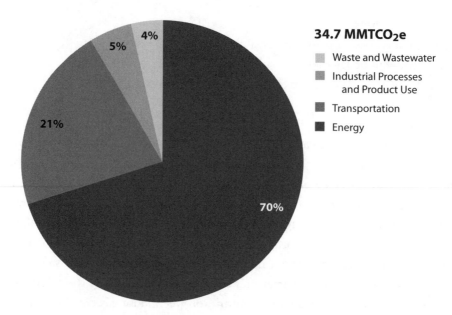

34.7 MMTCO$_2$e

▨ Waste and Wastewater

▨ Industrial Processes
   and Product Use

▪ Transportation

▪ Energy

Figure 2.5b. Chicago's carbon emissions
In Chicago, about 70 percent of all carbon emissions come from building energy use, with another 20 percent or so from transportation sources. This is why most green city agendas focus heavily on greening buildings and the built environment, as well as fleets and transportation systems. Figure courtesy of the Center for Neighborhood Technology (CNT).

the vast majority of carbon emissions come from buildings and transportation, which together typically constitute 75 percent or more of the carbon footprint. In Seattle, for example, transportation sources contribute about 60 percent of the city's carbon profile, and buildings contribute another 20 percent.[25] In Denver, where the majority of the electricity comes from fossil fuels, transportation contributes just 30 percent, while buildings represent 50 percent.[26] In Chicago, about 90 percent of all carbon emissions come from a combination of transportation sources (cars, trucks, buses, and other mobile sources) and the energy used in residential, commercial, and industrial buildings.[27] So it's not surprising that most green city agendas focus heavily on greening buildings and the built environment, as well as fleets and transportation systems.

Build Shared Ownership and Responsibility
One key to success for green city leaders and their teams is to avoid, at all costs, becoming the sole owner of all things green: the more that a sense of ownership and responsibility is shared across the government and the community, the better. One of the best strategies for building the requisite ownership and responsibility is to find and cultivate green

champions within and across departments—people with the expertise, experience, and passion for solving problems and finding solutions. It is critical to engage these champions, as well as elected officials, department directors, and key staff, in the process of setting priorities and developing and implementing solutions. Dennis Murphey, Kansas City's chief environmental officer, says that the development of the city's Climate Protection Plan "made city staff and community members realize that we could help *them* be successful. Whether they were focused on reducing greenhouse gas emissions or improving the financial bottom line or making Kansas City a more attractive place for young, creative people, they understood the plan could result in multiple benefits, and that brought more people under the tent."

Make Bets—but Hedge Them

It may be easier for municipal governments to take risks and experiment with new ideas than it is for state and federal governments, but that's not to say that it's easy. City actions and expenditures tend to come under a media microscope, and reporters like to play "Gotcha!" This can make elected officials and others in city government risk averse, lest some embarrassing failed experiment cost them their pride, political capital, or their jobs. So risks need to be carefully managed. In North Carolina, the City of Raleigh's leadership on electric vehicle (EV) infrastructure is a good example: green city leaders were well aware of the risks of being an early adopter of EV technology, but they worked to minimize and manage those risks by securing early and strong support from elected officials and the business community and by sharing ownership, responsibility, and risk across departments. (See "Case in Point: Greening City Fleets in Raleigh" in this chapter.)

Use the City Budget Process to Advance the Green City Agenda

Municipal budgets tend to be tight, short-term (usually one or two years), and developed through a fragmented, department-by-department process that engenders territoriality and discourages integrated solutions. There can be intense competition for limited discretionary funds, and if green city solutions entail up-front costs that can't be recovered within a single budget cycle, they are at a distinct disadvantage. Green city leaders need to find ways to transform the city's budget process from a challenge into an opportunity. (See chapter 5 for more on this topic.)

Successful efforts to lead by example share the following characteristics:

- They flow from, and are nested within, a broader green city framework that enjoys deep and wide support.
- They feature clear goals and targets and a system for regularly tracking and reporting on progress and for holding people accountable.

- They often start small—and then go to scale.
- They tend to be incubated, then integrated.
- They see the adoption of a policy as the beginning, not the end.
- They are sustained and consistently improved.
- They lead from the inside out.

They flow from, and are nested within, a broader green city framework that enjoys deep and wide support. The most successful "walking the talk" efforts don't come out of the blue but are part of an overarching framework or green city agenda. The best initiatives are (1) built in a highly collaborative way; (2) embedded in a citywide performance management system so that appropriate departments, directors, and staff are held accountable; and (3) integrated so that internally and externally focused initiatives are mutually supportive—for example, a municipal building efficiency retrofitting program that is tied to a local workforce training program.

They feature clear goals and targets and a system for regularly tracking and reporting on progress and for holding people accountable. Clear goals and targets are essential. Well-crafted "stretch goals" that are possible but not easy, such as Seattle City Light's goal of net zero emissions within five years, usually work best because they push the envelope without pushing anybody over the edge, thus inspiring action ("We can do it!") rather than resignation ("It will never work!"). Then progress needs to be tracked and reported, and people and agencies need to be held accountable for the results, because even artfully crafted goals are meaningless if they aren't systematically pursued. When it comes to green city agendas, what gets measured is what gets managed. This is especially important in a world in which responsibilities for implementation are highly decentralized. (See chapter 6 for more on this topic.)

They often start small—and then go to scale. As Seattle green city leader Ray Hoffman puts it: "When in doubt, pilot. The most important thing is to get your foot in the door." Starting small, showing early successes, and allowing stakeholders to get comfortable with new ideas is a good recipe for long-term success. "You start with the agencies that have some interest and some capacity, you help them achieve some success, and you go from there," says Jim Hunt, former chief of energy and environmental services for the City of Boston. "Success breeds success."

They tend to be incubated, then integrated. The most successful programs are often initiated and coordinated by a central environment or sustainability office but are soon embedded into the mission and work plan of the appropriate "line department," which takes responsibility for implementing it over the long term as well as tracking and reporting on progress. A key role of green city leaders is to be on the lookout for the best opportunity to get a new plan or program off the ground and then find a long-term home for the program, which may also entail helping the adoptive department secure the additional resources necessary to assume this new responsibility.

For example, Seattle's Clean and Green Fleet program was initiated and led by the city's Office of Sustainability and Environment (OSE) in partnership with the Fleets and Facilities Department (FFD), which manages 3,200 cars and trucks. Within two years primary responsibility for the program was transferred to the FFD, and the OSE worked through the city budget process to help the FFD secure additional resources to hire a green fleet coordinator.

They see the adoption of a policy as the beginning, not the end. There's no way around it—change is hard, and leadership-by-example initiatives that make it easy for city employees to understand and to participate tend to be the most successful. Santa Monica's green purchasing Easy Guides are a great example: they explain to employees in nontechnical terms the potentially negative health effects of conventional products and the benefits of greener alternatives, which are often verified by a third party. "We try to put it into human terms so that everybody from fleet managers to purchasing agents can understand the requirements and why they are important," says Shannon Parry, Santa Monica's deputy sustainability officer.

They are sustained and consistently improved. Green city leaders know that sitting on their laurels usually means losing ground and falling behind in the friendly race among cities to the great green top. The best green city initiatives are sustained over time—across budget and electoral cycles—and continually updated and improved. This is not likely to happen unless the initiative has been institutionalized in a city department and embraced as standard operating procedure so that city staff can no longer imagine doing it any other way. When the City of Seattle adopted its original Green Building Policy in 2002, for example, it was the first US city to do so. But several years later, Seattle found itself behind other cities in terms of the boldness of its policy and the robustness of its results. So in 2010 the city raised its bar, adopting a new policy that established more ambitious goals, including LEED Gold-Plus certification for new city buildings and a fresh set of strategies, including the ambitious Living Building Pilot Program discussed earlier.

They lead from the inside out. All of these initiatives demonstrate the art of starting where you are, doing what you can, getting some experience under your belt, and experiencing some success before taking the show on the road.

For example, green city leaders in Flagstaff, Arizona, decided to begin by focusing on the ways that climate change could affect the city's ability to deliver services and on how to better prepare for and manage these impacts. This allowed them to get something done in a shorter time frame (one year instead of three) and to gain the experience and capacity that they felt they needed to effectively engage their residents and businesses in a community-wide adaptation effort. (See "Case in Point: Assessing Climate Risk and Resilience in Flagstaff" in this chapter.)

"It's vital for cities to lead by example and to do things first," concludes Laura Spanjian, Houston's sustainability director. "It shows their credibility, it shows what can be done, and it shows leadership. And then you can take what you've done inside the city and start working with nonprofits and the private sector to convince the broader public to do some of the things you've already been doing. Almost everything we've done—from energy-efficient buildings to electric vehicles—is the result of an initiative that started with the city and caught fire, and then the momentum carried it over into the private sector."

CASE IN POINT:

Assessing Climate Risk and Resilience in Flagstaff

When the Schultz forest fire burned through 15,000 acres above the small city of Flagstaff, Arizona, in 2010, it provided city leaders with a lesson on just how vulnerable the city was to natural disaster. High winds fueled the fire, destroying nearly all vegetation on the mountain slopes, and in the months that followed, flooding from severe storms sent mud cascading down the denuded mountainsides and deep into the city—even into the garages and kitchens of some Flagstaff homes. The experience made the idea of climate variability and the risks and likelihood of extreme heat, drought, wildfires, and flooding seem very tangible, causing elected officials and staff to think hard about the need to reduce the city's vulnerability by identifying ways the city could cope.

Flagstaff's Sustainability Program staff proposed a vulnerability and risk assessment as a first step. Their argument was straightforward: the city needed to be prepared because an ounce of prevention was worth a pound of cure. The World Bank's Global Facility for Disaster Reduction and Recovery had concluded in a 2011 study that $1 spent on predisaster hazard mitigation could prevent the expenditure of $4 for postdisaster reconstruction. Sustainability staff then designed an engagement process that allowed all departments to work together to assess the risk, the probable impact on their ability to deliver services, and the resources required for the increased demand in services likely to result from extreme weather incidents. This highly successful initiative proved that even small cities, working internally with limited resources, could create an effective internal adaptation planning process.

Figure 2.6. Schultz fire, Flagstaff, Arizona
The Schultz fire burned through 15,000 acres above Flagstaff, and then rain poured down the denuded hillsides and flooded the city, making the threat of climate variability and the need to reduce vulnerability seem very real. Photo by Brady Smith. Courtesy of USDA Forest Service, Coconino National Forest.

The Inside Story

An opportunity to begin this process presented itself in 2011 when ICLEI—Local Governments for Sustainability, an international association of local governments that have made a commitment to sustainable development—invited cities to help beta test ICLEI's new climate change vulnerability assessment process. The City of Flagstaff accepted, and ICLEI staff came to the city to stage a half-day workshop on ways to measure and reduce vulnerability to climate change. Flagstaff's city manager invited representatives from the departments that would most likely be affected, including public health, energy, forest health, storm-water control, water, transportation, emergency services, long-term planning, and finance, as well as the sustainability program.

ICLEI recommended that Flagstaff undertake a community-wide resilience preparedness study and planning process, estimated to take about thirty-six months. Stephanie Smith, the city's sustainability specialist, thought this was too much time, given the sense of urgency felt by some in city government, and she proposed two modifications: she wanted to start with an internal study, rather than a community-wide process, that would take no longer than a year and would allow the city to come up with a plan before involving the rest of the community. She believed that once city departments had organized themselves around the issues, reached consensus on the risks, and developed internal leadership, it would be easier to meaningfully and effectively engage in a broader participation process.

Smith and her colleagues in the sustainability program brought together a core team of department heads and staff to support and engage in the effort, believing this would allow them to focus on strategies that were within the city's authority, therefore enhancing the likelihood that they would work. Smith also believed the city would be better off creating a process to incorporate the consideration of climate preparedness into all key decisions rather than crafting a comprehensive adaptation plan. "We didn't want to go through an extensive planning process," Smith says. "From day one we were very implementation-focused. We wanted to take stock of disaster preparedness efforts that were already in practice as well as understand new adaptation strategies."

Sustainability program staff guided the city through a one-year process to build consensus around answers to questions such as the following: If a department's operations were interrupted, what was the size of the population likely to be affected? Would the impact be life threatening? What would responding to such a disaster cost? Speculations about the causes of climate change were kept out of the discussion. The core team agreed that it was clear that the operations of city departments including public safety and public works were already affected by extreme weather—for example, the fire and storms discussed earlier—and that it was best to focus on assessing the impacts of droughts, wildfires, flooding, and winter storms and the resources that would be needed to enable departments to continue delivering services. "We focused on the impacts and not the science," Smith says.

The core team identified 115 impacts, including the need for backup generators, increased use of public facilities, increased demands on the city's fleet, and reductions in the integrity of pavement and culverts. The accuracy of this assessment of vulnerabilities depended on the collective expertise of the core team sitting around the table, and members worked together, assigning scores to the operations of each department. Each city function was ranked for sensitivity to climate change and capacity to adapt to climate change. City functions that received a low score for sensitivity to climate change and a high score for capacity to adapt, for example, were deemed to have low vulnerability to climate change.

The team approach was deemed especially valuable in bringing all departments on board, identifying crosscutting concerns, and building broad support for further resilience and preparedness planning as well as leveraging the risk-reduction strategies that were already in place. The city manager said that he saw this effort as an insurance policy against the impact of extreme weather occurrences, including fires and floods. All department heads agreed that the broad participation and even the disagreements during their discussions produced a stronger analysis, and they said they enjoyed the opportunity to work together on something as important as ensuring a prosperous future for Flagstaff. Proof of their buy-in was the fact that although the team began by meeting for an hour every other week, members voluntarily extended their work sessions to ninety minutes and then agreed also to meet in smaller working groups.

Results to Date

Upon completion of this process, the core team immediately recommended that the Flagstaff City Council adopt the study as public record, as well as statements about the importance of climate preparedness. The council did adopt a resolution that included a broad commitment to make incremental progress toward a culture of resilience by ensuring that considerations of climate preparedness be integrated at key decision points and by providing ongoing staff education. "We are already more resilient than we were eighteen months ago," Smith says, "because the team process has allowed us to take our blinders off. City leaders now understand the interdependence of city systems."

The city has yet to begin the very hard work of implementing the resolution. Smith hopes that the core team will be expanded and a process will be created to institutionalize the consideration of resilience in all plans, projects, and policy development. She also wants departments, especially those that are likely to be most affected by climate variability, to develop work plans and adopt performance measures. Smith has recommended that all departments report to the city's budget team and explain how they intend to meet the objectives of the council's resolution. Last but not least, the city still intends to engage the community, probably when the comprehensive plan and hazard mitigation plans are updated.

Key Factors for Success

Specific decisions and dynamics that have helped make the City of Flagstaff's efforts to better understand and manage climate-related risks very effective to date include the following.

Having the support of senior leadership. The fact that the city manager himself invited department directors to attend the first workshop indicated to them that he believed it was an important process deserving of their support. This greatly enhanced the success of the initiative and was key to getting buy-in.

Avoiding unnecessary controversy. The core team was able to undertake the vulnerability assessment and resilience-planning effort without reaching agreement on the causes of climate change, and this helped keep the process on track. Everyone was able to agree that climate is in fact changing and that the city must be better prepared.

Creating a core team. The core team allowed department heads to work together, break down departmental silos, achieve common understanding, and ultimately own the process and its conclusions. Sustainability staff believe that it's critical to keep this team together and to expand it over the next few years.

Taking time up front to set the stage. Smith says it was worthwhile to take extra time at the beginning to make sure that everyone was on the same page about why the city was undertaking this process.

Being willing to adapt the process. The process was continually adapted to reflect emerging interests and concerns, and Smith says this kept the process relevant and helped keep members engaged.

CASE IN POINT:

Greening City Fleets in Raleigh

A solar-powered electric vehicle charging station sits in front of the convention center in Raleigh, North Carolina, and Assistant City Manager Julian Prosser insists it's not just a passing green fad but the wave of the future—in Raleigh and beyond. Vehicle-to-grid technologies, he says, will one day allow the power stored in electric vehicles (EVs) to be fed back into the electric grid so that utilities can avoid buying expensive peak-hour energy. "In my opinion, that's the holy grail," Prosser says. The convention center's charging station is just one of nearly thirty installed so far in Raleigh, which, together with the rest of the Research Triangle region of North Carolina, has emerged as a world leader in electric vehicle readiness, thanks to clear and strong support from policy makers, solid strategic partnerships with key stakeholders, and green city leaders who knew how to turn yesterday's pitfalls into today's success.

The Inside Story

The City of Raleigh began dabbling in greener fuels back in the 1990s, when the director of Raleigh's solid waste services department approached Prosser, who was the fleet manager at the time, and told him of his interest in switching to biodiesel. They began using that cleaner fuel in the city's garbage trucks and had a good experience, and "that gave us courage to go further," says Prosser. They converted much of the rest of the city's diesel fleet to biodiesel. When the gas-electric hybrid technology came along, Prosser took a similar approach: he purchased a few vehicles to see how they would do. "I was looking for ways to reduce our cost of operations," Prosser recalls. "At first, people thought the hybrids were too expensive. But we tried a couple and found that they made good sense cost-wise."

The city also began experimenting with plug-in hybrids, encouraged by a local non-profit organization called the Plug-In Hybrid Coalition of the Carolinas, which had funding from power companies and saw electric vehicles as a way to efficiently use off-peak power, since cars would often be recharged overnight. "We saw the potential to reduce our dependence on foreign oil and all that goes along with that, including the cost of sending our young men and women into dangerous places to protect supplies," Prosser says. "It just seemed to me that there was a huge advantage to the city to look into EVs."

Raleigh bought a few more hybrids, converted them to plug-ins, augmented their battery capacity, and "played with that for a few years," Prosser says. Along the way, the city developed a stronger partnership with Progress Energy, the privately owned utility that supplies Raleigh's electricity. Progress Energy recognized the opportunity to sell off-peak electricity to this emerging market. The utility was working toward its own green power supply goal of reaching at least 12.5 percent renewable energy sources by 2021—a goal established by North Carolina's Renewable Portfolio Standard. This state regulation, requiring increased production from renewable sources, is the first such standard in the southeastern United States. "That gave them an incentive to work more collaboratively with local governments," Prosser says.

It was Progress Energy that in 2008 convened a group of key EV stakeholders, including the City of Raleigh and Nissan, to push the idea that the Raleigh region should participate in the Rocky Mountain Institute's Project Get Ready, a national initiative to help US cities get ready for plug-in vehicles. By this time, the city had established an ambitious goal of reducing its fleet's fossil fuel use to 20 percent below 2006 levels by 2011. The goal had been recommended by the Environmental Advisory Board, an all-volunteer board staffed by Prosser and Paula Thomas, the City of Raleigh's sustainability initiatives manager. The mayor and city manager both embraced the goal, and the city council adopted it unanimously. "The field had been cleared and plowed," Prosser says. "We saw EVs and Project Get Ready as a big opportunity to help us meet this goal."

The city joined Project Get Ready and established a broad-based interdepartmental team that consisted of senior staff from the transportation, planning, development and permitting, public affairs, and other departments. Team members tackled a range of complex challenges, including where to put charging stations and how to permit, finance, install, and maintain them. They educated residents about the benefits of EVs, worked with auto dealers to encourage them to offer EVs, and explored EV-related business and job creation opportunities. But being an early adopter is challenging, and the EV industry hadn't yet settled on a standard plug, even though it was clear that nobody would buy EVs or install charging stations until that decision was made. "We knew we had to wait," says Paula Thomas, who led the interdepartmental team. "That bought us time to work out some wrinkles and gear up. Once the standard plug decision was made, we were ready to hit the ground running, and we did."

They started by installing two charging stations in front of city hall. Several companies responded to the city's request for proposals, with bids ranging from $17,000 to $72,000, "an indication that nobody had any idea what these stations were going to cost," Thomas says. The team selected a local company and built rigorous requirements into the contract for data collection and sharing so that the city could track usage and use the data to set prices and promote the program. "We want to push out those findings so

Figure 2.7. Electric vehicles, Raleigh, North Carolina
Raleigh and the Research Triangle region of North Carolina have emerged as world leaders in electric vehicle readiness, thanks to clear and strong support from policy makers, cross-sector partnerships, and green city leadership by example.

that we can show people that adoption rates are picking up as the cars become available and prices come down," says Thomas.

The success of those first two charging stations provided the city with the experience and confidence to install an additional twenty-seven stations around the city. Funding for this first phase came from $300,000 in federal grants, including an Energy Efficiency and Conservation Block Grant, and from the city budget, including an allocation from a sustainability innovation fund established by the city manager and awarded competitively to departments looking to advance innovative green solutions.

Results to Date

By the end of 2012, Raleigh had installed twenty-nine EV charging stations, eleven for city fleet use and eighteen public stations where users pay for parking but not electricity. The city has purchased a number of EVs for its own fleet, including three all-electric vehicles and nine plug-in hybrids. The first two charging stations at city hall were followed by a third in front of the convention center, to maximize visibility. The city is supporting the installation of charging stations throughout the community, working with Progress Energy and a nonprofit advocacy group called Advanced Energy to help homeowners install residential chargers, and streamlining the permitting process so that it takes only two days to process a home-based charging station permit, from application to inspection.

In addition, green city leaders in Raleigh have identified and are addressing a number of barriers to EV adoption, providing training for contractors and inspectors, for example, and making adjustments to building and electrical codes as well as ordinances related to signage and parking. The city also has produced two instructional videos on installing EV charging stations and posted them on its website, and it offers free training workshops for electrical contractors.

Challenges

There have been many challenges along the way, most of them related to managing the risks associated with being an early adopter. "Is this technology going to survive? Have we stepped out too far and too fast? Are we going to see 'Death of the Electric Car: Part 2'? Is this effort going to fall flat on its face? We get a lot of questions like that," says Thomas. "And the truth is, we don't know. But we've done a lot to minimize and manage the concerns." The interdepartmental team that Thomas leads has been central to that risk management strategy. "We created that team to talk explicitly about the risk and to get broad buy-in. That was one way of spreading the risk. We learned together, we experimented together, and so we were invested together when it came time to roll this out."

Securing the early support of business leaders such as Progress Energy and the

Greater Raleigh Chamber of Commerce—by emphasizing the economic development potential along with the environmental benefits—was very important, as was securing outside funding for the initial capital investment, which didn't put too much additional pressure on an already constrained city budget. The role of the Rocky Mountain Institute as third-party convener was an important risk reducer as well. The well-respected national nonprofit organization brought expertise, technical support, and credibility to the effort.

Key Factors for Success

What accounts for the effectiveness of Raleigh's green fleet program? The following seven factors have a lot to do with it.

Strong top-level support. The clear mandate from the mayor, city manager, and city council—especially a unanimously adopted city council resolution embracing the goal of reducing the city fleet's energy consumption by 20 percent by 2011—has been critical to the success of the project so far. "You can have your champions in the departments and the community, but unless you have that strong support from the highest levels of your organization, it's hard," Thomas says.

Piloting, proving, pursuing. Prosser and Thomas were careful to start with relatively small steps and to bring others (via the interdepartmental Project Get Ready team) along every step of the way. "We didn't bite off too much," says Thomas. "We started with two EV charging stations. Once people stopped laughing, we were more comfortable moving ahead and expanding the infrastructure system and buying some more vehicles. Now all of the department directors want one—the police chief, the fire chief, the finance director, everybody. Even the people who didn't even know EVs existed are now clamoring for one. And that's what you want."

Applying lessons learned. Green city leaders were systematic about integrating into their EV initiative green fleet management lessons learned twenty years earlier, when the city's investment in compressed natural gas vehicles got too far ahead of the availability of fueling infrastructure. "Back then, we were trying to push on a rope," Prosser says, referring to the city's decision to invest in vehicles before sufficient fueling infrastructure was in place. "We were not as strategic as we are today, and we learned a bit from that!"

An economic development frame. Framing the initiative in terms of its potential to save money and create economic opportunities as well as protect the environment helped bring the utility and the business community on board early, which was critical. In Raleigh, it costs only about $3 to fully charge an electric vehicle and travel 100 miles, compared with about $14 to drive the same distance in a traditional gasoline-powered vehicle, assuming mileage of 25 miles per gallon and gas priced at $3.50 per gallon. "People could see that this wasn't solely a green idea—that it wasn't just some environmental zealot pushing her own agenda," Thomas says.

Aligning with the priorities of others. Raleigh's green city leaders saw and seized the opportunity to align with the interests and priorities of three other key groups: the federal government, which had laid out a bold goal for EV adoption nationally and provided funding through the Energy Efficiency and Conservation Block Grant Program; Progress Energy, which needed to move in a greener direction as a result of new state standards; and the Rocky Mountain Institute, which was on the lookout for cities willing to be early adopters of EV technologies and participate in its Project Get Ready.

Partnership and collaboration. The Project Get Ready team that Thomas assembled, with a range of department directors as well as key external stakeholders such as Progress Energy and auto industry representatives, was an effective way to build a sense of shared ownership and responsibility—including responsibility for the risks. Project Get Ready created an important learning network of early-adopter cities, EV manufacturers, electricity providers, and other experts from the academic and nonprofit sectors. As Project Get Ready's director, Matt Mattila, puts it: "There is no substitute for shared learning when building and pursuing an EV-readiness strategy."

Building on long-standing local assets. The Research Triangle region of North Carolina, which includes the cities of Raleigh, Chapel Hill, and Durham, as well as three great universities and many innovative technology companies, has a rich history of technological innovation, which Raleigh's green city leaders were able to take advantage of. "We are expected to be open to new technologies," Prosser says. "We're building on a great legacy here."

3.

Leading in the Community
Using City Assets, Policy, Partnerships, and Persuasion

"To advance urban sustainability, we have to get it out into the culture of the community. Residents, neighborhoods, blocks, and businesses small and large. Public-private partnerships. Bringing people together to collaborate on ideas, but also to pool resources and dollars. To really move forward, we have to partner even more."

—Brendan Shane, director,
Office of Policy and Sustainability,
Department of the Environment,
Washington, DC

Salt Lake City, Utah, nestled cozily between the Wasatch Range and the Great Salt Lake, offers residents gorgeous scenery and easy access to world-class hiking, biking, skiing, and other recreational opportunities. But there is one big downside to living there: meteorological conditions often trap pollution close to the ground within the valley, especially in the wintertime, creating some of the worst air quality in the United States. To address this concern, Vicki Bennett, sustainability director for Salt Lake City, and other green city leaders created the Clear the Air Challenge, a public-private partnership and social marketing campaign that provides information and incentives to encourage residents and businesses to voluntarily cut back on driving.

Individuals and companies form teams that choose from a menu of TravelWise strategies listed on the city's website—including switching to public transit, biking, walking, carpooling, and using cleaner vehicles and fuels. Incentives include free bus passes, bike accessories, and other prizes. Participants track and report their car trips and the miles saved and share stories and tips with others on the Clear the Air Challenge website. Those with the greatest reductions in driving and emissions are recognized on the city's website and at an annual awards ceremony, where they can win bus passes, bikes, ski weekends, and hotel stays.

The pilot program has produced results. More than 9,000 individuals and institutions

Figure 3.1. Salt Lake City transit and bike rack
Salt Lake City's Clear the Air Challenge is a full-blown regional public-private partnership to promote green transportation choices. It is being aggressively promoted by the Salt Lake City Chamber of Commerce, whose 7,700 member businesses employ nearly half of the state's total workforce. Photo by Eric Pancer / Flickr user: vxla.

participated during the first two years of the initiative, reducing vehicle miles traveled by an estimated 3.6 million, thereby reducing associated emissions by about 1,600 tons. But during that first phase Bennett and her team realized that a much bigger, broader effort was needed to match the scale of the problem. With the help of a grant from the US Environmental Protection Agency's Climate Showcase Communities Program, the city ramped up efforts to promote the program to the other sixteen cities and towns along the Wasatch Front, as well as Salt Lake County, Salt Lake City's chamber of commerce, and other stakeholders. Within a year or so, the program blossomed into a full-blown regional-scale public-private partnership, with eight mayors, the county executive, the governor, and the chamber of commerce officially signing on to the challenge.

The chamber—whose 7,700 member businesses employ 500,000 people, nearly half of the state's total workforce—emerged as one of the program's biggest champions, aggressively promoting business participation in the Clear the Air Challenge and launching its own Clean Air Champions initiative to promote and recognize voluntary clean air practices by its members. In addition, the chamber agreed to lead the challenge when grant funding ran out. "Poor air quality hinders corporate relocation efforts, places additional regulatory burdens on business, increases health care costs, and places Utah's federal highway funding at risk," reads the chamber's website. "The business community can make a difference."

Although leading by example, as described in chapter 2, is a necessary and foundational first step toward greening cities, it is far from sufficient. The carbon footprint of most municipal governments, even in big cities, is relatively small compared with a community's total footprint. The annual carbon emissions associated with municipal operations in Seattle, for example, are about 240,000 metric tons, only 3.5 percent of the city's total emissions. In Denver, city operations account for about 3 percent of the total, compared with Boston at 5 percent, and New York City at 6 percent.

To be successful, green city leaders must find innovative and effective ways to address that much larger challenge, which means engaging individuals, households, and neighborhoods; businesses and business groups; major employers; institutions such as school districts, universities, hospitals, ports, and military bases; and other governments. This is a daunting task for many reasons, and severely constrained resources and lack of control are on the top of that list. In fact, many of the solutions with potential to have the biggest impact are well beyond the city's authority.

In the end, what's required is widespread behavioral change on the part of individuals and institutions—a complex and difficult challenge around which an entire field of research and practice has emerged. Cities are highly complex economic, ecological, and social systems—replete with a wide range of stakeholders, perspectives, and interests that are sometimes in conflict—all nested within even more complex regional, national, and global systems. The ability of municipalities to fully understand—let alone influence—those interrelated systems is limited. But that is the challenge that green city leaders face.

This chapter explores how green city leaders are working to meet this critical challenge. It describes four leading strategies, illustrated with real-world examples of cities that are working to effect broad and lasting change. The strategies are (1) deploying the city's own assets and investments; (2) using city policy to encourage and sometimes require green behavior; (3) developing partnerships across departments and jurisdictions and with businesses, neighborhood groups, and nonprofit organizations; and (4) using the city's powers of persuasion—from the old-school bully pulpit to sophisticated new media and social marketing campaigns.

Strategically Deploying City Assets and Investments

Perhaps city government's most potent tool for cultivating green communities is the strategic deployment of its own financial investments and physical assets—such as city-owned land and streets—to enable and encourage green practices by residents and businesses. Direct investments can promote green practices by making them easier, more convenient, and more affordable for residents and businesses. Large-scale infrastructure investments in public transit, bike-sharing programs, and wider sidewalks, for example, make it easier and safer for people to drive less, while curbside organics pickup programs make it easier to compost and recycle.

New York City's Sustainable Streets strategic plan, a key element of PlaNYC that was adopted in 2008, is a good illustration of how a mix of policies and investments can lead the community toward a darker shade of green. Key elements of the strategic plan include a public plaza program; a "complete streets" policy requiring that all street-building and renovation projects consider and include—where appropriate—improvements for pedestrians and bicyclists; and a new street design manual that calls for the reconfiguring of streets for pedestrians and bicyclists and that sets new standards for landscaping. The transformation of Broadway, one of New York's most iconic and crowded streets, is a compelling example of what the program seeks to achieve. In February 2009 the city turned it into a car-free public plaza with chairs, tables, and planters—virtually overnight. An evaluation in January 2011 found that these changes to the street reduced traffic speeds—and therefore improved the safety of pedestrians and bicyclists—by about 17 percent. Perhaps even more important, 74 percent of visitors surveyed reported that their experience of Times Square was much improved.[1]

Similarly, through both the Sustainable Streets plan and its Bicycle Master Plan, New York City has adopted a complete streets policy and invested in infrastructure, including the installation of 255 miles of new bike lanes from 2008 to 2012—more than doubling the number of bike lanes—as well as 15 miles of separated bike lanes and 5,000 bike racks. Together, these policies and investments have dramatically increased bicycle commuting in the city—by 26 percent from 2008 to 2009, by another 13 percent from 2009 to 2010, and by an additional 7 percent from 2010 to 2011. Moreover, pedestrian and bicycling fatalities in 2009–2010 were the lowest since the city began collecting data, in 1910.[2]

Strategic investment in urban infrastructure can spur private investment that quickly dwarfs the public investment in terms of dollars spent. Investment in the streetcar systems of both Portland and Seattle, for example, catalyzed private investment many times the amount of the public investment—in compact, walkable development in downtown neighborhoods that have become very popular. Seattle, for example, committed to three major infrastructure investments to catalyze redevelopment of the South Lake Union neighborhood, adjacent to downtown: $31 million for a twelve-acre park on the southern tip of Lake Union; $55 million for a mile-long streetcar line linking the neighborhood to the downtown business core; and $164 million for street improvements to fix the so-called Mercer Mess, a tangle of traffic along Mercer Avenue, a four-lane road running through the heart of the neighborhood.

One-third of the park's cost, about $10 million, was contributed by Vulcan, a development company owned by Microsoft cofounder Paul Allen, the largest private landowner in the neighborhood. Half the costs of the streetcar were paid through a newly formed local improvement district that assessed the property owners, major institutions, and businesses located along the streetcar route.

These initial public and private investments in infrastructure unlocked billions of dollars' worth of private investment in development. For example, in 2012 Amazon decided to move its main campus to the neighborhood and invest $1.6 billion. "Initially I was skeptical about some of the grand plans to transform South Lake Union into a regional public health and technology powerhouse," says Seattle City Council member Richard Conlin, chair of the council's Planning, Land Use, and Sustainability Committee. "But the numbers demonstrate that targeted public investments and forward-thinking policy decisions actually did make a tremendous difference in shaping the future of that neighborhood."[3]

Smaller-scale investments can also help cultivate green practices and green communities, such as programs that provide residents with free compact fluorescent lightbulbs and faucet aerators and programs that provide homeowners with free or low-cost energy audits and weatherization services. Seattle's Community Action Projects are one example of how more and more cities are investing directly in neighborhood-based greening initiatives. The city awards small contracts to residents and businesses willing to partner with the city on climate action projects, as discussed in more detail below. Another example, the RainWise Program run by Seattle Public Utilities, encourages households to manage rainwater more sustainably by installing rain barrels, cisterns, and rain gardens. The city pays residents up to $4,000 to install rain gardens if they live in neighborhoods that drain into waterways experiencing combined sewer overflow problems.

Many cities are catalyzing green city solutions simply by making municipal assets such as vacant lots or even data sets available to organizations and individuals to implement green projects—from neighborhood groups that want to transform blighted blocks into green oases to young software developers who want to apply their high-tech talents for the greater good. The City of Lawrence, Kansas, launched its Common Ground Program in 2011 after inventorying the vacant and underutilized lots it owned; the city then invited community groups, nonprofit organizations, schools, and others to take over the lots and turn them into community gardens, student-run farms, or other green neighborhood projects. The City of Baltimore's Adopt-A-Lot Program leases vacant city lots to neighborhood groups interested in turning them into community gardens; nearly 800 lots had been adopted by the end of 2010. Similar programs exist in Cleveland; New York; Providence; and many other cities.

A growing number of cities are also sharing previously firewalled civic data in order to make government more transparent and to encourage creative and computer-savvy members of the community to develop websites and smart phone applications that improve environmental quality and quality of life. In the summer of 2012, for example, the Mayor's Office of Long-Term Planning and Sustainability and NYC Digital, part of the Mayor's Office of Media and Entertainment, organized the Reinvent Green Hackathon. The event called on "the expertise, dedication and stamina of the talented technology and design community . . . to help build digital tools and applications to support New Yorkers in leading greener, greater lives."[4]

More than a dozen new city data sets were released to kick off the thirty-hour Hackathon, during which thirteen teams of software developers donated about 1,000 hours of time to design projects ranging from apps to help locate public recycling cans and local farm markets to www.greenerneighbor.com, a website that ranks New York's boroughs in a friendly competition to be "green, greener, greenest."

Leading through Policy

In Texas, San Antonio's Mission Verde plan features a mix of policies and investments that are together increasing the energy efficiency of homes and businesses and attracting clean energy and other green businesses to the community. (See "Case in Point: Growing Green Businesses and Jobs in San Antonio" in chapter 5.) El Paso's Smart Code project is helping to reverse decades of sprawl-type development by changing zoning to require the development of higher-density mixed-use communities near bus and rail stations that are friendly to bicyclists, pedestrians, and transit users. (See "Case in Point: Returning to Green City Roots and Loving El Paso" in this chapter.) And in Vancouver, British Columbia, green city leaders are using a mix of policy, technical assistance, and education to encourage households and businesses to compost food scraps and move the community toward zero waste. (See the case in point about Vancouver's Zero Waste Initiative at www .guidetogreeningcities.org.)

Well-crafted policies such as these include incentives, regulations, and everything in between and can serve as a fulcrum for leveraging green cities. Garnering support for and winning passage of these green city policies almost always entails a difficult and time-consuming process, especially when new regulatory requirements are involved. But the payoff can be large and long-lasting because well-designed and thoughtfully executed policies can change the rules of the game, set a new bar, and establish a "new normal" that might forever change the way the community lives and does business.

Economic incentives—policies that financially reward green practices and discourage less green ones—can be especially effective. These include tolling heavily traveled roads and bridges and charging higher rates per unit for using more resources such as electricity or water—paying only $1 per gallon for the first hundred gallons of water, for example, but $3 per gallon after that—and levying higher fees for garbage pickup than for recycling and composting services. Seattle residents get a choice of three sizes of garbage cans, for example, and the fee for the smallest, the twelve-gallon "micro-can," is about 30 percent lower than the fee for the regular thirty-two-gallon can. Meanwhile, an unlimited amount of recycling and composting is allowed for curbside pickup, and the cost is built into the base garbage rate. These price signals, together with other factors, including a robust community education campaign, have transformed the way Seattle residents manage trash over the past twenty-five years.

Sometimes the best thing a city government can do to promote green practices in the community is to simply get out of the way. Cities that take a hard and honest look at their policies, practices, and programs against the backdrop of their green city goals and objectives often discover that outdated codes, requirements, and prohibitions are interfering with the adoption of green practices. Salt Lake City's Sustainable Code Revision Project is one of the most comprehensive examples. First, the city identified and summarized sustainability goals, policies, and initiatives; then it initiated a systematic comparison of these goals with current zoning and division ordinances in order to identify gaps, weaknesses, and opportunities.

The comparison resulted in forty proposed policy changes, including recommendations to remove barriers to green infrastructure, such as the use of pervious pavement and rain barrels on residential property; to adopt regulations that preserve solar access; to remove unnecessary restrictions on community gardens; and to allow accessory dwelling units, sometimes called mother-in-law apartments or granny flats. The city has already passed legislation removing barriers to urban farming and on-site residential solar and wind installations, and several other changes are in the works.[5]

New York City's Greener, Greater Buildings Plan (GGBP), a key element of PlaNYC, the city's sustainability agenda, is another good example of how policy can foster green practices. The heart of the GGBP, which has been hailed by some as "the nation's most comprehensive plan to reduce energy use and greenhouse gas emissions in existing buildings,"[6] is a suite of four laws signed by Mayor Michael Bloomberg in December 2009. The laws establish a tighter energy code for building renovations; mandate benchmarking and public disclosure of buildings' energy and water consumption; require buildings larger than 50,000 square feet to undergo an energy audit and to retune systems every ten years through a retro-commissioning process; and require the upgrading of building lighting to current energy efficiency standards and the submittal of monthly electricity usage statements to metered tenants.

As of April 2012, more than 8,000 large privately owned buildings and 3,000 city-owned buildings had benchmarked their energy usage in compliance with the plan. When the plan is fully implemented, it is projected to save $700 million in energy costs, create nearly 18,000 construction and building-related jobs, and reduce greenhouse gas emissions by about 5 percent. This is, states the plan, "the largest single advance the city can take to meet our goal of reducing citywide greenhouse gas emissions 30 percent by 2030."[7]

Of course there have been, and continue to be, many challenges. Initially there was confusion among building owners about what the new energy usage benchmarking requirement meant and how they should comply, and it has been challenging for them to work with the utility to obtain comprehensive building energy use data. Experience with the GGBP to date, including the implementation challenges, yields some important lessons about how city policy can be used effectively:

1. *Focus.* Early on, green city leaders made a strategic decision to focus the new requirements on very large buildings only—city-owned buildings of at least 10,000 square feet and privately owned buildings of at least 50,000 square feet. Although this amounted to only about 15,000 of the approximately one million buildings in the city, it meant the policy covered about half of the total square footage of buildings in the city, which were responsible for nearly half of the greenhouse gas emissions attributed to buildings. The focus on the biggest buildings should have a significant effect and should

also reduce the complexity of the process by reducing the number of stakeholders. "It involved a relatively small number of building owners, and they tended to be the more knowledgeable and sophisticated," explains David Bragdon, former director of the Mayor's Office of Long-Term Planning and Sustainability.

2. *Engage stakeholders and credible third parties from the get-go.* Purely top-down command-and-control approaches are rarely as effective as they were in the early stages of the environmental movement. New York's GGBP, for example, was developed in collaboration with a small number of prominent developers, building owners, and managers; commercial lenders; the New York State Energy Research and Development Authority (NYSERDA); and two well-respected and knowledgeable nonprofit organizations—the Natural Resources Defense Council's Institute for Market Transformation and the local chapter of the US Green Building Council, named the Urban Green Council.

3. *Facilitate and support implementation by affected parties.* Green city leaders in New York gave building owners the tools and support, including financial assistance, that they needed to effectively implement the four laws that are the heart of the GGBP. The city used $37 million of federal government stimulus funding from the Energy Efficiency and Conservation Block Grant Program to provide low-interest loans to building owners for energy efficiency upgrades. City leaders worked with the Urban Green Council and others to train building owners and managers in use of the US Environmental Protection Agency's Energy Star Portfolio Manager tool to meet the GGBP's benchmarking requirement. The Urban Green Council created a checklist of the steps required to comply, and the city provided half-day training sessions, established a call center, and created a website featuring the checklist and other resources. The city also established a workforce development working group called Amalgamated Green, which included representatives from real estate, labor, and workforce training, to identify the skills required to fill the jobs that would be created and to develop a training program to meet those needs.

Leading through Partnerships

Local governments and stakeholders are realizing they need each other to be successful because nobody can do it alone, that partnership is a more successful strategy than confrontation, and that no single person, organization, or sector—whether government, business, or nonprofit—has the human or financial resources to meet the challenge of greening a city alone. These resource constraints require green city leaders to pool ideas and investments across agencies, sectors, and jurisdictions and to find innovative ways to improve the efficiency of human and institutional as well as technical systems—such as building design and construction, energy supply and distribution, and transportation

Figure 3.2. Putnam Triangle Plaza, New York
The New York City Department of Transportation transformed Putnam Avenue into a pedestrian-friendly public plaza in partnership with the Fulton Area Business Alliance. Putnam Triangle Plaza has proven to be the boon to neighborhood businesses that the alliance hoped it would be. Photo courtesy of the New York City Department of Transportation.

networks. Strategic partnerships are the name of the green city game, including partnerships among city agencies; between city governments and the community—its institutions, nonprofit organizations, businesses, and neighborhoods—and among cities, other jurisdictions, and regional agencies. Each is addressed briefly below.

Partnering across City Departments
Greening the city requires integrated solutions that, in turn, require integrated action across multiple departments. One particularly effective strategy for green city leaders is to partner closely with those departments that have the most leverage, in terms of both greening their own facilities and operations and helping residents and businesses go green. A parks department, for example, typically manages facilities throughout the city and can green its own operations by transitioning from the use of pesticides to integrated

pest management, for example, and by improving the energy efficiency of its vehicles and buildings. Leading by example in this way, publicizing the effort, and then encouraging park visitors to adopt similar green practices—by posting anti-idling signs in parking lots, for example—can have a big impact on behavior in the community. Similarly, the building and permitting department is the city's main interface with the development industry, and the economic development office is the city's primary liaison with the business community. Fully integrating green practices and green solutions into the way these departments perform those roles can have a significant influence on development and business practices community-wide.

Partnering with Neighborhood Groups and Nonprofit Organizations

Historically, local governments and nonprofit organizations have tended to have combative relationships: local governments believe advocates are demanding too much, and advocates believe cities aren't delivering enough. But that is changing. Increasingly, governments and nonprofits are working together to bring about change. This may be partly because more environmental advocates are going to work in city government, but it's also because local governments and nonprofit organizations realize they need each other: each has skills and assets that can help the other succeed.

Nonprofit organizations, for example, can bring technical expertise to the table, as the Urban Green Council did with the development and implementation of New York's Greener, Greater Buildings Plan. Nonprofits can help build community support—and therefore political support—for city policies and programs, and they can offer fundraising prowess as well. In some cities, neighborhood-based groups are becoming more involved in promoting green solutions both in their neighborhoods and citywide. In Seattle, for example, neighborhoods are forming their own sustainability groups—Sustainable Ballard, Sustainable West Seattle, Sustainable Northeast Seattle, and others—fueled in part by the encouragement and support of a nonprofit network called SCALLOPS (Sustainable Communities All Over Puget Sound), which supports these groups through education, peer learning, and technical assistance. In order to support and build on this grassroots energy and enthusiasm, the City of Seattle has earmarked a portion of its Neighborhood Matching Fund for environmental projects, including climate protection. The fund provides neighborhood groups with $1,000 to $100,000 for community-driven projects that are matched by volunteer labor, professional resources, or other resources from the neighborhood.

More recently, the city's Office of Sustainability and Environment (OSE) launched a program called Community Climate Action Projects, the latest phase of Seattle Climate Action Now, a multifaceted community engagement and action campaign initiated by the city in 2006. Through this new program, the OSE awards small contracts of up to $7,000 to nonprofit organizations for projects that address the climate impacts of transportation, energy, waste, or food choices. Says OSE director Jill Simmons, "The idea is to help them do work with and for us. It's really about how the city can partner and work with existing networks and the momentum and excitement that is already out there, rather than trying to create it in-house."

The first request for proposals generated nearly twenty applications. The seven projects selected for funding included a targeted campaign to recruit women to ride together on established bike routes and a program to train community advocates to help their neighbors identify and make the right energy efficiency improvements to their homes.

Partnering with Business

When it comes to greening cities, the lines between the goals and agendas of the public and private sectors are blurring. SustainAbility, a London-based corporate sustainability consulting firm, put it this way: "We see the sustainability agendas for business and cities intersecting in interesting, meaningful and increasingly vital ways. For cities, businesses bring the skills and technologies needed to address a growing array of sustainability challenges. For companies, cities are critical to operations, increasingly central to the lives of both customers and employees, crucial platforms for innovation and, in turn, potential catalysts for long-term prosperity and sustainability."[8]

There is growing interest in both the public and private sectors in sharing ideas, talent, and resources to advance mutually supporting green solutions, but realizing that potential remains challenging. There is a sort of cultural divide between the public and private sectors, in part because leaders in each tend to have different types of training, hold different worldviews, and speak different languages. "There's a myth at the city, especially at the lower staff level, that we're not supposed to partner with the private sector," says Lucia Athens, formerly green building program manager in Seattle and now chief sustainability officer for the City of Austin, Texas. "We're trying to do some myth-busting and provide some guidance on how to do good public-private partnerships, and what the rules are and aren't."

There is lingering confusion and controversy about how closely the two sectors *should* work together. For example, when former Seattle mayor Greg Nickels and other city leaders embarked on an initiative in the mid-2000s to transform South Lake Union from a difficult-to-navigate low-density neighborhood of car dealerships, surface parking lots, and low-rise apartment buildings into a world-class hub for biotechnology and sustainable urban living, they were repeatedly criticized for being "in bed with Paul Allen," cofounder of Microsoft and the major property owner in South Lake Union. City council member Richard Conlin noted, during the council's review of Nickels's redevelopment plans for the neighborhood, "Clearly we've got two emotional pitches. One says biotech is the best thing since sliced bread and the other says it (the mayor's strategy) is all for the benefit of Paul Allen. We need to get away from the emotional polarization and make rational decisions."[9] Today, South Lake Union is widely regarded as a leading example of green urban infill development and a successful public-private partnership.

Despite the challenges, effective public-private partnerships are emerging, including Salt Lake City's Clear the Air Challenge, mentioned at the beginning of this chapter, which is a partnership between several local governments and a regional chamber of commerce. The electric vehicle initiative in Raleigh, North Carolina, is a collaboration between city government, a large privately owned utility, and major electric vehicle manufacturers to install charging infrastructure and promote the use of electric vehicles community-wide. (See "Case in Point: Greening City Fleets in Raleigh" in chapter 2.) In North Carolina, Envision Charlotte is a partnership between the city and Duke Energy, Cisco Systems, and Verizon Wireless to increase the energy efficiency of privately owned buildings and then to address water and waste management challenges.

Named Smart Energy Now, this program has organized a voluntary network of the owners and managers of about seventy buildings in Uptown Charlotte who want to reduce their collective energy use by 20 percent over five years and create the most environmentally sustainable urban core in the United States. Smart energy technologies have been installed in all the buildings, allowing owners and operators to better track energy usage and identify opportunities for improvement. Information-sharing kiosks have been placed in the lobbies of all buildings to inform the people who live and work there, as well as visitors, about this effort and to encourage them to participate. Volunteer "energy champions" have been identified in each building and trained to spread the word about the importance of managing energy use.[10]

City governments are also partnering directly with local businesses. Renew Boston, a home weatherization program initiated by the City of Boston but implemented by a small start-up company called Next Step Living, provides no-cost energy audits and upgrades to homeowners, especially to low- and middle-income households. "We used existing utility rebate programs and stimulus funding from the federal government and then partnered with community-based organizations to bring retrofitting to scale in every neighborhood of our city," explains Jim Hunt, Boston's former chief of environmental and energy services. In one year, the program completed 7,000 comprehensive home energy audits, including minor energy efficiency improvements such as lighting upgrades, and 2,000 complete home weatherization jobs. "We more than doubled residential energy efficiency through this program," Hunt says, "and we did it by targeting hard-to-reach, hard-to-serve populations."

Initially the city had hired Next Step Living to run a small pilot project, but when the city won a large Energy Efficiency and Conservation Block Grant from the US Department of Energy, it scaled up the program and chose Next Step Living as the prime contractor. "They grew their company from five employees to more than 350 employees," says Hunt. "They located their headquarters in our Innovation District, and they committed to hiring local people who reflect the diversity and talent of our city."

The Renew Boston partnership also involved two large investor-owned utilities, NSTAR and National Grid. "We have a long history of working with them on a host of issues," Hunt says. "They understand that by working with us they're helping themselves. Their customers are our customers. They're helping us help their customers and our constituents, and we're working collectively to help them achieve their energy efficiency–related regulatory goals and requirements. So it's a win-win-win."

Box 3.1. Tips for Working with the Business Community on Green City Solutions

- Speak their language by articulating and accentuating the economic benefits of green city solutions, such as cost savings, new business opportunities, improved employee morale and retention, and increased competitiveness. San Antonio's Mission Verde plan is a leading example of this approach.

- Engage businesses and business groups directly in the development of green city solutions by having private sector representatives serve on key commissions, advisory groups, and task forces. The Boston Green Ribbon Commission, for example, is a group of about thirty of the region's largest and most influential companies and universities working together on strategies for funding and implementing the city's Climate Action Plan.

- Create collaborative solutions in which the city, businesses, and community organizations can work together toward a common goal. The Clear the Air Challenge in the Salt Lake City region and Envision Charlotte are good examples of this.

- Recognition can be especially important to companies looking to tout and market their green reputations and credentials. The Houston Green Office Challenge and Santa Monica's Green Business Certification Program are leading examples.

Collaborating at the Regional Scale

Regional partnerships are also on the rise as local and regional governments, including counties and metropolitan planning organizations, recognize the need to pool information, ideas, and resources in order to address the scope, scale, and complexity of the challenges by implementing smart growth initiatives, green economic development, and climate resilience planning. Partnerships on this scale are difficult and time-consuming to create, manage, and sustain—as is evidenced, for example, by the difficulties the Denver Transit-Oriented Development (TOD) Fund had in transitioning from a program that served the city to one that served the region. (See "Case in Point: Financing Affordable Housing along Transit Lines in Denver" in chapter 5.) But successful examples include the Corridors of Opportunity initiative in the Twin Cities. This complex, multistakeholder regional partnership is developing and implementing a large-scale green solution: a regional transportation system that simultaneously promotes economic development, increases social equity, and reduces carbon emissions and other environmental impacts.

The effort is led by the Metropolitan Council, the region's metropolitan planning organization, but it is governed by a consortium including the Cities of Minneapolis and St. Paul, Hennepin and Ramsey Counties, the state, and leaders from the business, nonprofit, and philanthropic communities. With funding from several local and national foundations and the Sustainable Communities Regional Planning Grant Program of the US Department of Housing and Urban Development (HUD), green city—and green region—leaders are using the emerging light-rail and bus rapid transit network as a focus for integrating and aligning policies and investments in the areas of planning and development, housing, transportation, and economic development.[11]

The Southeast Florida Regional Climate Change Compact is another excellent example of four politically diverse urban counties with more than one hundred local jurisdictions joining together to develop and implement a regional strategy to reduce carbon emissions and manage climate impacts.[12] (See "Case in Point: Southeast Florida Regional Climate Compact" at www.guidetogreeningcities.org.) And in Western North Carolina, under the leadership of a regional green economic development agency called AdvantageGreen, the City of Asheville and other local governments are working with surrounding rural communities to transform the region, once dominated by the tobacco industry, into a national and global hub for the production and consumption of healthy foods and natural products.[13] (See "Case in Point: Greening Economic Development in Western North Carolina" at www.guidetogreeningcities.org.)

Cross-City Collaboration

Cities are also beginning to collaborate more with one another, sharing information, ideas, success stories, lessons learned, and other tricks of the trade through organizations such as the Urban Sustainability Directors Network, which is a network of sustainability directors from more than one hundred North American cities, and the C40 Cities Climate Leadership Group, a network of more than sixty of the world's largest cities. The U.S. Conference of Mayors Climate Protection Agreement, initiated by former Seattle mayor Greg Nickels in 2005, is a leading example of cities pushing one another to reduce their carbon emissions and pushing together for stronger national action on climate change. (See "Case in Point: Mobilizing a National Movement of Mayors" at www .guidetogreeningcities.org.)

Box 3.2. How Green City Leaders Can Hone Their Collaborative Skills and Capacities

Creating green cities requires unprecedented degrees of collaboration across municipal agencies, community sectors, and levels of government. But strong collaborative skills don't come naturally to most. "Collaboration is like a muscle," Colorado's governor, John Hickenlooper, says in describing his efforts to forge a regional economic development partnership when he was the mayor of Denver. "The more you exercise it, the stronger it gets."

David Fairman and Patrick Field of the Consensus Building Institute—a leading provider of training and technical assistance in negotiation, consensus building, and dispute resolution—offer the following advice to green city leaders and others looking to hone their capacity to collaborate:

- Try collaboration on smaller, more concrete initiatives before trying it on bigger, riskier efforts. Ground capacity building in ambitious but achievable one- to three-year initiatives that have broad support, and use the momentum to learn by doing.

- Look at comparable urban areas that have taken on similar challenges, and bring in peers to help with learning and strategy.

- Invest in formal training. Send cross-departmental teams for training on collaboration and negotiation; the ability to collaborate will depend on skills across departments, not just within the department that's most excited about sustainability.

- Think about being a collaborative efficiency expert. Sustainability ought to be about uncovering new and unexpected efficiencies.

- Be patient, build trust and relationships, and assume that it won't happen overnight. Collaboration is not just a skill but a culture, so one has to think about these efforts as long-term cultural change, not just goodwill and good ideas.

Leading through Persuasion

The art of persuasion is an important tool in the "cultivating green cities" toolbox. In many places, green city leaders are using grand visions, bold goals, and sophisticated branding campaigns as a rallying cry to motivate their communities. For example, Philadelphia,

Pennsylvania; Vancouver, British Columbia; and several other cities have declared their intent to be "North America's greenest city." Seattle is striving to be "carbon neutral" by 2030. San Francisco has set a goal of "zero waste" by 2020. Calgary, Alberta, set and met its goal of using 100 percent renewable energy to power not just municipal operations but all of its homes and businesses. Phoenix, Arizona, wants to become the "smartest energy city in the world." Cleveland, Ohio, aspires to be "a green city on a blue lake." Asheville, North Carolina, touts itself as "the world's first Foodtopian society." Boston, Massachusetts, has a new campaign called Greenovate Boston. These kinds of well-branded initiatives can be very effective in getting people and institutions to focus on a shared vision or common goal and then getting them excited about working individually and collectively toward it. These initiatives are especially effective when coupled with city leadership by example and policies and programs that allow residents and businesses to participate.

San Francisco's Environment Now is an interesting example of a much more targeted approach to outreach and education that directly engages households and businesses in meeting green community goals by providing information and assistance through "credible messengers"—other residents and businesses—rather than government officials. The program also advances social equity goals by providing workforce training, job opportunities, and career pathways for young people in underserved neighborhoods. About twenty young people, many selected from disadvantaged communities, are employed by the San Francisco Department of the Environment (SF Environment) for two years, during which time they are trained in the city's green programs and in general workforce skills, including communications, customer service, and computer literacy. These young people then engage residents throughout the city but especially in neighborhoods that are struggling to meet green community goals related to waste reduction and energy efficiency, for example. "It's one of the most inspiring things that we do," says Melanie Nutter, director of SF Environment, which runs the program.

Programs that challenge, recognize, and reward residents and businesses for going green can also be very effective. The Houston Green Office Challenge engages private property owners, managers, and tenants in an effort to set and meet energy and water efficiency goals, as well as vehicle emission and other waste reduction goals, using a "green office scorecard" to assess and track progress. In 2011, owners, managers, and tenants of buildings representing about 75 million square feet of office space participated in the program and were recognized for their efforts in the media and at an annual awards ceremony hosted by the mayor.

Santa Monica's Green Business Certification Program is "a voluntary program that encourages businesses to implement proactive actions that are good for their bottom line and the environment."[14] The program is a partnership between the City of Santa Monica, the Santa Monica Chamber of Commerce, the Santa Monica Convention and Visitors Bureau, and the nonprofit organization Sustainable Works, which administers the program. Businesses must meet a rigorous checklist of green practices focused on conserving resources, preventing pollution, and minimizing waste. If they pass an on-site verification process, they are certified as green and can display a window decal. About twenty businesses are certified annually, and certification is good for two years.

The program has grown rapidly, and the awards ceremony has become a huge event that draws hundreds of people and a lot of media attention. Dean Kubani, director of the city's Office of Sustainability and the Environment, believes that it has changed the way that the business community views green. "The Convention and Visitors Bureau now sells Santa Monica to tourists as a green destination," Kubani says. "They're directing tourists to shop at green businesses and to see green buildings, rooftop solar installations, and electric vehicle chargers—there is a lot of stuff that visitors can see. Green has become a great selling point." The chamber of commerce has seen the green light as well. Kubani says that downtown businesses now call themselves the "Green Light District." "Businesses were antagonistic in the beginning, but now they get it. The positive feedback and public relations helped a lot."

Other cities are implementing sophisticated community-based social marketing (CBSM) campaigns, which have grown in popularity as green city leaders have come to understand that simply providing information about why behavior should change is usually not enough to bring about the desired changes. CBSM uses the findings of social psychology to provide a better understanding of barriers to change and to find ways of overcoming them. In their book *Social Marketing to Protect the Environment: What Works*, Doug McKenzie-Mohr and colleagues note that CBSM campaigns begin by prioritizing the behaviors to change according to their potential impact, removing barriers to the behavior that is desired and enhancing the benefits of this behavior, and then piloting a behavior change strategy and evaluating the results before taking the strategy to scale.[15] CBSM tactics used to bring about behavioral change include making the change convenient; creating "benign peer pressure" to change; providing "trusted messengers" to advocate for the change; requiring public commitments to change and providing prompts, reminders, and positive feedback; and fostering competition and providing rewards.

For example, cities can make it easier for residents to recycle by making sure bins are in convenient locations. They can post signs prompting parents to turn off their car engines while waiting to pick up children at school. They can encourage reductions in energy use by showing residents whether they are using more or less than their neighbors. They can encourage employees to stop printing out e-mail by making it easy for them to store messages in archives for reference. All of these ideas illustrate the tactics of CBSM.

And these tactics can be quite effective. For example, when Action Research, a recognized expert on CBSM, surveyed government employees in Albany, New York, to find out why participation was low in the city's vanpool program, employees said they wanted to see visible support for the program from a high-level leader, not just the environment office. Action Research recommended that change and also suggested that posters used to raise awareness of the program show people who look like city employees and include testimonials from city employees. In addition, the company recommended implementing the campaign through the human resources department, which was skilled at describing benefits to employees. Once these changes were implemented, participation in the vanpool program increased and the fleet grew from just two vans to eighteen.[16]

When the Halifax Regional Municipality, Nova Scotia, piloted a curbside organics collection program with 2,000 families, the campaign used many CBSM techniques. When residents expressed concern that the carts used to collect the materials would be hard to maneuver, promotional brochures were created showing a ninety-year-old woman wheeling one of the carts. The city used community volunteers to make presentations about the program to neighbors. A kitchen container was provided to residents that had a handle and that was easy to clean in the kitchen sink, thereby helping to address the "yuck factor," and there was a sticker on the container indicating which wastes should go into it. People who lived in row houses or apartments who said they did not have room for a cart were allowed to share carts. By the time the pilot was over and the program was rolled out, people were calling a hotline to say they wanted to be first in line for the program, and over the first few years participation increased by 80 percent.

Sometimes the best way to facilitate broad change is to allow those individuals who have major concerns to opt out of it. For example, when the City of Fort Collins, Colorado, announced a plan to install smart energy meters at customers' homes to record their consumption of electricity and relay the information back to the utility for monitoring and billing purposes, some people pushed back because of privacy concerns. So the city launched an intensive communications campaign to assuage concerns and to allow residents to opt out of the program—but required them to pay a monthly charge to cover the additional cost of a manual meter reading.

The Best Recipe: A Portfolio Approach
The most effective greening initiatives tend to employ a mix of the four strategies discussed in this chapter: (1) deploying city assets and investments and leading through (2) policy, (3) partnerships, and (4) persuasion. As with investing money, when it comes to greening cities, a portfolio approach seems to work best. Philadelphia's Green City, Clean

Waters program is a good example: it includes city *investment* in green storm-water infrastructure on publicly owned lands, including parks and street rights-of-way. This investment is augmented by *policies* requiring or encouraging property owners—of homes, businesses, schools, and other institutions and facilities—to remove impervious pavement and replace it with something green. There is a new fee, for example, on private property owners based on the amount of impervious surface on their property, with credits given for those who remove and replace it.

Strategic *partnerships* are also a core element of the program. There is collaboration among city departments as well as with watershed-based partnerships that the city helped form and currently supports. These partnerships foster a sense of shared ownership and responsibility for the watersheds that residents and businesses live in and depend on. Moreover, the program's name, Green City, Clean Waters, is a positive and *persuasive* brand for Mayor Michael Nutter's broader vision of making Philadelphia "the greenest city in the United States"—and it is a compelling rallying cry. (See "Case in Point: Sewer Overflows and Sustainable Infrastructure in Philadelphia" in this chapter.)

The ultimate goal is for green principles and practices to become part of a community's identity, culture, and spirit. "One thing we're finding is that the investment that communities have made in sustainability is like an inoculation—a form of resilience against the inevitable pressure to take on or support unsustainable projects," says KC Golden, policy director of the Seattle-based environmental group Climate Solutions. As an example, he points to the battle under way in Bellingham, Washington, and other coastal communities in the Pacific Northwest over whether port facilities should be expanded to accommodate shipments of coal arriving from the Midwest for transport to China and elsewhere. "There's a very real sense in these communities that coal exports are an affront to their identity—even beyond the fact that they involve a lot of dust and noise. It's as if these shipments are a sort of alien invasion into a culture that prides itself on promoting sustainable prosperity. These communities have spent so much time affirming the idea of a sustainable future that the idea of becoming a big depot for coal exports just isn't taking root. People are invested in something that looks a whole lot better than that."

Toward Green *and* Equitable Solutions

Green city leaders must engage and serve everybody, not just those who already pay close attention to environmental challenges. There is a growing realization in cities across North America that environmental, economic, and social welfare goals and agendas are parts of the same whole. Jeremy Hays of Green for All, a national nonprofit working to build "an inclusive green economy," believes that inclusive planning processes tend to yield stronger results: "Green initiatives and plans that incorporate equity outcomes will enjoy broader constituencies of support, will be more likely to overcome political hurdles, and will be better positioned to address implementation challenges by leveraging a diverse base of committed problem solvers."

But developing and implementing agendas and initiatives in ways that engage and serve all segments of communities is extremely challenging for green city leaders, in large part because historically they have not seen it as a central part of their mission, and they often lack the training and tools needed to do the job. "Just like environmental protection and economic development, social equity has a distinct vocabulary, history, set of stakeholders, metrics, and tried practices and strategies," says Hays. "Part of the challenge that cities face when trying to implement social equity strategies is that leaders just aren't sure how to get the same level of experience and expertise in the equity field that they have in the environmental and economic areas." As a result, equity challenges, goals, and stakeholders often aren't included in green city efforts early enough or in sufficiently robust ways.

Hays offers the following advice to green city leaders looking to better build their capacity to achieve social equity goals and outcomes:

- Establish specific equity outcomes for green projects from the outset. Be as clear about the equity goals (e.g., increasing job opportunities for low-income residents) as about environmental ones (e.g., reducing carbon emissions).
- Be intentional about building capacity for social equity. Create project teams that include equity experts and professionals from city government as well as from the community at large.
- Build effective partnerships with local equity stakeholders. Create and support committees or commissions of community equity experts to help the city define and pursue equity outcomes. Engage influential social equity advocacy organizations in the development and implementation of green city agendas and initiatives.

Cities are deploying these and other strategies and taking steps in the right direction. "Community benefit agreements," which require development projects to provide benefits to the community that might include good jobs, affordable housing, social justice, and livable neighborhoods, are becoming more common elements of green city initiatives, especially those expected to generate significant development and economic activity. When the City of Portland designed its Clean Energy Works Portland pilot project in 2009, the city worked with a wide range of stakeholders to develop a community workforce agreement that channeled a percentage of the contracts and jobs created by the program to locally owned businesses and individuals from historically disadvantaged groups. More than thirty parties—contractors and employers, workforce development organizations, labor unions, and environmental groups—signed the agreement, which stipulated the following: 80 percent of employees would be hired from the local workforce; not less than 30 percent of the total trades and technical project hours would be performed by "historically disadvantaged or underrepresented people, including people of color, women, and low-income residents"; and not less than 20 percent of the total dollars would go to "businesses owned by historically disadvantaged or underrepresented people," including women and people of color.[17]

Similarly, a growing number of communities are using mapping tools such as an "equity atlas" or an "opportunities map" to better assess and understand equity-related challenges and opportunities and to craft green solutions that better meet those challenges and seize those opportunities. In Denver, for example, stakeholders worked together to produce an equity atlas that is helping policy makers ensure that the region's $6 billion investment in new public transit service results in greater access to housing, education, training, jobs, and other opportunities for all residents, including those who are economically disadvantaged.

Planners in the Gulf Coast region are using opportunity mapping to develop their regional sustainable development plan, with funding from HUD's Sustainable Communities Regional Planning Grant Program. The tool, produced by Ohio State University's Kirwan Institute, maps locations of "opportunity-providing" facilities such as high-performing schools, quality health-care and child-care facilities, job centers, and transit lines and the communities that need those opportunities the most, thereby identifying gaps that new land use, transportation, housing, and economic development plans and policies should address. "The planning process we would normally undertake does not fully endorse or incorporate social equity," says Elaine Wilkinson, executive director of the Gulf Regional Planning Commission in Gulfport, Missouri. She notes that it's an eye-opener to see the data—it makes it possible to understand why a population is disadvantaged and to see the whole region and how it's performing, not just the city or county.[18]

Full integration of social equity goals into the development and implementation of local sustainable development plans and projects was a requirement of HUD's Sustainable Communities Regional Planning Grant Program, which funded nearly 150 projects nationwide in 2010 and 2011 and which is a key component of the federal government's Sustainable Communities Initiative. Proposers were required to include one or more social equity advocacy organizations in their project consortium, and proposals were judged in part on the strength of their equity-related elements.

The Twin Cities region's Corridors of Opportunity project is a good example of the kind of projects that won funding. Its vision statement reads: "Transitways corridors will

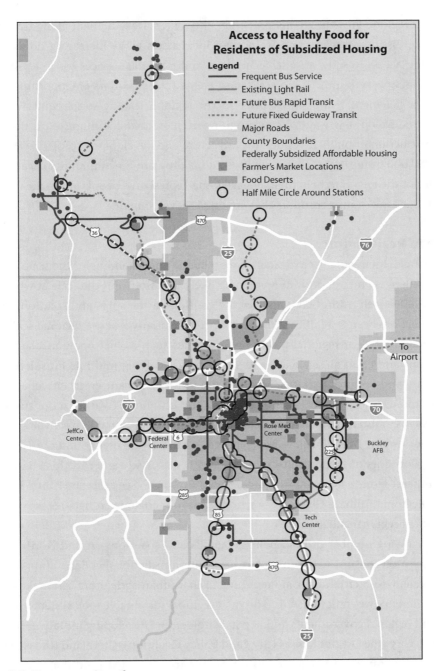

Figure 3.3. Denver equity atlas

Some green city leaders are using an "equity atlas" or similar mapping tool to help ensure that public policies and infrastructure investments such as transit lines connect low-income residents with schools, jobs, health care, housing, and other opportunities. Figure courtesy of Reconnecting America and Mile High Connects.

guide our region's growth, vitality and competitiveness. Development along transitways will create distinctive places and strengthen local assets while increasing ridership and expanding access to jobs, affordable housing and essential services for residents of all incomes and backgrounds."[19] Project leaders created the Corridors of Opportunity Community Engagement Team, led by three of the region's leading social equity advocacy groups, to develop new ways of engaging underrepresented communities in the design and construction of publicly funded infrastructure and development projects. This team won $750,000 from HUD for a competitive grants program for community organizations throughout the region to help them engage underrepresented people along the five light-rail and bus rapid transit corridors that are under development.

A Rise in Regionalism

Scale matters. Increasingly, city leaders have a better understanding of the scale at which green challenges and opportunities are most likely to unfold and the scale at which they are most effectively addressed, and they are crafting partnerships and solutions accordingly. There has been a significant increase in green initiatives at the regional scale, often led by major cities or regional government entities such as metropolitan planning organizations and clean air agencies, and sometimes involving multiple jurisdictions and the private and nonprofit sectors. Many of the most significant green city challenges—curbing sprawl and car dependence, greening the economy, creating more sustainable food systems, bolstering resilience to climate change—are regional in nature and must be tackled regionally. The Salt Lake City region's Clear the Air Challenge and the Twin Cities region's Corridors of Opportunity initiative, both discussed earlier in this chapter, and the Southeast Florida Regional Climate Change Compact (see "Case in Point: Southeast Florida Regional Climate Change Compact" at www.guidetogreeningcities.org) are great examples of regional collaboration.

The growing number of food policy councils and coalitions around North America is another indicator of the rise in cross-sector, interjurisdictional collaboration at the regional scale. Green city leaders are recognizing that urban agriculture can make an even bigger difference when nested within broader regional sustainable food system initiatives. Local and regional governments and key stakeholders are developing initiatives like these in Kansas City (the Greater Kansas City Food Policy Coalition), Cleveland (the Cleveland-Cuyahoga County Food Policy Coalition), Seattle (the Regional Food Policy Council of the Puget Sound Regional Council), and many other cities.

The Puget Sound area's Regional Food Policy Council was established in 2010 to develop "just and integrated policy and action recommendations that promote health, sustain and strengthen the local and regional food system, and engage and partner with agriculture, business, communities and governments in the four-county region."[20] Housed at the Puget Sound Regional Council (a regional land use, transportation, and economic development agency covering King, Snohomish, Pierce, and Kitsap Counties), the thirty-member council includes elected officials from all four counties (three county executives and one council member) and three of the cities (one mayor and two city council members), a tribal leader, regional public health and economic development officials, representatives from the food industry, and nonprofit organizations focused on everything from farmland preservation to social justice. In its first two years of operation the council completed several foundational projects, including a scan of existing food-related plans and policies in the region's sixty-five local jurisdictions, a web-based visualization tool describing food-related policy-making processes, and an equity assessment of the current food system.

Conclusion

There is a huge gap between the scope and complexity of the green city challenge and the levels of resources and control that cities have at their disposal to meet this challenge, and therefore it is critical that green city leaders identify and align with the priorities, aspirations, and resources of key community stakeholders. "Think of yourself as a small business," Susan Anderson, director of the City of Portland's Bureau of Planning and Sustainability, advises fellow green city leaders. "You should do a needs assessment of your 'customers,' including city agencies, businesses, developers, homeowners, and renters. You need to talk to them to find out what they want and what they're trying to do and then align what you're trying to do with their goals and objectives."

The art of alignment is time-consuming, at times even painstaking, but necessary and smart. It requires patience, persistence, and the ability and willingness to listen and learn and to relinquish some control and adapt. It entails proactively reaching out to key stakeholders in the community, including other governments, businesses and business groups, nonprofit organizations, neighborhood-based groups, and foundations. By spending time with leaders and staff in these other stakeholder organizations, green city leaders come to understand their perspectives and priorities, develop relationships and trust, and identify opportunities for collaboration. Where are the pockets of energy, passion, and leadership on which the city might build? Is there an innovative solution in the pipeline that the city could get behind, accelerate, and expand on? Where are the best opportunities for partnerships?

CASE IN POINT:

Returning to Green City Roots and Loving El Paso

After decades of debilitating sprawl, the City of El Paso, Texas, is returning to its green city roots, a transition sparked by fresh leadership, the rapid growth of a nearby US Army post, and increasing concerns about the adverse health effects of the conventional approach to development—including alarmingly high childhood obesity and asthma rates.

El Paso made a conscious choice to turn things around, and after a highly partici-patory two-year process in 2012, the city council unanimously adopted Plan El Paso, a master plan that is widely touted as one of the leading examples of green urbanism in the United States. Parts of the city are being rezoned to revitalize the downtown and create compact, mixed-use neighborhoods. Four bus rapid transit lines and several large-scale transit-oriented development projects are under way. And the city has been reorganized to facilitate alignment of its planning, permitting, environmental sustainability, and eco-nomic development agendas, policies, and investments.

The Inside Story

Three forces converged to catalyze this green renaissance. First, an influx of new leaders embraced a "green urbanism" paradigm—including several city council members, a city manager (Joyce Wilson), a comprehensive plan manager (Carlos Gallinar), and a sus-tainability manager (Marty Howell). Second, as this new leadership was settling in, Fort Bliss—a major army base partially within the city boundaries—was targeted for rapid ex-pansion under the US Army's Base Realignment and Closure program. The base's popula-tion would triple, and $6 billion would be spent on new construction, including five bri-gade complexes and a billion-dollar medical center—forcing the city to figure out how it could accommodate so much growth. El Paso's new leaders saw the opportunity to green this development by adopting a strong policy framework and working collaboratively with the army throughout the planning process.

Growing concerns about the increasing rates of obesity, asthma, and diabetes provided the third major impetus for redoing the city's comprehensive plan. Howell believes that obesity rates are due in part to the fact that children can't walk anywhere. "Kids can't walk to school, to the park, or to the neighbor's house—because they'd have to walk along busy roads where people are driving forty-five miles per hour, and they could die!" Local studies have correlated the increase in asthma rates with air pollution, and Howell also believes that "the transportation and development paradigm we've been following is the root cause."

To help address these concerns, Plan El Paso is instituting a new paradigm by revitalizing the downtown core, developing a central park on an abandoned rail yard, and redeveloping the infamous ASARCO site, former home of a massive copper-smelting operation. A key feature of the plan is the build-out of one of the most ambitious bus rapid transit systems in the United States, a $100 million network of four corridors radiating out from the city center. Plan El Paso also features an unusually robust public health section, emphasizing urban design that will create safe places to walk and bike, more recreational opportunities, and improved access to healthy food, community gardens, and farm markets.

PLAN FOR A CENTRAL PARK

A new park created by consolidating the tracks of an underutilized railyard would create a grand, unique amenity for Downtown living.

Plan El Paso: City of El Paso, Texas Comprehensive Plan

Figure 3.4. El Paso central park rendering

Growing concerns about waning economic competitiveness and public health challenges such as obesity, asthma, and diabetes inspired El Paso to plan for walkable neighborhoods. The revitalized downtown will also feature a multiline bus rapid transit system and a central park on an abandoned rail yard.

Results to Date

In March 2012, Plan El Paso was unanimously adopted by the El Paso City Council. It has gotten rave reviews, even winning the US Environmental Protection Agency's National Award for Smart Growth Achievement. The plan has already begun redirecting and reshaping development practices and patterns. Several areas of the city—including the ASARCO site and another site in the heart of El Paso that is envisioned as a 140-acre biomedical business park, to be called the Medical Center of the Americas—have been rezoned. Back in 2008, El Paso had adopted its Smart Code, one of the first "form-based" land use codes in the country, which emphasizes the design and form of buildings rather than their use, thereby encouraging a mix of shops, housing, businesses, parks, and open spaces, connected by streets that are welcoming to all users. But it was a voluntary option that wasn't often chosen by developers, whereas Plan El Paso makes it standard practice.

The bus rapid transit corridors are under development, with the first, the Mesa Line, slated to open by 2014. Two large-scale transit-oriented development projects are in the permitting process, and several others will be soon. These developments mark a major shift away from a low-density, car-oriented development approach.

The city has been reorganized to facilitate the "silo-busting" necessary to achieve more sustainable development patterns. Howell's sustainability shop has merged with the economic development unit, which is now under his leadership. The interrelated functions of the new Department of Economic Development and Sustainability, the planning department where Gallinar works, and the permitting department will be managed by the city's development director. "If cities are going to compete in the twenty-first century, it's not just about giving tax subsidies to companies to come to your city. Now it's about the quality of life you can provide through the built environment," says Gallinar. "The city is beginning to understand the importance of linking economic development and prosperity with parks, neighborhoods, the transportation system, and urban design."

Challenges

No transition as significant as this comes without challenges. It was hard to align key players in city government behind Plan El Paso's overarching vision, so new city manager Joyce Wilson issued an edict of sorts, directing key senior managers to get accredited by the Congress for the New Urbanism, a leading smart growth training and advocacy organization. More than one hundred senior staffers—deputy city managers, department directors and their deputies, and key external stakeholders, including utility and state transportation officials—went through the process. "Our city manager said, 'Enough! I want all of you on the same page. This is how we're going to talk to each other, and this is how we're going to do business,'" recalls Howell. "It was her way of building internal capacity. And it worked."

Green city leaders conducted robust market assessments that analyzed the relative benefits and costs of the new urbanist approach, which helped win the support of skeptical developers and the business community. "Some developers were suspicious," recalls Gallinar, "but by the end of the process, many people were thinking differently. The market studies showed that while costs were about the same, the new urbanist approach resulted in higher densities, more walkability, more connectivity, and more open space. So we were able to say that it makes sense to do greener, more sustainable development than the urban sprawl paradigm we'd become accustomed to in El Paso."

Engaging El Paso's large and diverse population of 750,000 residents in a meaningful conversation was another daunting challenge. Gallinar and his team developed a website that serves as a clearinghouse for timely information on projects and an advisory committee composed of a cross section of community representatives. They staged three intensive two-week-long charettes as well as hands-on public planning sessions that allowed residents and businesses to put their own ideas on the table. And they held more than 150 meetings with key stakeholders, including the school district, neighborhood associations, and the chamber of commerce. "Plan El Paso deputized the entire city as citizen planners," city officials wrote in an open letter to residents when Plan El Paso was finalized.

Key Factors for Success

The roots of Plan El Paso's success to date include the following:

Focusing on public health and economic development. Plan El Paso was framed in part as a public health improvement plan, which resonated deeply with a community increasingly concerned about the well-being of its children. And it was framed as an economic imperative that would lower infrastructure costs for the city and its taxpayers; reduce housing, health-care, and transportation costs for residents; and provide new opportunities for businesses.

Making planning relevant. Plan El Paso was framed as a strategy that really could improve quality of life, not just as a planning exercise. "The plan recognizes the indispensability of beauty, not as something separate and apart from life like pictures in a gallery, but beauty in homes, neighborhoods, civic buildings, streets, and public spaces," states the plan's introduction. "Plan El Paso aims not to return to a vanished time, but rather to grow a choiceworthy contemporary City based on cherished and enduring values."[21] The plan's logo is a sun rising behind a heart containing a picture of a green urban development, with the tagline "Love El Paso. Plan El Paso." Gallinar created both while daydreaming and doodling. "It really puts planning in the context of human emotions—where it belongs," Gallinar says. "The plan isn't about conceptual things like reducing carbon emissions—it is about preserving something that people love. There is a deep and abiding love of this place, and the logo connects with that."

LOVE EL PASO.
PLAN EL PASO.
PLAN THE FUTURE. NOW.

www.planelpaso.org

Figure 3.5. "Love El Paso" logo
The Plan El Paso logo puts planning in the context of human emotions: "It's not about conceptual things like reducing carbon emissions," says plan manager and logo creator Carlos Gallinar, "it's about a deep and abiding love of this place."

Using good data well. Green city leaders have used data effectively to make their case. For example, the city used the Center for Neighborhood Technology's Housing and Transportation Affordability Index to show that older neighborhoods where destinations were closer together and more easily accessible by foot and bicycle were much more affordable than newer neighborhoods where housing was supposed to be more affordable but residents ended up spending as much as 80 percent of their household budgets on housing and transportation combined.

Forging strategic partnerships. The growth of Fort Bliss was a major impetus for Plan El Paso, and the base's own ambitious green goals—to achieve net zero energy, water, and waste by 2015—are aligned with the plan. "Fort Bliss has been a great partner," Gallinar says, adding that the army is planting 10,000 trees, installing a huge solar power array, and building the largest desalination plant in the country. He says that the Texas Department of Transportation, which was initially wary of the new approach to development, become another key partner, thanks in part to the Congress for the New Urbanism's accreditation process. "Now we are at the point where people across many levels of government and the private sector are starting to talk the same language," says Gallinar.

CASE IN POINT:

Sewer Overflows and
Sustainable Infrastructure in Philadelphia

Maintaining infrastructure is a challenge for most cities because costs are high and funding is scarce. Cities must improve their sewer systems, however, because the US Environmental Protection Agency (EPA) is enforcing the federal Clean Water Act requirement that municipalities reduce combined sewer overflows—the storm-water and sewage mixture that is discharged directly into streams and rivers after heavy rainfalls. The cost of compliance, which generally requires the construction of "gray infrastructure" such as concrete tunnels, can be billions of dollars, which many cities cannot afford.

Howard Neukrug, now the commissioner of the Philadelphia Water Department, was a deputy commissioner during the period about which this case study is written, and he championed an integrated and green approach to reducing sewer overflows that brought the 2,000-employee department and the entire City of Philadelphia into the new age of sustainable infrastructure. Neukrug had begun advocating for comprehensive, multistakeholder solutions as director of the Office of Watersheds when he saw the potential for an integrated solution to sewer overflows. He reasoned that if the city combined green infrastructure—such as trees, bioswales, rain gardens, and permeable pavement—with restoration and preservation of stream corridors and upgrades to treatment plants, it could save billions of dollars at the same time that it achieved wide-ranging environmental, economic, and social benefits. "We recognized the utter futility of the gray option as not just unaffordable but inefficient and anti-sustainable," he says.

In September 2009, the city announced the Green City, Clean Waters plan, a $2 billion, twenty-five-year proposal to green one-third of the city's impervious surfaces and reduce the volume of combined sewer overflows by half. Moreover, the plan sought to maximize the environmental return on every dollar spent by transforming urban rivers and stream corridors, preserving and restoring habitat for aquatic species, and improving public health and neighborhood quality of life. In short, the plan would transform Philadelphia into a sustainable twenty-first-century city.

The Inside Story

The City of Philadelphia estimated that meeting the Clean Water Act mandate by increasing the capacity of its sewer system with new tanks and tunnels could cost $8–$10 billion. Neukrug believed there was a cheaper alternative—to reduce the need for storm-water management by keeping rainwater out of the sewer system—and argued that it was better

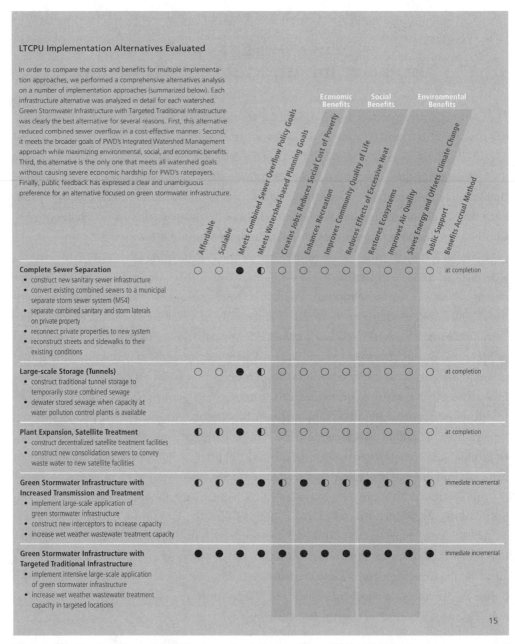

Figure 3.6. Evaluation of implementation alternatives, Philadelphia long-term control plan update

After evaluating a number of approaches, the Philadelphia Water Department determined that green infrastructure solutions would, over a period of forty-five years, provide the city with more in environmental, economic, and social benefits than they would cost to design, build, and operate. Figure from the Philadelphia Water Department, "Green City, Clean Waters," Summary Report.

to "conserve the rainwater, reuse it, recycle it, and let it infiltrate into the ground where it lands." In order to determine the potential of this strategy, the water department studied the distribution of impervious surfaces in sewer system drainage areas and then assessed the capacity of green infrastructure to absorb these overflows.

The study found that in order to achieve the scale required to absorb overflows, every city department, resident, and business would have to seek out greening opportunities whenever undertaking construction projects. These actions would need to include large-scale green storm-water infrastructure on public and private land and a large-scale street tree program, as well as the conversion of vacant and abandoned land to open space—to help manage storm water by preventing it from becoming runoff. Success would depend on building a high level of awareness among the public and private sectors and residents, and it would require new rules, design standards, regulations, incentives, and programs. But the ancillary benefits would include more and better open space, cleaner waterways, and improved access to more recreational opportunities. And the street trees would help green and beautify neighborhoods.

Box 3.3. Breakdown of Impervious Cover within the Philadelphia Combined Sewer System Drainage Area

Green streets: 38%

Green homes: 20%

Green industry, business, commerce, and institutions: 16%

Green open space: 10%

Green alleys, driveways, and walkways: 6%

Green parking: 5%

Green public facilities: 3%

Green schools: 2%

Neukrug, perhaps in part because of his training as an engineer, was able to make a compelling case for this paradigm shift from gray to green infrastructure. He and his staff created models and tools for decision making that compared the capital, operating, and management costs of gray and green infrastructure over their life cycles, enabling staff to show that "green storm-water infrastructure with targeted traditional infrastructure" was the most cost-effective way to reduce combined sewer overflows. This was an approach that would also help the city meet the broader goals of watershed management without

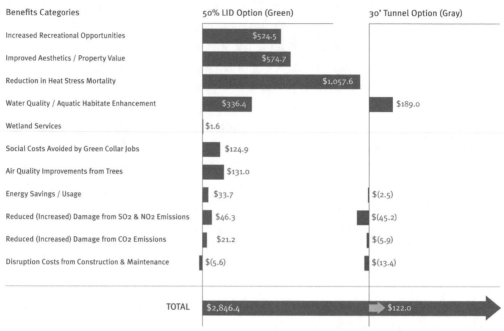

Benefits of CSO Options: Cumulative Through 2049 in millions of US Dollars

Benefits Categories	50% LID Option (Green)	30' Tunnel Option (Gray)
Increased Recreational Opportunities	$524.5	
Improved Aesthetics / Property Value	$574.7	
Reduction in Heat Stress Mortality	$1,057.6	
Water Quality / Aquatic Habitate Enhancement	$336.4	$189.0
Wetland Services	$1.6	
Social Costs Avoided by Green Collar Jobs	$124.9	
Air Quality Improvements from Trees	$131.0	
Energy Savings / Usage	$33.7	$(2.5)
Reduced (Increased) Damage from SO2 & NO2 Emissions	$46.3	$(45.2)
Reduced (Increased) Damage from CO2 Emissions	$21.2	$(5.9)
Disruption Costs from Construction & Maintenance	$(5.6)	$(13.4)
TOTAL	$2,846.4	$122.0

Figure 3.7. Benefits of combined sewer overflow options through 2049, Philadelphia
Philadelphia's triple bottom line analysis of green infrastructure solutions quantified benefits including additional recreational user-days on waterways, reduction of premature deaths and asthma attacks, increased property values, poverty reduction from green jobs, and energy savings. Figure from Philadelphia Water Department, "Philadelphia Combined Sewer Overflow Long Term Control Plan Update," Supplemental Documentation, vol. 2, "Triple Bottom Line Analysis," 2009.

causing ratepayers significant economic hardship, and it would maximize environmental, social, and economic benefits.

The Philadelphia Water Department was already prepared to take this comprehensive approach to green infrastructure. A decade earlier, the department had taken responsibility for protecting and enhancing the watershed's rivers and streams, ensuring the water was clean, and minimizing the threat of flooding. Partnerships had been created with other city departments, residents, businesses, and environmental and community groups, who became stewards of each watershed. Because of this engagement, the department learned how to align and manage diverse stakeholders around multiple goals, and staff discovered allies for their new green infrastructure initiative.

It wasn't easy to win support for Green City, Clean Waters in the beginning, however, because it required coordinating the activities of so many partners—planners, engineers, landscape architects, architects, artists and other designers, developers, community groups, watershed partnerships, and most city departments. "We had to coax, cajole, nudge, facilitate, demonstrate, discuss, argue, and, generally, outlast our naysayers," Neukrug says. But the people of Philadelphia were won over in the end because they understood that the plan would help create greener neighborhoods.

Part of making the case for this innovative plan was showing that it was fundable, which was going to require new as well as traditional financing mechanisms, including revenue bonds, new water and wastewater charges, and 100 percent leverage of private investment, achieved in part through new development regulations that went into effect in 2006 and a new "impervious cover charge with credit system" that went into effect in 2010. The impervious cover charge bills commercial property owners on the basis of the gross area of a land parcel and its impervious surface area rather than on its metered water usage. Property owners can get a credit against their fees by retrofitting their properties with green infrastructure. A residential credit program is also under consideration. The city has explored a variety of other creative funding approaches, building on its goal of making storm water a currency in private financial markets.[22]

Still, in spite of the strong evidence of both feasibility and benefits, Neukrug likely would not have succeeded if a new deputy mayor had not become a champion. Many people, even in Neukrug's department, viewed him as a renegade, and he was largely unknown in Mayor Michael Nutter's office. Moreover, the EPA wasn't sure that it would accept a green infrastructure plan to achieve compliance with the Clean Water Act because that would set a precedent for an approach that was unproven.

That was when Rina Cutler was appointed to the position of deputy mayor of transportation and utilities. She immediately saw the opportunity to break down departmental silos and promote innovation, and her appointment raised the profile of the water department. Cutler helped the mayor understand that in order to comply with the Clean Water Act, the city would have to undertake a major public works project, and she was able to convince him that the green infrastructure plan would cost significantly less and also maximize the benefits for residents and the environment. Mayor Nutter became an advocate for the program, helped convince Philadelphia's congressional delegation of the value of the green approach, and helped make the case to the EPA—which finally approved the plan. But this was just the beginning of what would become a long haul.

In order to quickly learn what worked, demonstrate results, and broaden the plan's constituency, the water department proposed tracking all benefits, including economic (new jobs and income, increases in property values); social (more recreational user-days, reductions in heat-related fatalities); and environmental (reductions in premature deaths, avoided illness, and missed days of work or school; reductions in energy usage; gallons of combined sewage overflows avoided; acres of wetland restored; and stream miles restored). The water department set up a process to systematically evaluate the results achieved by dozens of green infrastructure pilots and to make necessary modifications.

Results to Date

It was a major achievement for the Green City, Clean Waters initiative to win approval from both the EPA and Pennsylvania regulators, and it set a precedent for other cities. Chris Crockett, the water department's deputy commissioner of planning and environmental services, said in 2012 that the city was well on its way to meeting a five-year goal of creating 744 "greened acres," which are acres of impervious cover that are modified to capture at least the first inch of runoff that otherwise would be managed by storm-water infrastructure. A greened acre stops 80–90 percent of this runoff.

Challenges

One of the biggest challenges has been managing high expectations for the project, especially when sewage-laden storm-water overflows are expected to continue for some years. Many green infrastructure technologies that have worked as pilot projects have not been tried at the much larger scale of a big city such as Philadelphia. Efforts were hampered at the beginning by the fact that other city agencies had a hard time breaking out of their traditional roles as providers of narrowly defined services in order to work together toward the plan's broader goals. It will continue to be difficult to explain to the water department's ratepayers why their rates keep increasing—with green infrastructure just as with gray infrastructure.

Key Factors for Success

Transforming a major, older city's long-standing approach to managing storm water is no easy task, to say the least. The factors contributing to Philadelphia's effectiveness to date include the following.

Building a culture for holistic solutions. The seeds for Green City, Clean Waters were planted almost a decade earlier, when the Philadelphia Water Department adopted a watersheds approach that addressed many needs at once, including the need for cleaner water and more recreational opportunities as well as the need to reduce storm-water overflows.

Strong leadership at the top. The success of the program was greatly enhanced because Mayor Nutter was such a strong advocate and ultimately because EPA administrator Lisa Jackson embraced the opportunity to do something that was innovative but did not require the approval of the United States Congress.

Investing in improvements that win public support. The city won over community leaders by tapping into residents' desire to make neighborhoods better and healthier by making them greener and to expand neighborhood parks. The benefits of the green infrastructure approach became apparent early on as improvements began, and the demonstration projects that were used to inform the strategy and cost analysis increased everyone's familiarity with the program and the belief that it was good for neighborhoods.

Figure 3.8. Green roof, downtown Philadelphia
The green roof at PECO Energy headquarters in downtown Philadelphia captures 60–70 percent of rainwater that falls on it; plantings keep summer temperatures on the roof sixty to eighty degrees lower. Photo by Paul Rider.

Mixing carrots and sticks. In order for the city to achieve the fundamental behavioral changes necessary for success, both regulations and incentives were needed to encourage the greening of all repair, replacement, and construction projects. Allowing commercial property owners to reduce their impervious cover charge fee by investing in green infrastructure is an example of a carrot and stick bundled together.

Creating performance metrics that drive learning and adaptation. Having a quantitative measure of success, a "greened acre," is a boon for progress measurement and learning at many scales. The City of Philadelphia can assess whether individual green infrastructure projects achieve the goal of greening acres and, if not, revise technologies. It can assess whether each of its program areas (schools, roads, etc.) is producing its share of greened acres and, if not, revise outreach or incentives for that sector. The greened acre is a single metric that can focus the efforts of residents, businesses, and city government on achieving the goals of the plan.

4.

The Green City Leader

"In most roles in government, you are delivering a service. Our role is innovating, coming up with new ideas that benefit the rest of the city and county. On the flip side, in hard times we are seen as something extra, rather than necessary for government to operate. We have to be adding value at all times."

—Paul Young, administrator,
Memphis and Shelby County
Office of Sustainability, Tennessee

The stories in this book share a common factor for success: the green city leader. Jim Hunt, former chief of environmental and energy services for the City of Boston, led an effort that reduced utility costs by 30 percent and enabled the city to purchase 12 percent of its energy supply from wind farms. Maggie Ullman, sustainability program manager for the City of Asheville, North Carolina, helped her city's finance department create its Green Capital Improvement Program, which took advantage of the savings achieved through sustainability measures such as the installation of light-emitting diode (LED) streetlights. Adam Freed, who was deputy director of the New York City Mayor's Office of Long-Term Planning and Sustainability, brought together the local water utility, parks department, and transportation department to pursue green infrastructure as a new approach to managing sewer overflows. All of them advanced sustainability in countless small ways that gradually added up to systemic change.

Greening cities is all about making the case, building coalitions, breaking down silos, solving thorny problems, championing innovative and integrated solutions, and demonstrating performance. It requires consistent, skilled, ongoing change making, whether it is companies or governments that are being greened. When the public relations firm VOX Global, together with Weinreb Group Sustainability Recruiting and the University of California, Berkeley, surveyed thirty-two corporate sustainability leaders in 2012, the respondents said that their key roles were as "connector," "collaborator," and "catalyst."[1] Green city leaders in the public sector have the same roles, and they have proven that they can move easily between the public and private sectors. In fact, many of the green city leaders quoted in this chapter have moved on to take positions in corporate sustainability departments, utilities, consulting firms, and nongovernmental organizations.

Without these green champions, initiatives for greening cities tend to get lost in the shuffle. When David Cicilline, the mayor of Providence, Rhode Island, hired Matt Stark as director of policy and legislative affairs in 2008, he asked him to finalize "Greenprint: Providence," his guiding document for sustainability activities, and to help implement its recommendations. "As I sorted through these responsibilities," Stark says, "it became clear I was going to have to find partners across many departments and the community. I was going to have to attach sustainability to high-profile issues like workforce development or education and to support other members of the administration on their initiatives. It was going to take a lot of work, and it would need dedicated staff to do it." So Stark began to build the case for hiring Providence's first sustainability director.

In 2011, the City of Providence approved the creation of a four-person sustainability office. Stark had made the case that this was an opportunity to organize a citywide system to reduce energy consumption and costs and to improve access to energy performance data. He argued that energy efficiency could become a springboard for other resource-saving initiatives—such as recycling and green fleet management. He said the office could enter into community-wide sustainability partnerships, which were important to the mayor—who wanted to involve both government and the community on sustainability issues.[2] The sustainability director who was hired, Sheila Dormody, has successfully advanced all of these goals and the mayor's "Greenprint."

This chapter examines how the job of green city leader emerged, how it has come to be defined, and the two most important roles of green city leaders—organizing support and embedding sustainability in business practice.

Emergence of the Green City Leader

By 2012, more than 300 US and Canadian cities and counties had hired a sustainability champion, someone charged with fostering new green policies, programs, and frameworks for decision making. This is still a new occupation, and job titles vary widely. Some champions' job titles speak to their roles, such as green urbanist, chief sustainability officer, sustainability coordinator, environmental or energy or sustainability manager, facilities and sustainability manager, director of sustainability and strategic planning, director of sustainability and long-term planning, and climate and sustainability program coordinator. Others have the responsibility for sustainability even though this is not reflected in their titles, such as manager of urban design, director of environmental planning, environmental initiatives program manager, director of natural resources, director of environmental quality, and even city planner. In this book, we refer to all the people who fill these jobs as green city leaders.

The green city leader is an agent of change within government and in the community. Win-win arrangements that advance the green agenda happen because green city leaders build relationships, find funding, bring together stakeholders across city functions, pilot new approaches and then cultivate champions for these approaches, analyze the benefits, and communicate the results. They champion the development of city sustainability plans, which allows them to get agreement on goals and priorities. They nurture other green champions across the city so that they can get help in leveraging sustainability efforts. They facilitate collaborations across departments, which helps them break down the silos to find solutions with more cobenefits. They engage community and business groups, thereby cultivating new support and resources. They directly manage green initiatives and programs, and they incubate new programs that aren't yet owned by any department. They analyze policy and coordinate the measurement and monitoring of results, which helps them build their case. And they communicate everywhere and all the time, even about small successes.

One of the unique roles of sustainability leaders is that they must identify approaches that simultaneously benefit many city departments—from water to transportation to economic development—and leverage their resources. For example, as green city leaders in the New York City Mayor's Office of Long-Term Planning and Sustainability studied how to help the water utility comply with the Clean Water Act requirement to reduce sewer overflows, they looked to green infrastructure—which replaces impervious surfaces with

Figure 4.1. Ecotrust roof blooms, Portland, Oregon
The green roof of Portland's Ecotrust Building (Jean Vollum Natural Capital Center), together with street-level landscaping, filters and absorbs most, if not all, of the site's rainwater, eliminating runoff into the overburdened Willamette River.

technologies such as pervious pavement and rain gardens in order to capture more rainwater where it falls and keep it out of sewers.

Adam Freed and other green city leaders in New York City noted that roads managed by the Department of Transportation constituted a large share of city-owned land covered with impervious pavement. But it was the parks department that had expertise with green surfaces. So Freed formed a sustainable storm-water management working group that included the mayor's office and the transportation and parks departments; the working group came up with a plan for thirty green infrastructure pilot projects throughout the city. These pilot projects led to the development of a comprehensive plan, which still is overseen by the same working group.[3]

The major challenge for green city leaders is that they must influence people and organizations over which they have little authority and no control, and they must do it with very few resources. They succeed by nurturing, motivating, empowering, brokering, solving problems, leveraging hidden assets, and eliminating obstacles. They figure out what other city leaders need to achieve their goals and then help them succeed in ways that also advance the green agenda. They are, says author, speaker, and entrepreneur Joel Makower, the founder of GreenBiz.com, "chief translation officers." They advocate for "lean production" rather than "zero waste." They propose ways to reduce "energy spend," not "greenhouse gas emissions."[4]

Late in 2011, Roy Brooke, director of sustainability for the City of Victoria, British Columbia, wanted to use city resources to support a program to help businesses measure and reduce their carbon footprint. His successful request to the city council, made during a time of austerity and budget cutting, emphasized the cost savings to local businesses, the economic development benefits, and the new partnerships and leverage.[5]

More often than not, green city leaders succeed in advancing green initiatives by talking about cost savings and economic benefits. This is why Andrew Watterson, former chief of sustainability for the City of Cleveland, Ohio, mapped every city government cost and revenue center and found many green projects that saved money, earning the trust and support of his colleagues in government.[6] The analysis to make this case can be very complex, however, as it was when Howard Neukrug, then a junior member of the Philadelphia Water Department staff and now the commissioner, showed that combining the installation of green infrastructure with stream corridor restoration and preservation and upgrades to treatment plants would cost billions of dollars less than building more tunnels to reduce sewer overflows.[7] This was how Neukrug was able to tip the balance in favor of green infrastructure—by accounting for all the benefits, to stream corridors, habitat for aquatic species, public health, and neighborhood quality of life. (See "Case in Point: Sewer Overflows and Sustainable Infrastructure in Philadelphia" in chapter 3.)

Green city leaders become masters at identifying cobenefits. Paul Krutko, who as chief development officer for the City of San Jose, California, was an early leader of the San Jose Green Vision plan, made it his business to find ways to transform green challenges into economic opportunities. When the city needed to reduce the high cost of electricity and maintenance for streetlights, he proposed a new lighting policy that would not only reduce costs and greenhouse gas emissions but also help build local markets for innovations in light-emitting diode (LED) lighting, smart communications technology, and electric vehicle infrastructure—and generate funds for city services.[8]

Green city leaders also open doors by solving their colleagues' problems. John Coleman, who was sustainability director for the City of Fayetteville, Arkansas, made it his business to listen to the problems of other city staff members and look for ways to be of service. What he found, for example, was that maintenance staff wanted to reduce the burden of maintaining aging heating, ventilation, and air-conditioning equipment. So he helped them secure a performance contract to replace the equipment, and then he gave credit for the success of the project to the maintenance staff, thereby building a base for continued collaboration.[9]

Coleman and many other green city leaders also raise funds for other departments to make it easier for them to undertake new, green approaches. In 2010, one of Coleman's top priorities was to raise $500,000 in grants for city sustainability programs, and he was successful.[10] Securing new sources of project funding benefits the city budget while also creating new stakeholders who participate in and benefit from the funded projects. Fund-raising and achieving cost savings really helps build a constituency for the green city leader. In 2011, when the Cincinnati city manager proposed eliminating the Office of Environmental Quality, many government and community groups rallied in support of the office, pointing out that it had landed $20 million in grants and saved $2 million per year in operating efficiencies, whereas its elimination would save only $200,000 per year. Good results and good records helped make a successful case for maintaining the Office of Environmental Quality and its greening mission.[11]

Green city leaders nurture long-term relationships with their city partners on greening initiatives by allowing them to take credit for successes and to be in the limelight. Mandy Mahoney, former director of sustainability for the City of Atlanta, Georgia, made spreading the credit around a core part of her work ethic. "The system changes because people change," she says. "It's not about taking the credit, but making the unsung heroes get the credit that they need to feel supported."[12] Sharing the limelight is also a good way to build stronger buy-in from the city organization's leaders. Simple gestures such as having them talk to the media or to speak about initiatives at conferences can further build their ownership and commitment.[13]

Even when they pilot innovative programs, green city leaders look for others to manage these programs and to get credit for successes. Sometimes there is a magnificent greening opportunity without an obvious home or champion, and this is why green city leaders master the art of "incubation, then integration"—first showing what can be done but then finding homes for successful projects and programs as quickly as possible. Effective green city leaders may create new initiatives, but they find ways to embed them as soon as possible in the work plans of other departments or commissions and in budgets and performance management systems.

Once green city leaders in San Antonio, Texas, had championed the successful launch of the Mission Verde green economic development plan, they made sure it had a permanent home—in this case outside of city government, where it had broad community support. (See "Case in Point: Growing Green Businesses and Jobs in San Antonio" in chapter 5.) Similarly, one of Chicago's green city leaders led the initial trials for permeable alleys but worked with the Chicago Department of Transportation to take on the technology once it was proven, stepping into the background to keep it on the department's radar and move it toward broader public and private adoption. (See "Case in Point: Permeable Pavement and the Green Alley Program in Chicago" in this chapter.) By spreading credit and ownership, green city leaders take the first step in institutionalizing the greening of cities.

This kind of change making requires a broad set of skills. The most important "content knowledge," many green city leaders say, is energy management, probably because many green city leaders initially proved their value to cities by saving them money by reducing energy usage and cost.[14] However, green city leaders also benefit from knowledge about a wide array of topics related to sustainability, including models and programs for urban sustainability, climate change science, environmental management, and social behavior change. They benefit from an understanding of fields that help them manage change in cities, including public administration, public policy development, public financing, project management, systems analysis, strategic planning, collaborative problem solving, and performance management.

Purview of the Green City Leader

During the past two decades, most green city leaders have focused on greening their cities' building, energy, transportation, water, and food infrastructure and embedding green concerns in decision-making processes. However, their roles are evolving toward the promotion of a broader triple bottom line approach to sustainability that integrates environmental, economic, and social goals. Few have concretely defined triple bottom line sustainability, instead taking a simpler first step of asking how each project and investment can enhance environmental quality, economic vitality, and social equity and quality of life. For example, the City of Calgary, Alberta, uses its Triple Bottom Line Policy Framework appraisal tool to help decision makers explore the social, economic, and environmental impacts of proposed policies and plans. Under this approach, sustainability is about balancing social, economic, and environmental goals as well as embracing a longer-term time horizon that allows for consideration of the welfare of future generations.[15]

Location of the Green City Leader

Green city leaders are emerging at many levels of local government and in different locations. Green city leaders who are part of the mayor's or city manager's office are well positioned to organize across departments and agencies and in the community. But it is valuable also to have green city leaders fostering change from within departments at the same time because they have more staff support and more resources and they better understand the culture and rules of departments.

Seattle is one of many cities that have had green city leaders in many departments as well as in the mayor's office. In 2009, Seattle mayor Greg Nickels saw climate protection as a big tent that should also include economic development and social justice, so champions of these issues were included in meetings too. In Providence, as discussed earlier, green city leaders already operating within departments helped drive the creation of a central sustainability office because they saw how it could advance their goals. For example, the city's purchasing and properties manager often tried to take a green pathway, installing solar projects when it was cost-effective, retrofitting city hall, and building the first school to be certified by the Collaborative for High Performance Schools, which promotes healthy, green schools. The manager had no way to document changes in city building energy use, but he knew that the mayor's sustainability office would track energy use and performance over time. He supported the idea of hiring a sustainability director and even served on the search committee. Other department directors—including the directors of parks and recreation and public works—also understood that having a sustainability office could help advance their goals for tree planting, community gardens, access to healthy foods, and recycling.[16]

Organizing Support for a Green City

Successful green city leaders never go it alone. Building partnerships and community support is a critical path to success, even in those cities that have built up staff and even entire departments of sustainability. City leaders dedicate much of their time and effort to building political support, cultivating internal green champions, and pursuing community partnerships.

From their first day on the job, green city leaders begin to reach out to key stakeholders to understand which greening goals and plans are most important, the barriers they will face, and the ways that the green city leader can help *them* to succeed. It is through these conversations that the green city leader discovers which actions have strong support internally and in the broader community and can produce the most cobenefits, which actions can bring recognition to and build on what they have already accomplished, which actions are likely to have the fewest barriers moving forward, and which actions will build generative relationships for the sustainability director. This process never stops.

Building Political Support

The most important contributor to a green city leader's success in advancing green initiatives is having strong support from government leaders.[17] Cities with supportive elected officials and managers report a significantly higher rate of success in funding programs, expanding the sustainability office, collaborating with other cities, and establishing core infrastructure for sustainability, such as performance management systems. A supportive mayor who advocates for greening the city will spur action. One who charges internal leaders to collaborate on greening and sets aside time and resources for them secures a bigger impact. One who rewards employees for green innovation and successes will spur even more change.

Cities that report low support for sustainability from elected officials and managers also make progress, but it is more difficult. Green city leaders with less internal support have to depend more on community support, effectively message the potential impact that sustainability can have on issues of political and community concern, and point out the other communities in the region that are already taking action.[18] Community support helps build mayoral support because political leaders care about how they are viewed by constituents and colleagues.

Targeting issues that are of high interest to political leadership is effective practice in all contexts. Many mayors have come to support a broad sustainability agenda over time after initially caring only about one narrow issue, such as beautification or public health. Green city leaders find ways to make connections to their mayor's agenda, whether that agenda is about bikes or birds. The challenge is to find ways to advance the priorities of elected officials and at the same time influence these priorities so that they advance the greening of the city. When Chicago mayor Richard Daley expressed significant concern about the cleanliness of construction sites during a construction boom in the mid-2000s, one of this book's coauthors, Sadhu Johnston, then the mayor's chief environmental officer, developed a construction site recycling law mandating that a minimum of 50 percent of the waste from large construction sites be recycled. Construction site recycling hadn't been the focus of the mayor's request, but he was pleased to see that this policy achieved his goal of cleaning up construction sites while also keeping millions of pounds of waste out of the landfill. Green city leaders can be most successful when they deliver success for their mayors while also influencing them to expand their priorities to incorporate the green agenda.

Sometimes green city leaders pursue programs or initiatives that are a priority for their mayor or city manager even if they are a poor fit with sustainability program goals. Concerned about water quality in the Great Lakes, Mayor Daley directed his environmental staff to develop programs to reduce the amount of pharmaceutical drugs that were showing up in the sewer system. Neither the city's Zero Waste Chicago plan nor the city's Water Agenda prioritized removing pharmaceuticals, so staff developed a program that enabled residents to drop off these drugs at specially designed containers at police stations. The staff delivered results for the mayor while advancing their broader waste program.

A green city leader who is located close to leadership in the mayor's or city manager's

Figure 4.2. Jurisdiction over action plan, Vancouver, British Columbia
Vancouver's Greenest City 2020 Action Plan is ambitious, but the city doesn't control all of the factors that will lead to its successful implementation. So city staff assessed their jurisdiction of the plan's implementation, and the city council adopted plans that are based on their greatest areas of leverage. Figure courtesy of the City of Vancouver.

office—as are the chief sustainability officers in New Haven, Connecticut; Chicago; New York City; Los Angeles; Seattle; and Fayetteville, Arkansas—may find it easier to sustain political support and engage senior officials across departments. The downside is that political appointees can be the first to go when the mayor or city council changes. Holding a cabinet position can also help green city leaders solidify support, as it has in Portland, Oregon, and Montreal, where green champions head departments of planning and sustainability.

Even when the green city leader is in the most challenging location—deep within a department and with little exposure or power—there is opportunity. Some cities have started out by locating the green city leader in a department but then have moved the position to the mayor's office. In Cleveland, Andrew Watterson started the city's first sustainability office from the water department. Because Watterson kept the mayor informed about the progress he was making, the cost savings he had produced, and the relation-ships he had built, the mayor invited him to move to the mayor's office.[19] The best alter-native may be to have green city leaders in both the mayor's office and the city manager's office, where they can convene all departments, and to have them serve in high-level positions within one or more departments so that they have staff and can run programs. San Francisco; Vancouver, British Columbia; Kansas City, Missouri; Denver; and many other cities have this dual structure. The success of any of these arrangements depends on strong relationships and trust.

Building Internal Support

It is the aspiration of most green city leaders to cultivate new green approaches and then embed them in other city departments and functions. This is why they nurture green champions, organize green teams, and work to build a green employee culture.

Nurturing Green Champions

Most green city leaders need the help of green champions throughout local government. These are the motivated early adopters who already organize initiatives to use less paper or procure green products. Usually what the green champions need most is encourage-ment, support, and recognition, or, as in the City of Providence, Rhode Island, which was discussed earlier, they may need better performance measurement so they can demon-strate results. They may also need mayoral support for a more ambitious goal or a change in procurement policy to allow them to purchase an innovative local technology. Or they may need their department head to allocate time for their green initiatives. The prize for empowering the early adopters is a cadre of green champions that stretches across the city, helping to undertake more initiatives, engage more employees, and unearth more partners and resources.

If green champions cannot be found, green city leaders need to work with depart-ment heads to hire additional staff. Sadhu Johnston felt that the City of Chicago needed at least one dedicated green staff member serving the parks board, school board, wa-ter department, transportation department, airport, facilities department, and purchas-ing department to ensure these areas had internal leadership on greening issues.[20] Steve Nicholas, another coauthor of this book and previously sustainability director for the City of Seattle, found that adding staff in other city departments was one of his most potent change strategies. He and his team actively sought and helped secure a position for a green fleet coordinator in the Fleets and Facilities Department, a green purchasing coor-dinator in the Department of Finance and Administrative Services, a sustainability coor-dinator in Parks and Recreation, a sustainable transportation manager in the Department of Transportation, a green affordable housing coordinator in the Office of Housing, and a green business champion in the Office of Economic Development.

Building a Green Team

Internal green teams, which bring together representatives from multiple government departments and sister agencies, can empower green champions or stifle them. When a green team is effective, team members help one another solve problems, break down silos, and take on large-scale initiatives. Unfortunately, it is much easier to create a green team than to sustain one. Many start with great anticipation and then die a slow death.

Successful green teams take on few and concrete goals, help members choose tasks that reflect their strengths and talents, set aside time for members to work on these tasks, track progress, publicly celebrate the successes of individual team members and the team, and build on these successes.[21] It is easier to sustain a green team that has high-level support from the mayor's or city manager's office. Recognition of green team members by the mayor is a reward that can also deepen support from senior managers. Recognition can be a sign on the door, a star on a badge, or increased time set aside for the work of the green team. Green teams are also easier to sustain if they have meaningful goals and an engaging process. John Coleman, former sustainability director for Fayetteville, Arkansas, staffed an employee sustainability team made up of one person from each city department. This was one of his core responsibilities, and the mayor's office supported the idea that each department should send staff members to meetings. The first project the team took on was an energy competition between buildings. It worked well to start with one small project and achieve a quick success because team members had little time to give, but this project was less successful at engaging the team than was the second attempt.

The Fayetteville green team really came together when members collaborated on a plan of action. In 2009, the team helped to develop a report on sustainability goals and metrics for various city operations; the report recognized what departments were already doing for sustainability and identified the next steps with high potential for success. Each member of a small subcommittee went out to a few departments to collect ideas and data, which were then adopted by the full green team. The team continued to meet six times a year, with two members reporting at each meeting on progress toward meeting the goals. Coleman also arranged for team members to report to the public on the city's television channel and also to make presentations at department directors' meetings attended by the mayor.[22]

Fostering a Government-wide Green Culture

Green city leaders eventually have to reach beyond the green team to engage all employees as green champions. Green messages don't work for most employees—except in cities with a deeply ingrained green culture—especially when speed and efficiency are the primary measures of job performance. The risk of trying something new can be high, and most people won't take this risk without a directive from top-level leadership. The key lessons from green city leaders who have reached "beyond the choir" are about the importance of securing top-level leadership, identifying champions and persuaders in each department, and relying on peer-to-peer engagement to drive action.

Employee engagement is the key to building a green culture. Green city leaders figure out how to provide a variety of opportunities for staff engagement through committees, work groups, educational opportunities, and department liaisons. They find ways to publicly recognize participants, and they find ways to help them undertake projects they care about that have green benefits. Sustainability program leaders in Albuquerque, New Mexico, created the Sustainability Awareness Training Program to educate staff and walk them through simple activities such as calculating their carbon footprint. Then staff members were asked to make a commitment to change one thing to reduce that footprint.

In Florida, the Sarasota County Green Champion Program provides certification to employees who complete a multicourse sustainability curriculum, recognizing that although policies and programs are important, employees are the most critical piece of the campaign to achieve sustainability. Courses in the curriculum include Introduction to Sustainability, Policies, and Commitments; Sustainability in the Workplace; Drive Green; Green at Home; Sustainable Health and Wellness; Social Sustainability; Sustainable Landscaping and Water; Healthy Eating for a Healthy Planet; and Incentives for Home Energy Improvement. This information helps employees lead by example and share information with their peers. The program's first graduating class certified thirty-four green champions. The goal is to certify 10 percent of all employees.

Green city leaders frequently recognize staff for their sustainability work. John Stokes, as sustainability leader for the City of Fort Collins, Colorado, urged peers to "carve out the doable. Measure success and failure. Overcommunicate with the organization. And, most important, recognize achievement."

Green city leaders also build education and engagement into green initiatives. Departments in the City of San Francisco achieved an 80 percent reduction in waste that otherwise would have gone into a landfill through incentives, policy, education, and engagement. The city appointed zero waste coordinators at almost every city facility to serve as ambassadors for waste prevention, recycling, composting, and green purchasing in their departments. These coordinators work with the city's Department of the Environment to ensure that their departments are modeling the best waste reduction and buying choices, to monitor compliance with existing waste reduction programs, and to create new programs where appropriate. To support their efforts, the Department of the Environment developed comprehensive educational programs and trained more than 10,000 employ-ees, custodians, property managers, and purchasers on the benefits and procedures of waste prevention, recycling, and composting.[23]

But education often fails to translate into behavioral change unless green city leaders also identify and remove barriers to action. People may print e-mail because they don't know how to access their messages in an archive. They may print memos and mark them up because they don't know how to use the "track changes" feature to edit on the com-puter. They may not recycle because they don't have convenient access to bins. They may not bike to work because they think it takes too much time or they think the physical exertion could make them perspire and there are no showers. Community-based social marketing is one tool that green city leaders use to identify and eliminate these barriers and communicate about the benefits of taking action.

Building Partnerships with Community Institutions

The most profound greening will take place out in the community but only if there is broad public involvement, and one of the best ways to involve the public is to partner with respected community institutions (see chapter 3). This is why the Baltimore Office of Sustainability, in partnership with the Baltimore Community Foundation, launched the Baltimore Neighborhood Energy Challenge in August 2009 to motivate households to reduce energy use. It is also why Boston's sustainability director worked with the Barr Foundation to convene the Boston Green Ribbon Commission, which included leaders from business, education, health care, civic society, finance, real estate, professional ser-vices, tourism, and other sectors, to support the outcomes of the city's Climate Action Plan—including getting 150 large commercial and industrial enterprises to adopt internal strategies to reduce their greenhouse gas emissions by 25 percent by 2020. Sustainability commissions are most effective when they take responsibility for achieving specific goals. As with internal green teams, they need to have work plans and performance goals that foster participation and inspire action.

Even internal leadership-by-example initiatives can require external support, espe-cially when decisions involve spending money or changing policy. One reason the City of Providence, Rhode Island, created a sustainability office was that both environmental groups and organized labor supported the idea.[24] Ann Arbor's community-wide environ-mental commission, which was written into city code, drove the hiring of an environ-mental coordinator.[25] The City of Cleveland's first sustainability coordinator position was paid for by the George Gund Foundation and the Cleveland Foundation and was spear-headed by EcoCity Cleveland, a nonprofit environmental organization.

Green city leaders often advocate for the creation of sustainability commissions that

Figure 4.3. Talk Green to Us forum, Vancouver, British Columbia, 2010
Vancouver mayor Gregor Robertson and other green city leaders participated in a forum in which the top five voted-on ideas from the city's online engagement were presented, discussed, and then integrated into the city's formally adopted Greenest City 2020 Action Plan. Photo courtesy of the City of Vancouver.

bring together key community leaders who are willing to help advance green initiatives. These commissions can add stature to sustainability efforts, enhance mayoral support, and attract new resources. But even when there is a great commission, green city leaders must also join the coalitions and committees that have been created in the community and find ways to help them succeed. They can extend the reach of these initiatives by bringing city assets to the efforts, whether this means help with permitting, access to land, or moral support.

Fostering Community-wide Change Makers

Green city leaders spend an increasing share of their time grappling with how to activate the broader community in greening efforts, using a tool kit that includes broad engagement, transparency, accountability, and empowerment. Green city leaders are also pushing the boundaries on ways to reach stakeholders. ImagineCalgary was an eighteen-month public engagement project launched in January 2005 and involving more than 18,000 Calgarians who contributed ideas, making it one of the largest community visioning processes of its kind. And green city leaders are pushing boundaries on transparency and accountability. New York City mayor Michael Bloomberg's PlaNYC, released in 2007, provides annual progress reports to the public, and the city attributes some of the plan's success to this sharing of data and results.

Green city leaders are also moving beyond consultation to authentic engagement. In 2011, New York City's Office of the Mayor launched Change by Us NYC, a website designed to enable New Yorkers to find or initiate projects and build teams that can make the city a better place in which to live. The site, created by a media design firm named Local Projects and run by the city, also connects project leaders to public and nonprofit programs that can help. Change by Us NYC offers small grants to New Yorkers who are organizing around issues that relate to city goals; as of May 2013 it had spurred development of more than 3,500 ideas and 450 projects.[26] Similarly, the City of Vancouver, British Columbia, and the Vancouver Foundation together created the Greenest City Fund, a four-year, $2 million fund to support community-led green projects that address goals in the Greenest City 2020 Action Plan. Minigrant programs for community projects are proliferating in other cities too.

Embedding Sustainability in Government Practice

Green city leaders face a daunting task in making sustainability the default way of doing business. They need to achieve quick results, but they need to do so in a way that helps embed sustainability thinking in decision-making processes. They need to be seen as an asset by all departments without getting overwhelmed by demand for their involvement. They have chosen to build their case by saving resources and money, but they also need to prepare their city leaders for changes that involve increased risk and cost. They have to appeal to what matters most to potential partners while also showing them how their goals connect to other goals. James Joerke, former sustainability director of Johnson County, Kansas, says green city leaders must "lead with common sense value creation, but always hint at the bigger picture—environmental quality, economic vitality, social equity."[27]

While significant change can result from sustained incremental projects that focus on what people already care about, these incremental steps will not take a city all the way to sustainability. Roy Brooke, director of sustainability for the City of Victoria, British Columbia, explained it this way in an op-ed that appeared on www.iPolitics.ca on July 4, 2012: "Sustainability used to focus on saving energy and wasting less. Such efforts remain vitally important, and offer scores of opportunities to increase efficiency and profits. However, these . . . initiatives are really about doing less bad. . . . Scale is the challenge now . . . many more connected, pervasive and coordinated projects are needed; systems are needed."[28]

Making sustainability the default approach is a disruptive endeavor. It requires a change in the understanding of problems (e.g., climate change), tools (e.g., life-cycle analysis), solutions (e.g., distributed), and measures of success (e.g., resilience). It requires a commitment to more holistic approaches and innovation across the public, private, and nonprofit sectors.[29]

The national nonprofit Innovation Network for Communities created its Four Stages for Sustainability Checklist after talking to eighty members of the Urban Sustainability Directors Network who described their progression toward making sustainability the default driver and the measure of success for local government. The four stages in the schema are (1) setting vision and direction, (2) engaging and empowering stakeholders, (3) capturing results in performance management systems, and (4) embedding sustainability in continuous improvement. Even while green city leaders work on early wins, they need to look for opportunities to move through these stages.

First Stage: Setting Vision and Direction

This first stage of institutionalizing sustainability is about establishing goals and raising visibility: elected officials articulate the vision and the case for sustainability and local government's role in making it happen. The city identifies and announces the first sustainability initiatives or blueprint for action and develops a budget for green initiative development. Internal communications and education programs begin to promote sustainability projects. Elected officials and managers communicate with the public about the vision and early initiatives. The mayor may create a sustainability office or function with staff and funding to help accomplish the vision.

St. Louis, Missouri's, triple bottom line sustainability planning process, completed in late 2012, has contributed to a major increase in understanding of and support for sustainability among public officials and the community. According to Catherine Werner, the city's sustainability director, the planning process increased the understanding of the triple bottom line approach to sustainability, buy-in for the resulting plan, and commitment to tracking implementation and progress.

Second Stage: Engaging and Empowering Stakeholders

The second stage of institutionalizing sustainability is largely about broadening involvement, support, and collaboration. Departments come together to design crosscutting projects while also beginning to develop their own sustainability goals, plans, and budgets. Interdepartmental green teams take on projects, such as employee behavior change around recycling, water conservation, energy saving, and commuting, which allow the city to lead by example. Government officials partner with civic organizations on community-wide plans and initiatives and community-based education. Local governments increasingly coordinate with other communities in the region, sometimes establishing regional structures for sharing information and undertaking projects.

When the City of Chicago decided in 2008 to create the Chicago Climate Action Plan for mitigation and adaptation, green city leaders built an entire engagement apparatus that included more than 500 local and regional leaders, many of whom became champions for implementing the goals of the plan. (See the case in point on the CCAP at www .guidetogreeningcities.org.) In 2010, the City of Chicago joined with the Chicago Metropolitan Agency for Planning, utility companies, other local governments, and citizen advocacy groups in creating Energy Impact Illinois, which received a $25 million grant from the US Department of Energy to build a comprehensive, sustainable energy efficiency retrofit program for commercial, industrial, and residential buildings.

Third Stage: Capturing Results in Performance Management Systems

The third stage of institutionalizing sustainability involves integrating sustainability goals into performance management systems and tracking and rewarding performance. Sustainability goals are embedded in budgets and work plans. Elected officials establish goals and metrics and ask for progress reports by department—government-wide and community-wide. Progress indicators are shared with all stakeholders and the community. The departmental sustainability goals are embedded in job descriptions and staff performance evaluations. Community partnerships also have measurable goals, and government and community groups together develop and broadly share a community-wide sustainability dashboard (see chapter 6).

Gayle Prest, sustainability director for the City of Minneapolis, tried from the very beginning to integrate sustainability into every department and activity. She knew that "the way this was really going to work was if all these departments saw sustainability not as separate from their jobs but as the ultimate goal of their jobs." She decided not to create a sustainability plan, instead working across city departments to achieve a formal adoption of sustainability goals and agreement on the need for annual reporting on performance measures. All departments incorporated sustainability indicators into their five-year business plans and developed implementation plans. Comparing this with creating a sustainability plan that might just sit on the shelf, she noted, "It's much more important and effective to integrate sustainability into updates of existing transportation, storm water, and affordable housing plans."[30]

Fourth Stage: Embedding Sustainability in Continuous Improvement

The fourth stage of institutionalizing sustainability is about solidifying a green city culture, continuing to improve, and staying on the cutting edge. All levels of government produce sustainability improvement plans and budgets, and these reflect increasing levels of collaboration across departments. Employees continually contribute new ideas for leading by example and are rewarded for these ideas. Community members are involved in a variety of ongoing processes for creating, refining, and scaling green initiatives. Overarching progress is tracked, and plans are revised to ensure continued progress. Chapter 6 describes the performance management systems that emerge when sustainability has been institutionalized.

The integration of social, economic, and environmental sustainability departments in Fort Collins, Colorado, provides one good example. Fort Collins, as described earlier, has a Sustainability Program that tries to move beyond greening to a triple bottom line. Its city council approved the new Sustainability Services Area department in 2011 to increase coordination, accountability, and collaboration across the city functions and services that address the triple bottom line of economic health, environmental services, and social sustainability. The Sustainability Services Area includes offices for affordable housing and human services, economic health, and environmental services.

Building a Sustainability Field of Practice

The municipal sustainability field still is in an early stage of development. It faces unique tensions, including high stakes; high aspirations; massive technical, financial, and political barriers; and pressure to share only successes. As pointed out by the nonprofit Innovation Network for Communities, when a field is moving from vision to deep practice and measurable performance, networks to foster exchange and peer learning are valuable. They can foster convergence around common methods and tools and integration of practices.

In 2009, Sadhu Johnston, Amanda Eichel (now with the C40 Cities Climate Leadership Group), and Julia Parzen founded the Urban Sustainability Directors Network to help municipal sustainability leaders achieve more rapid proliferation and adoption of sustainability ideas through honest exchange in a safe environment. Since that time, USDN members have tripled the size of the network, built strong peer connections, and pursued a variety of collaborations to advance urban sustainability. Today, USDN is a network of about 120 North American municipal sustainability leaders and 400 of their staff members.

USDN members have worked together in user groups on dozens of sustainability topics, such as enhancing revenue models for bike sharing, integrating adaptation planning into city departments, exploring the benefits of eco-districts for advancing sustainability, adding an equity lens to sustainability project development, building urban food systems, partnering with federal agencies to advance sustainability, improving messaging about sustainability, developing ways to capture data on outcomes of investment in energy efficiency in multifamily housing, implementing best practices for sustainability indicators, developing a typology of effective approaches to fostering sustainable behavior, and developing asset maps of ways to advance sustainable economic development.

USDN members also collaborate by applying for grants from the USDN Innovation Fund, which was created by USDN members in 2009. Innovation Fund proposals from USDN members provide a "market test" of which innovations matter to cities and which are likely to be adopted. Since 2009, a steering committee of USDN members has awarded $700,000 to eighteen collaborative projects, and funding grows each year. More than half of all members have participated in developing a proposal. The types of projects supported by the fund range from a study of innovative waste diversion technologies and process systems that would help participating cities reach maximum diversion at the absolute lowest overall cost and environmental impact, to a design for the features and functions of a sustainable rental housing selection tool to be developed collaboratively between cities and universities.

To fund implementation of proven innovations, in 2012 USDN partnered with the Funders' Network for Smart Growth and Livable Communities to launch the Local Sustainability Matching Fund (LSMF). The purpose of the LSMF is to catalyze partnerships between municipal sustainability directors and local, place-based foundations to advance important community-based sustainability initiatives. The fund provides matching investments from national foundations on a competitive basis to build these partnerships.

Although USDN is a private peer network, all of the products of Innovation Grants are disseminated beyond the network. Part of the content of this book is drawn from USDN member discussions and projects over the past four years.

Conclusion

Some green city leaders say that their goal is to work themselves out of a job. As the vision and goals for achieving sustainability are embedded in various city departments, budgets, and performance management systems, sustainability directors have less to do. However, they continue to have an important role as brokers and facilitators of solutions that cross departments, city functions, and communities. To be successful in generating comprehensive, multidisciplinary solutions, cities will continue to need people who can be connectors and catalysts and who have the skills of sustainability directors.

CASE IN POINT:

Funding Sustainability through Savings in Asheville

Green city leaders are like alchemists: with few resources and not much in the way of institutionalized power, they conjure up results. They can do this by building relationships with colleagues who do have resources and power and by brainstorming with these colleagues on ways to address problems in other departments with solutions that also green city government. From the start, Maggie Ullman understood that her mission as manager of the Office of Sustainability in Asheville, North Carolina, was to make her job unnecessary by finding champions for sustainability among senior managers of other city departments. "Institutionalizing sustainability means implementing strategies that result in other people carrying the torch," says Ullman, "so that one day my job title is unnecessary."

The Inside Story

From her first day on the job in 2008, Ullman's approach to advancing sustainability in the City of Asheville was to be a problem solver and capacity builder for city project managers. She spent time with them and learned about their goals and the barriers they faced until she understood enough to begin to suggest creative ways to solve their problems that would also advance the sustainability agenda. This meant that she spent time with staff from many departments, waiting for the right moment when it was possible to find a win-win green solution. She was flexible about problem solving and willing to help other departments in any way she could, whether it was convening meetings, taking minutes, or writing grant proposals. Along the way, she built trust and earned a place on the problem-solving team.

Ullman used these efforts to build green capacity in other departments. She went out of her way to help her colleagues become knowledgeable about sustainability in a way that would allow them to become the experts, but from their own departments' perspectives. And she stayed in the background, making sure they got credit for the progress. In the process, some of these staff members were won over to the green approach and came to see the Office of Sustainability as a partner. For example, the Information Technology Services Department and the Office of Sustainability often partnered on finding resources during the budget process.

Ullman also worked with the city's fire chief to fund and complete energy efficiency projects in the city's fire stations, and the chief later asked if the Office of Sustainability and the fire department could continue working together to keep the momentum going once the buildings were retrofitted. They worked together to figure out how firefighters could help the city reach its sustainability goals. They decided that the Office of Sustainability would provide energy performance reports for each fire station, which the fire chief would use to demonstrate to the city council his department's commitment to policy goals, as well as the results of the department's energy conservation efforts.

After many successes working with various departments in this way, Ullman found an opportunity to advance sustainability and improve the efficiency of the city's budget management. Using the same collaborative consultation process, she reached out to senior leaders to ask where budget processes were producing suboptimal outcomes and offered to pull together working groups to come up with solutions. The senior leaders knew, on the basis of their experience with Ullman, that she was not trying to take over the process or get more money for the sustainability program. And they were all dissatisfied with the current budget processes.

Ullman found that she could help city departments modify budget priorities in ways that helped projects get funding and that advanced sustainability at the same time. She had built a relationship with the fleet manager and public works director after helping secure a grant for new compressed natural gas vehicles. The fleet division used an American Public Works Association (APWA) method to score vehicles and determine when they should be replaced, and Ullman stayed at the table during the procurement process to learn more about fleet decisions. The fleet manager knew that other departments were holding on to poorly working vehicles—even though these vehicles cost more to maintain and consumed more fuel—because they didn't want to be caught short when vehicles were out of commission.

Figure 4.4. Fleet maintenance building, Asheville, North Carolina
City departments in Asheville were holding on to older, poorly working vehicles—even though they cost more to maintain and consumed more fuel—because they didn't want to get caught short. Green city leaders figured out how to incentivize the right decisions, thereby encouraging city departments to dispose of old vehicles. Photo courtesy of the City of Asheville, North Carolina.

Ullman approached the leaders of the fleet division with an idea she thought could convince the departments to voluntarily reduce their total fleet size while also improving the fleet's environmental profile. She proposed that the division add some priorities to the APWA rating, and she convened a working group that came up with a way to incentivize the right decisions. If a department agreed to voluntarily retire two poorly functioning vehicles in exchange for one new vehicle, its request would be prioritized in the budget process, and the department would be more likely to get the vehicle. And if a department downsized its vehicles or chose more fuel-efficient vehicles, its request would also be prioritized. Many departments appreciated the new criteria and their new vehicles. Ullman recommended more ways to prioritize green procurement, not all of which have been adopted, but she says she will bring them back for consideration when they have broader support.

Cities rarely have enough money to fund all their capital needs, and this work helped Ullman better understand the challenges the city's budget director faced when prioritizing requests for funding. It was about this time that Ullman met with Asheville's chief financial officer to discuss a long-term strategy for funding green capital improvements, including the replacement of 9,000 streetlights with energy-efficient LED fixtures. In 2010, the Asheville City Council had adopted a goal of reducing the city government's carbon footprint by 20 percent over five years, and this was one of the recommended carbon reduction initiatives. In order to pay for this project at a time when capital budgets were declining, Ullman suggested that the city create a finance team to explore the idea of recycling the savings these green projects would produce, and she got the go-ahead.

Ullman assembled a team that included herself and the city's chief financial officer, budget manager, accounting manager, and assistant director of public works—key players who would understand financial, operational, and technical barriers. Ullman argued that recycling the savings wouldn't increase the city's budget because the projects would save more than they cost, and the margin could be used to help fund other capital projects. "Lightbulbs went off in people's heads," Ullman said, but the idea proved difficult to negotiate because it required changes in accounting and financial reporting, and it became clear that Ullman would have to wait and let the idea ripen.

When Ullman's boss moved into the position of chief financial officer, she approved the idea of creating what was named the Green Capital Improvement Program (Green CIP), which would create a new revenue stream from the savings of sustainability projects. This would allow the city to fund more projects more quickly by improving access to capital, which would in turn offset future costs by, for example, reducing deferred maintenance. If more sustainability projects were funded, the city could achieve its goals faster, meanwhile increasing the savings that the city could reinvest. "The fund created through the Green Capital Improvement Program merged new revenue and cost reductions," explains Ullman.

The city council endorsed this approach because staff could demonstrate it would help fund important policy initiatives that were unfunded, and staff could demonstrate reliable positive payback with detailed financial spreadsheets for each project. The table summarizes the Office of Sustainability's initial projections of cost, funding source, return on investment, and reductions in greenhouse gas emissions for all of the city's carbon reduction projects, including the Green CIP projects.[31]

The LED streetlight program, for example, was expected to generate $3.3 million in savings above and beyond what is required to retire the installation debt—money that will be available to fund other energy-saving initiatives. The city council agreed to leave the operations budget line item for the non-LED streetlights unchanged and to authorize the difference between that amount and the reduced cost of operating the LED streetlights to go to the Green CIP fund. The city council authorized what is essentially an internally managed energy performance contract for a minimum of thirteen years (the time required to retire the debt). In this way, the Green CIP is financed entirely through energy savings over time.

The Office of Sustainability has moved from the City Manager's Office to the Finance Department, where it manages the Green CIP. This relocation was part of an expansion of the Finance Department to include management services, and it proved fortuitous. This exposure to capital planning, budget planning, and internal workflow processes and staff has helped Ullman strengthen the sustainability program.

Results to Date

Asheville's Office of Sustainability has helped to incentivize green decisions and priorities and has created a green capital investment fund that provides an ongoing revenue stream for greening efforts. This has helped to institutionalize sustainability within the Finance Department, where all budget decisions are made. Ullman has built relationships with many departments, which continue to yield win-win project collaborations.

Challenges

Ullman anxiously watches utility bills to ensure that actual savings meet or exceed projected savings—she says that the measurement and verification of savings is the most stressful part of this project. Utility rate increases are hard to predict. As utility rates have gone up, savings have gone down, and Ullman hasn't been able to program as many capital projects. To make sure that savings are sufficient to cover debt service for

Table 4.1. Return on Investment (ROI) and Emissions Reductions of Carbon Reduction Projects, Asheville, North Carolina

Project	Five-Year Investment	Revenue Source	ROI (years)	Reduction
City hall lighting retrofit	$136,000	Grant	11.3	0.33%
Solar thermal power at stations 6 and 8	$21,000	Grant	7.8	0.05%
Computer server virtualization	$100,000	Grant	10.0	0.16%
North Fork Treatment Plant motor upgrades	$510,000	Grant	12.8	1.41%
Energy manager	$375,000	General Fund	1.0	1.80%
LED streetlights, phase 1	$290,000	Grant	6.1	0.79%
Clean Cities Grant for twenty-seven compressed natural gas vehicle retrofits	$425,326	Grant	1.0	1.14%
Civic center heating, ventilation, and air-conditioning retrofits	$130,000	Grant and Green CIP	26.0	0.23%
Transit bus replacements	$2,600,000	Grant	—	0.81%
LED streetlights, phase 2	$3,031,814	Green CIP	5.1	7.11%
City hall and public works building automation	$558,000	Green CIP	15.5	0.98%
Solar thermal power for ten fire stations	$130,000	Green CIP	8.7	0.23%
City hall window replacements	$500,000	CIP	62.5	0.15%
Insulation during roof replacements	$200,000	CIP	20.0	0.23%
Upgrading full diesel fleet to B20	$375,000	Green CIP	—	1.58%
Facilities maintenance staff	$500,000	Green CIP	5.0	1.95%
Sustainability outreach and education program	$250,000	Green CIP	5.0	1.70%
Other	—	Green CIP	—	0.30%
Total	**$10,132,140**			**20.95%**

Figure 4.5. Asheville streetlights
Asheville's LED streetlight program is expected to generate $3.3 million in savings above and beyond what is required to retire the debt from the project—money that will be available to fund other energy-saving initiatives. Photo by Greg Plachta.

the LED streetlights and to fund other sustainability projects, Ullman and her energy analyst regularly check that LED lights have been installed on schedule and that utility bills accurately reflect the LED light installations. If savings are less than projected, the City of Asheville must find money elsewhere in the budget to fund implementation of the sustainability program.

Key Factors for Success

Success in Asheville was solidly due to learning how and why decisions are made and funds are allocated. These are essentials for all change making.

Understanding why decisions are made. Ullman's success in Asheville is largely due to her interest in understanding the challenges faced by the city's departments and her ability to come up with creative solutions to their problems.

Solving problems with green solutions. Ullman came up with creative and workable solutions to challenges experienced by other departments that also advanced her sustainability agenda.

Catalyzing change. Ullman looked for ways to address the barriers that stood in the way of green decisions, whether this required money, information, or just more time.

Learning budget and finance skills. The Asheville City Council endorsed the Green CIP in part because staff presented the financial analysis that was needed to make the risk acceptable.

CASE IN POINT:

Permeable Pavement and the Green Alley Program in Chicago

Chicago has experienced extreme rain events that have overtaxed the city's combined sewer overflow system and required expensive sewer infrastructure upgrades. But building more sewers only exacerbated the problem, prompting the city to begin experimenting with faster, cheaper solutions, including the installation of permeable pavement in alleys. Permeable pavement, however, was both unfamiliar and unproven. "Getting over the hurdle of whether we could do this was only the first challenge,"[32] says Janet Attarian, project director for this initiative led by the Chicago Department of Transportation. "Costs were the second challenge, which we were able to meet only by working with our suppliers." Eventually, this led to the manufacturing of a permeable pavement product that cost the same as traditional pavement. Now most alley construction projects are built to allow rainfall in the city to filter into the ground under the alleyways—reducing local flooding, recharging the groundwater, and saving taxpayers money that would otherwise be spent treating storm water.

The Inside Story

Like many older cities, Chicago has a combined sewer overflow system that frequently backs up into basements or overflows into the natural waterways. These problems have gotten worse in recent decades as more and more land has been covered with impervious surfaces—approximately 25 percent of Chicago's surfaces are paved—and because of the increasing number of extreme storm events resulting from climate change. The conventional solution is to install sewer pipes under the street to catch the storm water and deliver it to the sewer system. But many alleys in Chicago didn't have street sewers, and transporting so much water could make the overflow problem worse.

Chicago's regional sewer district dealt with the issue by installing a huge underground storage system to hold the storm water until the storms pass and the treatment plants have regained capacity. But despite the investment of billions of dollars, the problem continued. To proactively address these problems, the city began experimenting with ways to keep the water out of the system, such as the use of rain barrels, green roofs, and other green infrastructure, including innovative pavement technologies.

Mayor Richard M. Daley had begun investigating green building techniques a decade before this discussion about permeable pavement, and he insisted that the city let nature do its job and allow rainwater to filter into the ground rather than being treated as waste in the sewer system. Despite the mayor's earlier successes with installing green roofs, disconnecting downspouts, and creating rain gardens, however, the city engineers and the private road-building contractors were skeptical. "Any good road designer knows that water is the enemy of the road—and that it was crazy for them to consider allowing rain to permeate the road," explains Attarian. "Neither the city nor the industry had experience in this area." But the mayor persevered and pushed his staff to explore other options.

Results to Date

The Chicago Department of Transportation began experimenting with alternative pavement in 2006, installing five green alleys in different parts of the city using different approaches and materials—including permeable pavement, pavers, French drains and infiltration basins, reflective surfaces, and recycled materials. An approach was chosen for each alley depending on the type of soil, the environmental challenges particular to the area, and other local conditions.

As stated in the city's "Green Alley Handbook," "While one solution to this problem is to install expensive connections to the City sewer system, the Green Alley Program also looks at other more sustainable solutions. In particular, where soil conditions are appropriate, water is allowed to infiltrate into the soils through permeable pavement or infiltration basins, instead of being directed into the sewer system or onto adjacent property. This not only solves a persistent problem, but it also provides an environmental benefit by cleaning and recharging the ground water. Furthermore, by not sending additional water to the combined sewer system a green alley can help alleviate basement and other flooding issues."[33]

The pilot project using permeable pavement worked well, was easy to install, and was durable enough to withstand a snowplow. It worked best in parts of the city that had sandy soils. By allowing rainwater to flow straight into the ground, permeable pavement reduces the problem of flooding without overtaxing the sewer system or requiring the construction of more sewer pipes or storage capacity. But although the innovative approach was promising, there were significant challenges, including a lack of experience among city staff and their industry partners, high costs, unknown maintenance needs, new design specifications, and skepticism among residents.

Figure 4.6. Green alley installation, Chicago
The City of Chicago experimented with five green alley installations using different approaches and materials depending on the soil, the environmental challenges, and other local conditions. Permeable pavement, which works best in sandy soils, allows rainwater to filter into the ground rather than flowing into pipes, which requires energy and chemicals to treat the water. Photo courtesy of the City of Chicago.

Despite the initial challenges, the City of Chicago established the Green Alley Program in order to continue to experiment and then expand the deployment of successful approaches, which became popular among residents and garnered considerable media attention. More than 200 green alleys have been built since 2006, and this green approach is now business as usual. "There is no non-green alley program," notes Janet Attarian. "When people call to ask for a green alley, I tell them that there's only one alley program."

The city has also begun installing permeable pavement on arterial streets. The first project was part of a major street renovation called the Pilsen Sustainable Street, which included permeable pavement, rain gardens, wind-powered lighting, and an additive called photocatalytic cement. The additive causes a chemical reaction between air pollutants and sunlight that has the effect of filtering the pollutants out of the air, and it also helps keep the cement white and thereby keeps the road cooler. Urged to do even more by Chicago's new mayor, Rahm Emanuel, Attarian and her staff are now applying what they

Figure 4.7. Permeable asphalt alley, Chicago
When permeable pavement was new to Chicago's construction industry, it cost three times as much as conventional paving approaches. City and industry representatives worked together to refine specifications, and within a year prices were equivalent to those for standard paving approaches. Photo courtesy of the City of Chicago.

have learned to the development of Sustainable Urban Infrastructure Guidelines and Policies for other city infrastructure investments.

Key Factors for Success

Challenging the fundamental approaches to road building and urban storm-water management didn't happen in Chicago without significant effort, and many lessons have been learned that can guide other cities in adopting permeable pavement or other changes to conventional approaches.

Adopt realistic design standards. Unrealistic design standards hindered early attempts to build green alleys. In the beginning, they were designed to withstand a hundred-year rain event—a storm with a 1 percent probability of occurring in any given year—even though conventional streets were not designed to such a high standard. When the standards were eventually lowered to a five-year rain event, installing the green alleys became cost-effective.

Help industry gain experience and comfort. The road construction industry was skeptical about permeable pavement in the beginning. But after much trial and error in the lab, the city worked with a private contractor who built the first green alley using a mobile mixer to refine the concrete on-site. While this approach required more effort, it was worth it, and the contractor was ultimately able to mix the concrete at its facility, which brought down the price.

Develop good specifications. City staff experimented with different concrete mixes in the lab in order to figure out which formulations worked best. Then the results were integrated into the design specifications when city staff was bidding contracts for construction. In this way, the city was able to help the industry develop a product that worked and at a price that was realistic.

Drive down costs. Because permeable pavement was new to the construction industry, the first five pilots were expensive. While conventional concrete cost $50 per cubic yard, permeable pavement cost $150 per cubic yard for the five pilots. Fortunately, there was no need to install sewer pipes below the permeable pavement, which yielded a cost savings. Because the city continued to work closely with the industry, by the second year of the program the price of permeable pavement per yard was the same as the price of conventional concrete. Moreover, the concrete suppliers realized this was an opportunity to diversify their product lines and to expand their market by offering green solutions.

Experiment with maintenance. Permeable pavement is porous, so it collects dirt and leaves; therefore, city staff also experimented with the maintenance program, finally determining that the pavement needed to be swept clean twice a year in order to remain porous.

5.
Getting Down to Business
Budgeting, Financing,
and Green Economic Development

*"We launched our city's green vision
as an economic development plan.
Being able to show benefits to livability,
job creation, and attracting a talented
workforce has helped us sell some pretty
difficult programs. Being green is part
of doing good business."*

—Jo Zientek, deputy director,
Environmental Services Department,
City of San Jose

In recent years, green city leaders have entered the business realm committed to securing the second leg of sustainability's three-legged stool: economic vitality. In Boston, they are partnering with business leaders on the Green Ribbon Commission to implement a climate action plan sector by sector. In Chicago and Houston, they are recognizing businesses that green their operations through the Green Office Challenge. In El Paso, Texas, and San Jose, California, they are providing city facilities as demonstration sites for new technologies. In Portland, Oregon, and Tucson, Arizona, they are helping launch new green business clusters. In Cincinnati, Ohio, and Asheville, North Carolina, they are partnering with finance and budget departments and are fully involved in calculating returns on investment, cost savings, and other benefits of advancing sustainability.

No doubt, government budget woes and the recession have accelerated the integration of economic issues into sustainability work, but the holistic approaches that green city leaders are championing have also pulled them in this direction. For example, they have made the case for green infrastructure by monetizing benefits that go beyond reduced flooding, such as recreational access for residents and the reuse of vacant land. When they have launched massive energy efficiency retrofit partnerships in their communities, they have worked with training institutions to produce a skilled workforce ready to do the work. They have recruited entrepreneurs to create new companies to process organic waste in order to advance recycling. They have increased the renewable energy share of the energy supply by taking advantage of new third-party financing mechanisms.

Green city leaders are moving from a green lens to a broader focus on the triple bottom line of balancing environmental, economic, and—increasingly—social goals. It's a natural progression that is gaining momentum because it makes it easier to justify and advance a great variety of green initiatives. This chapter explores the expanding roles of green city leaders in public finance and budgeting, private finance, and business and economic development.

The Role of the Green City Leader in Public Finance and Budgeting

Most of the first wave of green city leaders began their careers as environmental scientists, lawyers, or policy makers. They may have mastered public finance in order to find ways to implement sustainability plans that drive large-scale investments in energy efficiency, electric vehicles, waste reduction, urban food hubs, green infrastructure, distributed energy, renewable energy, and transit-oriented development.

Green city leaders have found key allies in their cities' budget, finance, and legal departments. Maggie Ullman, sustainability program manager for the City of Asheville, North Carolina, found that the Office of Sustainability and the budget department shared a more holistic view of the city than did most of the other departments in charge of one city function.[1] Larry Falkin, director of the City of Cincinnati's Office of Environmental Quality, concluded that "the sustainability office and budget office are natural allies most of the time, because they are focused beyond the current budget cycle on the long-term success of the city and city government, on mitigating risk, and on eliminating waste."[2]

Ullman, Falkin, and other green city leaders built partnerships with budget directors by respecting the budget process and helping budget directors to be successful in their jobs.

They learned not simply to pitch new ideas, which budget directors hear from every department every day, but rather to show how they would deliver cost savings and other benefits. They made their pitches at the right time in the budget-planning time line and followed budget procedures. And they solved problems for the budget director.

Ullman sees working with the budget director as basic customer service: because the budget director needs to balance the budget every year and gets caught between competing priorities, Ullman continuously looks for ways to help. She aligns her program goals around opportunities to increase revenue, attract grants, and decrease costs. For example, she introduced the idea of leasing the rooftops of government buildings for renewable energy installations, thereby providing a new revenue source for the City of Asheville. She successfully proposed ways to streamline the prioritization process for municipal capital investments and to align competing interests by incorporating additional green prioritization factors into capital decisions. She helped the budget office convene other departments to get their input and build support for these new approaches.[3] For example, building renovation projects now receive a higher ranking on the capital project list if they show a positive return on the investment from energy savings, as do vehicle purchases if they use alternative fuels that will produce a savings in operations.

Green city leaders have also found ways to become valued partners to other city departments in the budgeting process. Early in his tenure, John Coleman, former sustainability director of Fayetteville, Arkansas, and now a private sector energy consultant, was invited to sit in on higher-level city budget meetings as a professional development opportunity. As Coleman came to understand the budgeting process, he began to take a more proactive role in budget discussions. In one instance, he was able to successfully argue against eliminating funding for a solar thermal dryer for biosolids—processed wastewater solids that can be used as fertilizer—by preparing a more complete financial analysis. Coleman showed how the dryer could help the city create commercial-grade compost, which could then be sold and would also reduce the amount of waste sent to the landfill, thereby saving money on disposal fees.

Over time, Coleman assumed a role in the budget discussions of multiple departments, which allowed him to advocate for adding green features to projects—such as reducing waste and saving resources—before budget decisions were finalized. "Other department heads or staff members know that I'm thinking about more than just environmental issues—that I want to understand the process—and they're more comfortable with me in meetings because of that," he said at the time.[4] This kind of consistent access to the budget process allows green city leaders to find opportunities to advance their agendas at the same time they bring their expertise to bear on improving projects that other departments have prioritized.

Green city leaders in dozens of cities are using financial analysis to track and share their results over time, building credibility with mayors' offices and budget departments. In 2005, Boston's Environmental and Energy Services Department worked with the Office of Budget Management to centralize the city's electricity accounts, aggregate total city energy demand, and put a request for proposals out to bid for meeting the city's energy needs. The city saved 10 percent on electricity purchases under this new energy contract. Under Boston's Integrated Energy Management Plan, Jim Hunt, then head of the Environmental and Energy Services Department, and his team tracked and shared data on the continued savings from all of his office's energy efficiency projects, which amounted to millions of dollars per year. Later, the office began tracking energy savings from solar and wind installations, demonstrating that these projects were saving the city money by offsetting the use of utility-provided energy, taking advantage of incentives, and selling renewable energy credits, or RECs—certificates representing proof that the city had generated one megawatt-hour of electricity from an eligible renewable energy resource. Purchasers of RECs buy them from the city so that they can claim credit for the use of renewable energy—the city effectively monetizes what is otherwise only an environmental benefit. Through these efforts, the Environmental and Energy Services Department became a close partner of the Office of Budget Management and the Property and Construction Management Department in prioritizing energy projects.[5]

The capacity to produce sophisticated financial analyses has helped many green city leaders convince their cities to invest in sustainability projects not already in the budget. In 2008, for example, Larry Falkin, head of Cincinnati's Office of Environmental Quality (OEQ), proposed using energy service performance contracts to help the city reduce energy costs, although there were no funds in the capital budget for energy efficiency investments. Energy performance contracting allows a city to enter into an agreement with a private energy service company that will identify and evaluate energy-saving opportunities and then recommend a package of improvements that can be paid for through savings. The energy company will guarantee that savings meet or exceed annual payments to cover all project costs, and if they don't, the energy company will pay the difference. After a long collaborative development and learning process, the budget office agreed to invest $10 million to retrofit sixty-nine city buildings because the savings would be sufficient to pay off the debt.

When Cincinnati's OEQ wanted to enhance the city's recycling program, staff penciled out a conceptual plan to use $4 million in bonds to buy six-gallon recycling carts. These would allow to city to reduce the frequency of collection from weekly to biweekly, which would reduce hauling fees. This enhanced recycling program would also reduce disposal costs, thereby yielding a net savings over the current costs of waste collection. The city also rewarded residents for recycling, assigning points that could be redeemed at stores and restaurants. The OEQ pointed out that this enhanced recycling program was also a job creator—thirty-five jobs are created for every 10,000 tons recycled, and the recycling program was projected to recycle 13,000 tons. The budget office modified Falkin's assumptions but supported the project, using capital and Energy Efficiency and Conservation Block Grant (EECBG) funding to purchase the carts and using the projected savings to help balance the budget. Eventually Falkin was invited to join the capital committee, which reviews the city's six-year spending plans.

However, an ongoing commitment to be part of the budget process demands a great deal of time. Green city leaders are tracking both operating and capital budgets—which sometimes are developed and approved at the same time but sometimes are not—to identify opportunities for new green projects and to ensure that the city's existing green commitments are prioritized and acted upon. Green city leaders are involved in the budget process from the early internal negotiations through public input and the city council approval process in order to watch out for opportunities to mesh their priorities with those of other departments and to help those departments with their budget submissions. There is no substitute for continuously and clearly communicating priorities to the budget office and mayor and reminding policy makers when additional resources are required to make good on prior commitments, such as carbon reduction targets.

Funding Sustainability Staff

One of the challenges that green city leaders face is figuring out how to maintain their own positions and the positions of their staffs through the budget process. These positions are relatively new in city government, and they must compete with essential services during hard economic times, when budgets are cut. Initially, many of these positions were funded through government grants—cities typically used some of their federal EECBG funding. For several years, the City of Bellevue, Washington, received a grant for half the cost of hiring an energy efficiency manager from Puget Sound Energy with the goal of eventually funding the position through energy savings.[6] But green city leaders who are hired with money from programs such as these know that the clock is ticking and they must quickly prove their value by saving money and bringing in more grants.

Cities now support many of these positions with money from their general funds—a clear sign of institutional support—but positions wholly paid for out of general funds are still at risk during the budget process. Sustainability staff members try hard to diversify their funding sources in order to protect themselves from budget cuts and political change. In 2011, ICLEI—Local Governments for Sustainability compiled a summary of funding sources for sustainability staff in thirty-eight local governments in the United States and found that 55 percent were funded at least partially through general funds; 37 percent were funded through special fees or rebates, such as solid waste fees; 24 percent were funded through foundation grants and partnerships; 29 percent used EECBG or other federal stimulus funding; and 16 percent were funded with the cost savings they helped achieve.[7]

The optimal mix of funding sources depends on the local context and opportunities, but diversification of funding is essential. Funding for Seattle's Office of Sustainability and Environment involved a mix of money from the general fund, from electricity rates, and from water and solid waste disposal rates. This was possible because the office had established relationships with the electric utility and the water and waste utility. Moreover, the sustainability office and its partners went through a systematic process with the budget office and the legal department to highlight the linkages between the city's sustainability agenda and the missions of these two utilities.

Successful green city leaders always keep an eye out for revenue streams that can be used to advance the sustainability agenda. The province of British Columbia implemented a carbon tax in 2008 to encourage individuals, businesses, industry, and others to use less fossil fuel. The municipalities in British Columbia worked together to negotiate a refund from the province for the work they had done to support carbon reduction goals. When the City of Chicago was awarding a new contract for waste handling, green city leaders negotiated a per-ton fee that was then used to fund a nonprofit organization run by the city to support the city's greening initiatives. When the City of Chicago filed suit against its electric utility for not investing in infrastructure improvements and won, the city was able to allocate more than $100 million toward green energy initiatives, including Department of Environment staff focused on energy conservation.

Positions for energy managers and other staff members who are focused on energy conservation can be fully or partially paid for by energy utilities, since they have energy reduction targets that this staff can help deliver. For instance, BC Hydro, the clean energy company in Vancouver, British Columbia, pays half the salary of the energy manager in the city's facilities department, and FortisBC, the power and gas company, pays half the salary of a technical staff person who works on district energy systems.[8]

Foundations have also funded sustainability directors. In Cleveland, two local foundations funded the first sustainability director, Andrew Watterson, and foundations in Pittsburgh, Pennsylvania, helped launch that city's Office of Sustainability and Energy Efficiency.

Many cities rely on volunteers to make staffing more robust. The City of Oakland,

California, has had success in using volunteer interns to help develop funding proposals, manage social media, do climate research, develop photo libraries, design the city's sustainability report, and work on other projects. Oakland's sustainability coordinator, Garrett Fitzgerald, also helps other departments complete projects by finding them green volunteers. His office manages a combined job posting for other departments and performs the initial screening of applicants.[9]

Green city leaders often work with students on special projects, thus freeing up staff. These projects work well when they are a high enough priority for the city that staff can be assigned to provide oversight, and it's important to choose students who are prepared to do the work and to involve a professor who is trusted and can help manage the students. But even in the best circumstances, the cycle and tempo of the school year often don't match the urgency that cities face in meeting deadlines for delivering results.[10]

In spite of the challenges, many green city leaders have valuable ongoing student programs. Fort Collins, Colorado, offers a "revolving" internship each year for a student who helps staff events and who agrees to train an intern for the following year. Fort Collins also works with a class at a local business school. The students form teams to create marketing strategies for changing human behavior related to sustainability, with the winning team receiving $300 to implement the strategy. The New York City Mayor's Office of Long-Term Planning and Sustainability has benefited from a number of studies prepared by Columbia University students working under the direction of leading faculty members. And each year the City of Ann Arbor, Michigan, provides a list of topics of interest to key faculty members willing to supervise master's degree projects.

Vancouver has an interesting partnership with the University of British Columbia: the city provides tree trimmings to the university for a new wood gasification energy facility that heats and powers the campus, and the university pays a stipend to ten graduate students who work for city government during the summer. The City of Vancouver, British Columbia, also has a program called CityStudio, a partnership with the city's six post-secondary academic institutions. Students work full-time in the studio, which is located in city offices, but they work with city staff on projects and research that help advance Vancouver's Greenest City 2020 Action Plan.

Tapping Municipal Resource Savings

Some green city leaders have found a way to move beyond helping cut costs to capturing cost savings for additional sustainability projects. When water and energy use and the cost of waste disposal are reduced, sustainability offices have a good case to make for sharing some of the savings in order to continue to fund these sustainability initiatives. Some cities have set up funds that recycle savings from a single initiative, such as a municipal building energy efficiency program, while others have created comprehensive funds that recycle savings from all aspects of their climate action plan or other initiatives.

The City of Atlanta, Georgia, passed legislation in 2009 to establish a green revolving loan fund for the city's internal energy efficiency projects. Atlanta's Office of Sustainability develops memoranda of understanding with other city departments to establish that the sustainability office will finance energy efficiency projects for other departments out of the loan fund if the departments in turn deposit their savings back into the fund until they have returned the original investment and an annualized return not to exceed 20 percent. The repaid funds can then be used for new capital projects related to energy and water efficiency and renewable energy, as well as consulting services and salaries and benefits for staff. The fund was initially capitalized using federal EECBG funds.

The City of Ann Arbor, Michigan, created the $500,000 Municipal Energy Fund, which invested the money in energy efficiency projects in return for 80 percent of the savings realized over a period of five years. The $500,000 was invested in forty-six energy efficiency projects from 1998 to 2009, producing an $860,000 savings. The city accrued an 11 percent internal rate of return on this investment, and the fund has grown to $600,000. The city's Energy Office administers the fund with supervision from a three-person board composed of staff from the city's energy, environment, and parks departments.[11] The fund has become a model for other cities.

Asheville, North Carolina, sustainability program manager Maggie Ullman also created a revolving fund, which captures the savings from energy efficiency, renewable energy, fleet changes, and light-emitting diode (LED) lighting, as well as other projects that are part of the city's Green Capital Improvement Program (Green CIP). Under this plan, the annual savings from projects are captured and used to pay off the debt incurred during procurement for these projects, with the rest of the savings used to fund more Green CIP initiatives. This is essentially an internally managed energy performance contract, and the city council authorized it for a minimum of thirteen years—the time required to retire all the debt.[12] Ullman believes that the Asheville City Council endorsed this reinvestment of savings because she and others were able to produce a detailed financial model demonstrating reliable positive payback and they were able to show that the program would provide a funding strategy for multiple key policy initiatives that were unfunded. (See "Case in Point: Funding Sustainability through Savings in Asheville" in chapter 4.)

Even under the best circumstances, however, creating a revolving fund for municipal resource savings can be a hard sell, and some green city leaders have not been able to persuade their cities to create funds to recycle savings even though they have demonstrated savings. Even more difficult and disappointing is the situation of some green city leaders who have won access to the savings they helped produce only to see the money reprogrammed to cover budget deficits. It is challenging to keep the funds revolving, but the effort is worth it because highlighting the fact that there are savings underscores the financial benefits of resource efficiency.

Larry Falkin of Cincinnati's Office of Environmental Quality summarizes the key steps for the green city leader in the budget and funding process this way: "Include your budget analyst as a team member so they understand what you do and how your office works. Make sure your proposals make economic sense. Develop and present your own financial analysis. Be ready to adapt to meet the needs of the budget office. And be ready to step back if the time is not right for a project."[13]

Using Corporate Finance to Advance Sustainability

Green projects often don't fit traditional financial product requirements. They cross product lines, capture value that markets don't yet monetize, or can't yet demonstrate long-term performance results. One of the key strengths of green city leaders is their willingness to pursue innovative financing strategies, which has helped their cities commit to innovative sustainability projects. Sometimes this has involved the early adoption of new financing vehicles and sometimes even the development of new financing vehicles. Green city leaders have been at the forefront in developing and adopting several innovations, including the following:

- Property-assessed clean energy (PACE) programs allow residents and businesses to borrow money for energy efficiency or renewable energy projects and to pay back their loans through property assessments paid as an addition to their property tax bill.
- On-bill financing of energy efficiency improvements allows residents and businesses to borrow money and repay their loans through a line item on their monthly utility or tax bill.
- Renewable energy power purchase agreements enable property owners, including cities, to invite developers to build and own solar photovoltaic systems on their property and sell the power to them—customers don't need to make up-front capital investments or acquire the expertise to maintain the renewable energy facilities, and they are compensated for use of their property.
- Clean Renewable Energy Bonds, a type of federal tax credit bond, provide what is essentially an interest-free loan to finance renewable energy projects.
- Qualified Energy Conservation Bonds are another type of tax credit bond used to finance renewable energy and energy conservation projects.

While this willingness has helped expand the supply of capital for sustainable development, not all innovative financing approaches have worked. Green city leaders have at times overestimated the importance of financing to the building of new markets.

Financing isn't the only barrier or even the main barrier to greening cities, as a 2010 study of energy efficiency loan funds for the National Renewable Energy Laboratory pointed out.[14] This study concluded that it is less important to provide access to financing than it is to make it easy for consumers to understand the right steps to take to improve energy efficiency, to find the right contractor for the work, and to take advantage of all the incentives that are available. This is why many of the financing programs described in this chapter are part of multifaceted, comprehensive strategies.

Innovative Financing Strategies

Green city leaders have become valued partners in demonstrations of the financial viability of new financial products and new uses of existing products because they work close to the ground, where needs are defined and deals are made. They also understand that partnerships are essential. Through partnerships they are helping to build private markets for energy efficiency and renewable energy loans and bonds, improve vehicles for recapturing from developers the value of public investment in creating great places, refine federal investment programs to support more sustainable infrastructure, and restructure local fees to support sustainability. These efforts, it is hoped, are building relationships and successes to tackle bigger financing challenges.

Energy Efficiency Loan Funds

When cities across the United States started launching community-wide energy efficiency financing programs to take advantage of the American Recovery and Reinvestment Act of 2009, they discovered they were breaking hard ground. Energy efficiency projects had not yet proven their appeal to mainstream financial markets, as Sarah Hayes and colleagues from the American Council for an Energy-Efficient Economy concluded in a 2011 research report titled "What Have We Learned from Energy Efficiency Financing Programs?" Hayes concluded, "There is a lack of information, uniformity, and standards that [makes] it difficult for private lenders to evaluate the risk these types of loans present. The lack of uniformity also makes it difficult to package these small loans into larger portfolios for sale to larger financial institutions on the secondary market."

Some cities decided to help demonstrate the creditworthiness of energy efficiency loans by providing credit enhancements—loan loss reserves, subordinated debt, or loan guarantees—to lenders willing to step in and serve this fledgling market. Because community development financial institutions (CDFIs) were created expressly to serve these underserved markets, they were apt demonstration partners for green city leaders. In the United States alone, hundreds of CDFIs—including banks, credit unions, loan funds, venture capital funds, microenterprise development loan funds, and development corporations—provide $5 billion per year in loans, investments, and financial services.[15] The mission of many CDFIs is to prove that new markets deserve investment from mainstream financial institutions, and a group of CDFIs have come together to help standardize lending practices for energy efficiency loans to small businesses, rental buildings, and residents, which will lower borrowing costs. These CDFIs include Boston Community Capital, the Community Investment Company and the IFF (formerly the Illinois Facility Fund) in Chicago, Craft3 (formerly Enterprise Cascadia) in Seattle, the Grow America Fund in New York, the Low Income Investment Fund in San Francisco and Los Angeles, the Center for Community Self-Help in Charlotte, North Carolina, and the Reinvestment Fund in Baltimore and Philadelphia.

A variety of green city leaders have partnered with CDFI leaders to advance community energy efficiency. John Hazlett, past director of the Office of Sustainability in the City of Indianapolis, formed a CDFI partnership with the Indianapolis Neighborhood Housing Partnership (INHP), a twenty-two-year-old CDFI. The INHP generated a pool of capital to invest in energy efficiency loans by offering investors a $3 million loan loss reserve, funded by the City of Indianapolis, to cover the first 50 percent of losses that might be incurred. Banks were willing to invest in the pool because of the loan loss reserve, and proceeds of the pool are used to provide below-market-rate loans for energy upgrades for Indianapolis households earning up to 120 percent of area median income.[16] The INHP is collecting data on loan demand and performance in order to demonstrate the viability of this market to future investors, who eventually may be willing to invest with a lower loan loss reserve or none at all.

Boulder County's EnergySmart program launched a residential property-assessed clean energy (PACE) program in 2009, which allowed residents to borrow money through the county and pay it back as a property assessment. When the Federal Housing Finance Agency opposed residential PACE programs in July 2010—arguing that they constituted first liens over preexisting mortgages, thereby creating significant risks for lenders and other mortgage holders—Boulder County had to find a new solution. The new EnergySmart loan program, which is administered by Elevations Credit Union, finances energy efficiency upgrades and renewable energy projects in Boulder County and Denver, supported by an $8 million loan loss reserve funded by a federal grant. Elevations Credit Union is willing to make $35 million in loans because the loan loss reserve can cover a significant share of any losses. The credit union found the partnership attractive in part because it already had customers seeking energy loans and because borrowers must become members of the credit union to participate in the program.[17]

The cities of Madison and Milwaukee in Wisconsin were able to attract a lending partner willing to accept a much smaller loan loss reserve, hopefully a sign of greater confidence in this kind of loan. The two cities structured a $3 million loan loss reserve, which supports a loan pool of up to $50 million provided by Summit Credit Union. If loans default, the $3 million is available to cover part of the loss. If the loan portfolio has low losses, Summit Credit Union may not require a reserve in the future, and other lenders, satisfied with the performance of these loans, may enter the market too.[18]

Property-Assessed Clean Energy Financing (PACE) and On-Bill Financing

Cities also have been helping to build financial market and consumer receptivity to PACE programs. In 2008, the City of Berkeley, California, piloted Berkeley FIRST—which became the model for the PACE bond—to enable residents to undertake energy efficiency and renewable energy projects without needing to invest a lot of money up front. Loans for projects were secured by property liens and repaid by property owners as a voluntary special assessment on their property tax bill over a five- to twenty-year period. Berkeley FIRST was modeled on land-secured financing districts, a common approach to funding projects that serve a public purpose.[19] Many Berkeley property owners were reluctant to invest in energy improvements because they were not sure that they would own their buildings long enough to recoup their investment through energy savings. PACE allowed them to repay loans over a long period of time and transfer responsibility for repayment to new property owners if they sold the property before the loan was repaid.

In one approach to PACE, cities seek pooled bond financing to make loans to a set of projects. A second approach allows project proponents to arrange their own financing—which works well for larger projects. As noted earlier, the Federal Housing Finance Agency put the brakes on residential PACE programs in 2010. But commercial PACE programs are proliferating.

PACE programs for commercial building have been launched in Sacramento, San Francisco, and Los Angeles, California; Ann Arbor, Michigan; and Washington, DC. In late 2011, the City of San Francisco launched GreenFinanceSF for owners of commercial properties, and in October 2012 it closed its first $1.4 million in financing for energy efficiency and renewable energy upgrades. GreenFinanceSF uses the open market PACE model, which allows building owners to obtain financing from capital providers of their choice and to repay the cost of the upgrade over time through a voluntary special tax on their property tax bill. PACE is being used to fund a range of building upgrades, from high-efficiency lighting and heating, ventilation, and air-conditioning retrofits to installations of fuel cells and solar panels. Commercial PACE is still an early-stage financing mechanism, and cities are working together with financial institutions and nongovernmental organizations to address barriers and refine the models.

The City of Portland, Oregon, was an early adopter of on-bill financing, another early-stage financing mechanism for energy efficiency that allows borrowers to repay their loans through a line item on their monthly utility bills. When a borrower moves, the outstanding loan amount is transferred to new residents on the same meter. The City of Portland hoped that on-bill financing would increase participation in Clean Energy Works Oregon (CEWO), a comprehensive residential energy efficiency retrofitting program, because there would be no—or low—up-front costs, and energy savings could be used to cover loan repayments. On-bill financing is also attractive to energy efficiency investors who view the linkage to payment of utility bills as a form of security because most people pay their utility bills.[20] Portland on-bill financing also expands access to energy efficiency loans for credit-constrained customers, who benefit from modified underwriting that takes utility bill payment history into account.[21]

Figure 5.1. Clean Energy Works Oregon
Although city energy efficiency initiatives have yet to become game changers for local economies, Clean Energy Works Oregon has already created a significant number of high-quality green jobs that support families.

The City of Portland partnered with a CDFI named Craft3, formerly Enterprise Cascadia, to create CEWO. Craft3 is the loan underwriter and manager of the on-bill financing program. The local utility is compensated for being a conduit for repayment but does not take on the risk of nonpayment. The City of Portland contributed 20 percent of its EECBG dollars to create a $2.5 million, 10 percent loan loss reserve for the program in order to leverage state funding and senior debt.

According to the Environmental Energy Technologies Division of the Lawrence Berkeley National Laboratory, CEWO's unusual underwriting process, which includes not only a traditional credit score check but also a review of utility bill repayment history, is relatively low in cost and scalable. Using utility bill repayment history instead of the debt-to-income ratio lowers the cost of reviewing applications and may also increase the number of eligible borrowers. The Lawrence Berkeley National Laboratory also lauds the program's decision to permit borrowers to use part of loan proceeds for non-energy-related improvements, such as deferred maintenance. While it still is early in the life of this program, performance data on the first 1,180 loans for $14.7 million are promising. CEWO has had to reject only one-fifth the number of customers rejected by other loan programs and has to date achieved a low default rate.[22]

CREBs and PPAs for Renewable Energy Purchases

Green city leaders have been willing to experiment with and compare alternative financial products if this is what it takes to achieve sustainability goals. The City of Tucson, Arizona, wanted to figure out how to finance more solar installations at more city buildings in order to build a regional solar energy market. In 2008, there were few city examples to follow, so Tucson decided to explore both Clean Renewable Energy Bonds (CREBs) and a power purchase agreement (PPA) in order to compare the strengths and weaknesses of each approach. Tucson became the first issuer of CREBs in Arizona when it sold a thirteen-year, $7.6 million bond in 2009 to finance the construction of seven solar projects generating one megawatt of energy, enough to power about 1,000 homes. CREBs allow cities and other qualified entities to issue bonds and pay back only the principal because the investor receives federal tax credits instead of interest. The United States Congress created CREBs to lower costs of renewable energy for public entities, which cannot benefit from tax incentives. Congress also created a similar product, Qualified Energy Conservation Bonds, for broader purposes including energy efficiency and to help finance private sector projects.

Tucson also completed a PPA to construct a second one-megawatt solar photovoltaic energy facility. PPAs allow developers to build and own solar photovoltaic systems that are located on their customers' properties and sell the power back to the customer, which means customers don't need to make up-front capital investments or have the expertise required to install, operate, or maintain a renewable energy facility.[23] The developer takes advantage of tax credits, rebates, depreciation, and other incentives. PPAs are a private sector innovation that was quickly embraced by the public sector as a way to reduce the up-front cost of solar power. In less than a decade, PPAs have become the dominant approach to financing photovoltaic installations for schools and government and nonprofit entities, as well as for businesses.[24]

Figure 5.2. Tucson, Arizona, solar installation
Tucson's pursuit of innovative financing mechanisms for solar photovoltaics was part of a broader strategy to create a solar energy economic cluster in the city, which has 350 days of sunshine.

Tucson continues to explore an array of innovative financing mechanisms, including the trading of state solar tax credits and New Markets Tax Credits, which are designed to spur revitalization in low-income areas by providing tax credits to investors. In addition, Tucson requires all new city buildings to meet 5 percent of their energy demand with some form of solar power, so construction budgets have some solar capacity built in.[25]

TIFIA for Accelerated Investment in New Transit Infrastructure
Green city leaders have taken on the challenge of accelerating investments that can transform communities. Most of the financial innovations described in this chapter apply to

discrete projects, but cities also face the much bigger challenge of reinventing major infrastructure systems for water and transportation and doing it as soon as possible. Although sales taxes are one way to finance new or expanded transit systems, it takes decades to accumulate the taxes to pay for these systems. Accelerating these projects would allow cities to build out multiline transit systems more quickly and to more rapidly achieve benefits such as reductions in greenhouse gas emissions.

Los Angeles mayor Antonio Villaraigosa was largely responsible for the decision by Congress to scale up an existing federal program that allows cities to accelerate these capital projects. The mayor's goal was to enable Los Angeles to build all the transportation projects that would be funded over the course of a local thirty-year sales tax in ten years instead of thirty through financing from low-interest federal loans and federal tax credit bonds. In response to the advocacy of a coalition including Mayor Villaraigosa, Congress passed a two-year transportation bill that expanded the Transportation Infrastructure Finance and Innovation Act (TIFIA) to $1.7 billion over two years, enabling cities such as Los Angeles to obtain up to 49 percent of project funding through TIFIA loans at interest rates as low as 2.73 percent.[26] Other cities have expressed interest in emulating Los Angeles, including Minneapolis, Seattle, and Boston.

Value Capture to Fund Projects That Enhance Property Values

Green city leaders are tapping into the potential for sustainability initiatives to increase the attractiveness of communities and enhance their value. Across North America, cities are funding transit and other neighborhood improvements by recapturing some of the value these improvements create. As described in the next section of this chapter, researchers have shown that investment in transit and transit-oriented development can increase land and property value near transit stations. Tools that are used for value capture include tax increment financing, special assessments, impact fees, and shared profits from joint development.

The Atlanta BeltLine, a proposed network of public parks, multiuse trails, and transit created by repurposing twenty-two miles of historic railroad corridors encircling downtown Atlanta, is using a form of tax increment financing called a tax allocation district (TAD) to fund part of this initiative. Many of the properties within the Atlanta BeltLine TAD are underutilized or abandoned industrial properties. The City of Atlanta, Fulton County, and Atlanta Public Schools have agreed to continue to receive the 2005 level of tax revenue from properties within the Atlanta BeltLine TAD for twenty-five years, at which point the TAD will expire. As the Atlanta BeltLine spurs new development on the underutilized properties, these properties should generate additional property tax revenue. Bonds issued to pay for the capital investments for the BeltLine over the twenty-five-year project period will be paid back using the incremental tax revenue generated by the new development.[27]

Figure 5.3. Atlanta BeltLine race
The Atlanta BeltLine running series allows people to experience the historic twenty-two-mile railroad corridor and helps to build excitement and support for the project. It will ultimately connect forty-five in-town neighborhoods with a combination of rails, trails, green space, housing, and art. Photo by Chris Martin.

Using Storm-Water Fees to Advance Green Infrastructure
Green city leaders are also finding ways to finance major reinventions of infrastructure through fees that incentivize green property improvements. Part of the challenge of achieving the goals in the City of Philadelphia's Green City, Clean Waters plan has been the need

to find innovative funding and financing mechanisms. As explained in chapter 3 (see "Case in Point: Sewer Overflows and Sustainable Infrastructure in Philadelphia"), one such mechanism is an "impervious cover charge with credit system," which is a storm-water billing system for commercial property that bases fees on the gross area of a land parcel and its impervious surface area rather than on the metered water usage. Property owners can get a credit against their fees by retrofitting their properties with green infrastructure such as storm-water gardens or bioswales. The fee creates an incentive to invest in infrastructure that reduces storm-water runoff, which will help meet the goals of the Green City, Clean Waters plan. The Philadelphia Water Department compiled twenty-seven case studies showing that property owners could earn a return on their investment of 13 percent or more if they reduce runoff, counting reductions in their monthly storm-water fees.[28]

Some of the funding and financing mechanisms discussed here have become proven financial vehicles, and some are still in the pilot stage. To attract sufficient capital to fund a shift to more sustainable infrastructure will require massive financial innovation beyond the examples in this chapter. As described in chapter 3, this is likely to include dramatic expansion of public-private partnerships. Leading green cities will need to continue to seek out and test new state, federal, and private partnerships to green water, waste, energy, transportation, and other systems.

Business and Economic Development

Increasingly, green city leaders believe they can and must make the case that greening cities increases livability, attracts skilled workers and entrepreneurs, and launches new industries. New urbanist developer Christopher Leinberger has documented the increasing preference in America for mixed-use, transit-accessible neighborhoods and walkable places.[29] The National Association of Realtors found in one survey that 56 percent of home buyers preferred communities with amenities such as a mix of housing types, destinations within walking distance, public transportation options, and less parking.[30] For years, studies have shown that transit-oriented development increases property values by 10–20 percent and increases commercial activity too.[31, 32]

Research also has shown an increase in demand for bikeable neighborhoods and increased sales for businesses on streets with protected bike lanes. So it's not surprising that Minneapolis mayor R. T. Rybak and an increasing number of other mayors see biking as a cost-effective economic development strategy. "Biking is definitely part of our strategy to attract and retain businesses," Rybak told Citiwire.net in 2012. "We want young talent to come here and stay. And good biking is one of the least expensive ways to send that message."[33]

Green city leaders also have an increasingly persuasive case to make for the role of renewable energy, energy efficiency, zero waste, green infrastructure, and other green technologies in economic development. In a report titled "Sizing the Clean Economy: A National and Regional Green Jobs Assessment," the Brookings Institution estimated that 2.7 million workers were employed in the green economy in 2011, in both mature and new sectors. Brookings also estimated that 64 percent of current clean economy jobs and 75 percent of newer jobs—created from 2003 to 2010—were in the nation's one hundred largest metropolitan areas.[34]

The "2012 California Green Innovation Index," by the nonprofit organization Next 10, documents a high return on investments in energy efficiency and renewable energy. Per capita electricity consumption in California in 2012 remained close to 1990 levels, and the state led the nation in clean technology patent registrations. In 2011, the state earned 62 percent of total global venture capital investment in solar energy. From January 1995 to January 2010, 1,503 solar businesses were born in California, an increase of 171 percent. The report credits public policies for helping to drive investment in green tech research and development and providing certainty about the rules so that private investors will enter the market.[35]

Leading-edge cities are linking their visions for greening and for economic development. San Jose mayor Chuck Reed launched the San Jose Green Vision plan in 2007, committing to ten goals, among them retrofitting 50 million square feet of green buildings, installing 100,000 solar roofs, reducing per capita electricity use by half, becoming a zero waste city, recycling and reusing 100 percent of the city's water, moving to 100 percent renewable energy, and creating 25,000 clean tech jobs.[36] (See the San Jose case in point at www.guidetogreeningcities.org.) In 2009, the International Economic Development Council named the San Jose Green Vision plan the best in its class for the way it embraced clean tech innovation and livable communities. San Antonio's Mission Verde plan projects that its support for green and renewable energy projects and ventures will generate thousands of green jobs that span many industries.

While only a few cities have publicly staked their economic futures on sustainability so far, a growing number have moved beyond single green business projects and are instead fostering green tech business clusters. In the same way that financing has been a more effective tool as part of a comprehensive strategy, comprehensive economic development strategies are also emerging as a preferred approach. Business clusters are geographic concentrations of interconnected firms along with organizations that support them or help them coordinate their activities.[37] Clusters are valuable because they make it easy for businesses, government, universities, technology labs, and business assistance organizations to exchange ideas—they provide a flow of information that fosters innovation and entrepreneurship.

Figure 5.4. Newby Island Resource Recovery Park, San Jose, California
The City of San Jose used its purchasing power to help achieve sustainability goals, support the local economy, and create 289 jobs by contracting with a waste hauler that recovers more than 80 percent of all commercial waste.

Tucson's pursuit of innovative financing mechanisms for solar photovoltaics, described earlier in this chapter, was part of a broader strategy to create a solar energy economic cluster in Tucson. Tucson has 350 days of sunshine, a state renewable energy standard, utility incentives for solar power, a regional vision for energy, and a solar energy development plan. Stakeholders are working together in the Southern Arizona Regional Solar Partnership and the Tucson/Pima County Metropolitan Energy Commission. The city has created a solar research and innovation zone, and the University of Arizona is home to the Arizona Research Institute for Solar Energy. To enhance the potential for a solar cluster to emerge, the City of Tucson and Pima County installed more than 4 megawatts of solar photovoltaics on public facilities between 1999 and 2012. They tested the photovoltaic models of local suppliers, collected performance data, and took thousands of visitors on tours of test sites. In 2011, Tucson dedicated the largest multitechnology solar evaluation site in the United States, which produces up to 18.5 megawatts of power, enabling various technologies to perform side by side under identical operating conditions and maximizing local content. Developers are able to determine which systems are most efficient and economical for companies in the region. All of these steps are helping Tucson build a solar cluster.

Other cities are leveraging green policies to create or upgrade jobs within existing economic sectors. When New York City was ready to advance a nationally lauded legislative package requiring building energy audits and retrofits, the real estate sector said there were not enough trained auditors. The city had to prove that there would be a workforce to implement the law by inventorying existing training programs and then addressing impediments to getting people trained and hired. To achieve its goals for improving building energy performance, the City of New York also became a partner in the Green Supers program, a collaboration of labor unions, employers, building owners, and educators to train more than 2,000 building superintendents so they could create green building plans, help implement changes in their buildings, and document the resulting savings. A majority of the participating workers have documented one or more upgrades to their buildings.

City energy efficiency initiatives have produced a significant number of jobs, although they have not yet been game changers for local economies. What they have done, however, is show that the energy efficiency sector can create high-quality jobs that support families, and more of these jobs will be created as this sector grows. As described in chapter 3, Renew Boston, a home weatherization program initiated by the City of Boston and implemented by Next Step Living, completed 7,000 comprehensive home energy audits and 2,000 home weatherization projects. The number of Next Step Living employees hired locally grew from 5 to more than 350. Clean Energy Works Oregon, described earlier in this chapter, expects to employ 1,300 residents in family-supporting jobs by the end of 2013.

Green city leaders often focus as much on creating pathways to good middle-class jobs for disadvantaged workers as they do on creating green tech cluster development. This allows them to address social equity—the third leg of the sustainability stool. They are trying to promote equity by bringing a new lens to their project decision making, addressing concerns such as these:

- Inclusion. How does local government meaningfully include low-income communities and communities of color when establishing and carrying out its sustainability agenda? How does it enable low-income communities and communities of color to shape initiatives that will benefit their communities?
- Distribution of benefits and costs. How does local government ensure that policies minimize costs and maximize benefits to low-income communities and communities of color? How can policies be shaped to promote wealth creation and economic integration at the neighborhood level while preserving diversity?

The City of Cleveland became a partner in the Evergreen Cooperatives model as a means to create jobs in employee-owned businesses in disadvantaged communities by providing sustainable products and services to local educational and medical institutions.

Evergreen Cooperatives, which is located in Cleveland, includes a green laundry, a solar business, a business services company, and a food growers' cooperative. Founders envision a network of about ten cooperatives by 2015, owned and managed by about 500 local residents. The model draws from the experience of the Mondragon cooperatives in Spain, which also started small but grew to include 120 businesses with 90,000 employees. This complex and ambitious project, which breaks new ground in creating triple bottom line jobs, would not be possible without extensive foundation and business partnerships.[38]

The connection between greening cities and economic development is becoming increasingly clear and accepted. The rest of this chapter describes the roles of green city leaders in promoting economic development, as well as the roles of foundations and businesses, two key partners in this work.

Economic Development Roles for Green City Leaders

Green city leaders add value to efforts to promote local economic development in many ways. They advocate for policies that help create new markets, as they have in Boston for energy efficiency and in Philadelphia for green infrastructure. They use strategic procurement to help demonstrate new technologies, as they have in San Jose and Tucson. They create recognition and incentive programs for green businesses, as they have in Houston and Fort Collins. They support partnerships to reuse land and other assets with the goal of improving quality of life by encouraging transit-oriented development or park development, for example, as in Vancouver.

Green city leaders in Portland's Bureau of Planning and Sustainability helped the city recognize the green building economic cluster as a regional opportunity for economic development. In 1999, Portland's Energy Office (now the Bureau of Planning and Sustainability) launched the Green Building Initiative, which provided information, education, technical assistance, and financial resources for the green building industry. This initiative helped create demand and build the supplier base to meet this demand. The region grew to have leading architectural, design, and development firms that specialized in green buildings as well as a high number of LEED-certified buildings. The Oregon Economic and Community Development Department began convening industry leaders to identify how to support a green building cluster of manufacturing companies and suppliers. The State of Oregon funded the Oregon Built Environment and Sustainable Technologies Center, and leading green building companies started to attract customers from outside the region. Portland is seeing rapid employment growth in the green building sector, and the Portland Development Commission is actively looking for opportunities to bring more suppliers to Portland to provide products and services not yet locally available.[39]

James Nixon, a longtime sustainable economic development innovator, describes seven ways green city leaders can support economic development in a 2009 concept paper on the subject:[40]

1. Provide opportunities for businesses that specialize in environmental products and services (the clean tech business cluster) to test new products and gain new markets, which will encourage them to start up, locate, and grow in the region.
2. Create certifications for all businesses to become greener and at the same time save resources and money and to become more economically productive.
3. Create programs—such as incentives for energy- and water-efficient buildings or for clean energy—that also help businesses save resources and money.
4. Adopt policies and programs that create new green job opportunities, and align workforce training and educational resources to support this job creation.
5. Adopt policies and incentives for development that is mixed use, mixed income, walkable, energy and resource efficient, and transit oriented—qualities that are attractive to young skilled workers and entrepreneurs.
6. Promote improvements to regional physical infrastructure to provide energy, water, materials, buildings, and mobility in a way that is both ecologically and economically efficient.
7. Help brand the city and region as green or simply as a better place to live, work, and locate a business.

Green city leaders, except in the few cities where sustainability is part of the economic development department, generally don't have the lead role in economic development. In order to make a difference, they need to find partners and champions in local and regional economic development agencies, redevelopment authorities, chambers of commerce and other business organizations, universities, workforce development agencies, technology development agencies, and the like.

The challenge for green city leaders is getting a seat at the table where economic development strategy is formulated. This takes time and effort. Marty Howell, sustainability program manager for the City of El Paso, achieved the unusual success of being named the head of economic development in addition to sustainability. From day one Howell had seen economic development as an important contribution that his sustainability office could make, and he worked closely with other departments—including general services, facilities, fleet, and economic development—to build programs that would contribute to sustainability and the economy. He helped other departments create a green building challenge, an energy efficiency program, and a solar rebate program, bringing them new resources from federal recovery grants.

Over time, Howell came to spend about a third of his time working with the economic development department, which ran the solar rebate program and green business challenge. Through a clean energy initiative he began to build relationships with labor, university, and business leaders, and they began to work together on building this industrial sector in El Paso. He always asked economic development staff to participate in these meetings. He was brainstorming with local entrepreneurs who had ideas for green building and solar technologies, and he began connecting them with opportunities to demonstrate products at city facilities. About a year after the head of the economic development department left his position, Howell was asked to become the interim head of the department, and he is now the director of economic development and sustainability.

Green city leaders in other cities have established their value in economic development efforts by researching local economic development strategies, getting to know who the actors are, sitting in on economic development meetings, identifying ways to help economic development initiatives be more successful, and participating in small projects with economic development leaders to help build trust.[41]

The best way to speak "economic development" is to quantify the economic benefits of green initiatives. Chicago's Department of Environment analyzed the Chicago Climate Action Plan (CCAP) and found that the plan's climate change objectives will create 10,000–17,000 jobs by 2020, depending on the level of investment intensity, and will save a significant portion of the $7 billion residents and businesses spend annually on energy, water, waste, and fuel—meanwhile reducing carbon emissions and accelerating Chicago's leadership position in the global green economy. The department also completed an analysis of which sectors would produce these jobs and what it would take to create them. Washington, DC, and New York City have produced similar analyses.

Several cities have created models to analyze the economic impact of proposed green initiatives. Green city leaders in San Antonio, Texas, took advantage of federal recovery funding to create the City of San Antonio Sustainable Urban Economics Tool for assessing the effects of proposed policies and programs. Bill Barker and the Office of Environmental Policy worked with an external consulting team to develop the model, which quantifies the impact of sustainability goals on air quality, water, waste, energy, economic output, jobs, household spending, personal health, and tax dollars. For example, the model showed that a 10 percent reduction in vehicle miles traveled would result in the second largest onetime economic impact and the largest annual ongoing economic impact of all the policies tested, while a 5 percent increase in household energy efficiency would generate the most onetime economic impact. The Sustainable Urban Economics Tool helps make the case for proposed policies to elected officials and civic, business, and community groups, and it is fully transparent, allowing stakeholders to see the series of direct and indirect impacts of policies.[42]

Jim Hunt, who was chief of Boston's Environmental and Energy Services Department, worked closely with the Boston Redevelopment Authority to create a "triple bottom line calculator" that would help demonstrate the comparative sustainability benefits of proposed green projects and measure the performance of prioritized projects. The redevelopment authority developed standardized "conversion tables" for assessing the economic benefits (such as tax generation), environmental benefits (such as reduction in carbon dioxide emissions), and social benefits (such as health improvements) of projects including renewable energy, energy efficiency, and transportation infrastructure. This was one component of a broad collaboration between green and economic development leaders in city government.

Key Partners in Advancing Sustainable Economic Development

Green city leaders will not lead economic development in more than a handful of cities. They need to develop partnerships and collaborations. A challenge is finding the catalysts for these collaborations. Two promising catalysts are global corporations pursuing sustainability markets and foundations, which can be trusted conveners.

Major global corporations have indicated that they want to develop new relationships with cities to share the costs, risks, and benefits of broader innovation, and corporations also want to partner on larger-scale demonstration projects to build new communities, showcase and field-test new technologies, and cocreate customized technologies that address specific needs.

These "smart cities" partnerships could be highly beneficial to green city leaders trying to advance sustainable economic development. Business partners can help launch demonstration projects, drawing local research institutions into new partnerships related to smart city technology and helping to build the capacity of local small businesses. (See chapter 4 for a discussion of these partnerships.)

While some of these partnerships have been win-wins, many cities have found that it's hard to establish terms and performance goals that yield valuable results, and that the payoff is less than what they expected for the time invested. The key to success, based on Vancouver's experience, is identifying early in the process what the municipal or environmental problem is that the collaboration will solve and what each party will get out of it. It's also important that both the city and the business partner adequately resource and staff the collaboration.

Several cities have developed criteria for screening offers like these from corporations; the criteria include the existence of a business plan and a time line; a clear benefit to citizens and local businesses; clear expectations on the part of both partners; issues to resolve, whether legal, financial, or political; a clear reporting process to keep the city informed of the project's progress; an exit strategy should the project be unsuccessful; next steps for the corporation if the project is successful; a role for the city in communications about a successful project; identification of primary city and consultant staff; and local business partners and local product and service providers.

Green city leaders often find natural allies among the leaders of foundations, who also care about the competitiveness, economic vitality, and quality of life of cities, often with a particular interest in equity. Successful relationships extend far beyond funding—green city leaders and foundations can be important sources of intelligence for each other. Foundations tend to have relationships with business leaders who are willing to become innovation partners, funders, and advocates for sustainability initiatives. They also have a good sense of which nongovernmental organizations would be good partners for job training and small business development programs. Foundation program officers tend to follow what is happening in their fields, and they can help green city leaders stay at the front of the curve too. Moreover, foundations are natural conveners and have the standing to bring together a broad cross section of a community, including business and community leaders—a necessity for most sustainable economic development initiatives.

Foundation staff can also provide cover and visible support for politically sensitive initiatives. Chicago foundations offered financial support to the City of Chicago to implement energy efficiency programs and prepare workers for related jobs in exchange for performance requirements, which were helpful in keeping programs on target. Foundations can also help cities attract funding from other sources. When the City of Dubuque, Iowa, launched its Green and Healthy Homes Initiative, for example, the Community Foundation of Greater Dubuque reached out to local banks to find funding for the initiative and also introduced city staff to staff of national foundations.[43]

In return, green city leaders can be valuable partners for foundations. They can share their experiences in working with particular nongovernmental organizations, their insights about how city government works, and their opinions about whether proposed grant-funded programs are likely to succeed. They can also suggest ways that foundations can leverage city assets to achieve shared goals.

Beth Strommen, sustainability director for the City of Baltimore, Maryland, found a long-term partner in Cheryl Casciani, director of neighborhood sustainability at the Baltimore Community Foundation—not by asking for a grant but by exchanging valuable perspectives and information through an ongoing conversation. Strommen was able to offer Casciani information about how nongovernmental organization projects might tap into city services or use city property, for example, and ways that foundation support could be leveraged with government grant funding. Strommen also asked for Casciani's advice, and as a result of their collaboration Casciani was asked by former mayor Sheila Dixon to chair the newly created Baltimore Commission on Sustainability. Casciani is now serving a second term as chair, appointed by Mayor Stephanie Rawlings-Blake, and

Strommen and Casciani still meet every Wednesday morning to have coffee and brainstorm about ways to solve each other's problems as well as support efforts to implement the recommendations of the Baltimore Sustainability Plan.[44] The city and the community foundation have now partnered on several major initiatives. For example, the Baltimore Community Foundation is a lead partner in the city's Baltimore Energy Challenge, which asks volunteers to engage their neighbors in saving energy and cutting utility costs.

Conclusion

It is hard to advance a sustainability agenda, especially in difficult economic times. Packaging funding and financing is a crucial tactic that green city leaders use to build support for change. Green city leaders need a deep enough bench to be able to effectively analyze and communicate the benefits and risks of financing vehicles.

For the green city leader, advancing sustainable economic development is less a tactic than a mind-set. Green city leaders are urgently working to align environment and economy at every opportunity. As more and more cities commit to a triple bottom line approach to sustainability—a shift many green city leaders expect will happen in the next five years—they also may find it easier to make the case, build the partnerships, and amass the resources that are needed.

CASE IN POINT:

Growing Green Businesses and Jobs in San Antonio

Clean energy companies are flocking to San Antonio, bringing with them tax revenues and high-quality jobs, and green city leaders attribute much of the region's newfound allure to Mission Verde, the city's economic development–oriented sustainability plan. Unlike the vast majority of city greening plans, which tend to be about environmental initiatives that can help meet economic and social goals along the way, Mission Verde is rooted in sustainable economic development as a pathway to improved quality of life as well as enhanced environmental quality and social equity.

Several companies—including a smart meter manufacturer, an LED lighting installer, and a large solar power producer—have decided to locate in and around San Antonio in recent years because this plan has generated demand for their products and services and because the municipal energy utility has also made a strong commitment to clean energy solutions and the "new energy economy." "The smart meter company came here based on the fact that we're installing 130,000 of their meters. The lighting installer came based on the fact that we're installing 25,000 of their LED streetlights. The solar company is coming because we're purchasing all of the 400 megawatts of energy they will produce," says Laurence Doxsey, past director of San Antonio's Office of Sustainability. "Companies respond if you've got a deal for them."

This excerpt from the plan illustrates the way it was framed: "We live in a world of volatile energy prices, increasingly scarce resources, vigorous world competition and technological innovation," the plan begins.

> How we respond to these changes will define us as a city and determine the quality of our lives and our economic fate. . . .
>
> San Antonio cannot afford to be left behind. We must invest in green technology, energy conservation, renewable energy, efficient transportation, and smarter buildings. We must build a new energy infrastructure that transforms our city from reliance on centralized power to distributed power. We must create a multi-modal transportation system that is integrated and efficient. We must bring venture capital to invest in new green businesses and technology. We must conserve, create and grow. . . .
>
> We can position ourselves to compete successfully in a 21st Century global economy. We can transform our city and improve the lives of all San Antonians. With Mission Verde, we control our destiny.[45]

Larry Zinn, chief of staff to former San Antonio mayor Phil Hardberger, was a driving force behind Mission Verde. He says the goal was to find a common principle that would draw people together. "If you define sustainability only as an environmental goal, you're going to lose a lot of people. So we defined it as helping San Antonio position itself to compete in a twenty-first-century global economy, with sustainability as the theme. Economic development and job creation is a message that resonates with everyone."

The Inside Story

Mission Verde was initiated and led by Larry Zinn and Laurence Doxsey, who was hired in 2008 to oversee development and implementation of the plan. They engaged key stakeholders—the municipal energy and water utilities, key companies and business groups, workforce development agencies, and nonprofit organizations—to assess the local economy's assets, challenges, and opportunities, the workforce needs of current and future employers, and existing job training programs. The assessment showed huge potential for economic development in the areas of energy efficiency, renewable energy, and clean technology, and the plan was designed to tap that potential.

The mayor introduced the plan during his State of the City address in 2009 in front of an audience dominated by the Greater San Antonio Chamber of Commerce, and later that year he appointed the Green Jobs Leadership Council, chaired by Zinn and including key leaders in business and education, to promote its implementation. The plan laid out eleven major initiatives in six action areas—energy infrastructure, clean and green technology, sustainable buildings, transportation and land use, community outreach, and leadership by example—and near-term action steps for each.

Mission Verde was well received from the start, but the plan was slow to translate into on-the-ground action and change, in part because it was created from the top down—without broader, bottom-up engagement—and because the city government lacked the

Figure 5.5. Community garden, San Antonio, Texas
San Antonio's Mission Verde Center is a living laboratory for research and development that provides public school students with green skills training and internships—simultaneously developing new technologies and creating jobs and business opportunities. Photo by the Texas Center for Applied Technology (TCAT).

formal authority to implement it. The city council stepped in and formally adopted the plan in February 2010 and added elements related to conserving water, reducing waste, promoting compact infill development, implementing alternative transportation and fuels, increasing the urban forest canopy, and bolstering local food production. The new mayor, Julián Castro, fully embraced Mission Verde when he was elected in 2009, folding it into his San Antonio 2020 (SA2020) initiative and overseeing adoption of the city council resolution that expanded and formally adopted the plan. This marked a turning point in its influence.

Results to Date

The influx of clean technology companies suggests that Mission Verde is working. "We did the plan, the council adopted the resolution, and then the Greater San Antonio Chamber of Commerce and Economic Development Foundation really got behind it," says Doxsey. "At that point, companies started coming through the door left and right."

The city began adopting policies and programs that would improve quality of life in San Antonio while simultaneously encouraging green businesses and jobs by bolstering demand for products and services. These included strict energy and water codes for new construction, tax incentives for green building, weatherization assistance for low-income households, and lighting efficiency assistance for small businesses. The city also did energy efficiency retrofits of several municipal buildings and created the first bike-sharing program in Texas.

The mayor's Green Jobs Leadership Council was renamed the Mission Verde Alliance and became a stand-alone organization. "We were frustrated with all the meeting and planning and wanted to start doing," recalls Zinn. "But we couldn't get much done because we didn't have a budget or staff. So the city council created a separate entity and provided $100,000 to seed the effort." The University of Texas at San Antonio donated office space, and Bank of America provided additional funding to get the alliance up and running.

Zinn was appointed executive director and recruited a board of directors composed of influential public, private, and nonprofit leaders, including the mayor's new chief of staff, the president and chief executive officer of the Greater San Antonio Chamber of Commerce, the executive vice president and chief sustainability officer of CPS Energy, the executive director of the city's residential green building program, and the founder and chair of the San Antonio Clean Technology Forum. Doxsey says the alliance has been able to "facilitate the cross-fertilization necessary to drive the connections that new businesses are looking for," and it also helps screen new technologies that could play a role in creating jobs as well as increasing energy efficiency and renewable energy.

The Mission Verde Center was created as a living laboratory for research and development, education and green skills training, and the demonstration of new technologies. The city wanted to provide a learning environment for public school students and young people that would also accelerate the development and deployment of innovative energy and water technologies, create new business and job opportunities, and promote community understanding of and support for the adoption of energy efficiency and renewable energy innovations. Located in a decommissioned middle school in a low-income part of San Antonio, the center also illustrates how schools can be repurposed as facilities that can anchor the revitalization of low-income neighborhoods. The city invested $1.5 million of its Energy Efficiency and Conservation Block Grant funding in energy improvements to the campus, including lighting upgrades, reflective roofs, and geothermal and solar energy installations.

Challenges

Not everything has gone as planned, of course. A clean technology fund envisioned in Mission Verde has yet to materialize, for example, because of the weak economy. For similar reasons, the Mission Verde Center hasn't gained traction and grown as fast or as far as originally hoped. Budget constraints forced Alamo Colleges to cut back on planned green workforce training course offerings. And the initially slow pace of implementation for Mission Verde taught green city leaders in San Antonio a valuable lesson. "Make sure you don't leave your community out of the loop," says Laurence Doxsey, reflecting on Mission Verde's relatively top-down beginnings. "Don't leave the voters and the ratepayers behind."

Key Factors for Success

A number of factors account for Mission Verde's success so far.

An economic development orientation. Anchoring Mission Verde to economic opportunity helped to broaden ownership of the plan. "To get buy-in, you have to build an agenda that most people can relate to, and that is the economic agenda," says Doxsey. He adds that there were proponents for environmental and equity agendas, but these agendas were not deemed as having as much power to drive decisions about the future of the city and the policies and programs needed to provide a foundation for that future.

The art of alignment. Green city leaders aligned Mission Verde's goals and action agenda to address emerging global issues, such as the increasing volatility of energy prices, scarcity of resources, and innovations in clean technology. Mission Verde was also aligned with the priorities of federal stimulus funding, such as the Energy Efficiency and Conservation Block Grant Program, and with the commitments of the municipal energy utility to energy efficiency, renewable energy, and related job creation.

Strategic partnerships. The city collaborated closely with the private sector from the

Figure 5.6. Mission Verde Center solar power system
Reinforcing economic development and sustainability efforts focused on implementing renewable energy applications, San Antonio's Mission Verde Center stages open house demonstrations of solar electric and solar thermal energy. Photo by the Texas Center for Applied Technology (TCAT).

start, including the Greater San Antonio Chamber of Commerce and the San Antonio Clean Technology Forum, an alliance of several hundred representatives from the energy, utility, finance, government, and education and research sectors, as well as with workforce development institutions including Alamo Colleges, Texas A&M University, and the University of Texas at San Antonio.

A synchronized approach. One key aspect of the green economic development challenge is syncing up supply and demand for a well-trained green workforce. Some cities that were motivated to train a green workforce because of the availability of federal grants found that graduates could not find green jobs. San Antonio chose instead to begin by carefully assessing the region's current and potential workforce needs in close partnership with businesses and workforce development programs and then working with them to create and coordinate programs to meet those needs.

Incubation, then integration. The city developed Mission Verde but was eager to find a home for it outside government. Doxsey explains that the city believes the Mission Verde Alliance represents a broader cross section of the community and that, in an era of constrained government resources, taxpayers could criticize Mission Verde as an "auxiliary activity"—that is, beyond the scope of essential city services and therefore ineligible for funding.

CASE IN POINT:

Financing Affordable Housing along Transit Lines in Denver

Improving the quality and quantity of public transportation—from light-rail corridors to streetcar networks to bus rapid transit systems—is an important part of the green city agenda in North America, but experience has shown that there can be unintended consequences: transit construction and related improvements can activate the real estate market in neighborhoods around stations, and land and property values can escalate very quickly. If the right policies and programs aren't put in place in time, neighborhoods can gentrify, pushing out lower-income residents who already live in these places—the very people who are likely to need and use transit the most.

This is why the City and County of Denver and its partners created the Denver Transit-Oriented Development (TOD) Fund—to preserve and construct affordable housing around fifty-seven new transit stations funded by FasTracks, the region's ambitious $6.5 billion public transit expansion program. The Denver TOD Fund was the first public-private-nonprofit partnership in the United States created to buy and hold land near transit stations for affordable housing and other community assets such as libraries, day care centers, and open space. Other cities have followed Denver's pioneering work. "It's an evolving tool being used across the United States," says Dace West, director of Denver's Office of Strategic Partnerships, which along with the Denver Office of Economic Development coordinates the city's involvement in the Denver TOD Fund.

The Inside Story

Rapid and sprawling population growth in the Denver region has resulted in similarly rapid increases in traffic congestion, average commute times, and air pollution. Growth projections showed that the region should expect 1.5 million new residents by 2035, a 55 percent increase over thirty years. In response, the Regional Transportation District developed the FasTracks public transit plan, and in 2004 voters approved a sales tax increase to fund the program—launching one of the largest transit expansions in the United States.

From the start, Denver's leadership was concerned about affordable housing. Demand for housing within a half mile of light-rail stations was expected to more than triple to 150,000 households by 2030, and 40 percent of the demand was projected to come from low- and moderate-income households already spending about 60 percent of their income on the combined cost of housing and transportation. To promote green development—healthy, affordable, energy efficient, bike and pedestrian friendly, and mixed use—along these new light-rail and high-frequency bus corridors, the City of Denver adopted the Transit Oriented Development (TOD) Strategic Plan in 2006. It laid out development plans for specific transit stations and set priorities for infrastructure investments. In 2010, the city adopted a form-based land use code around stations to promote mixed-use development and helped create the Denver TOD Fund.

The fund is a partnership between Enterprise Community Partners, a national nonprofit organization that specializes in financing green and affordable housing,[46] the Urban Land Conservancy (ULC), a local nonprofit organization that "uses real estate as a tool to benefit urban communities,"[47] and the City and County of Denver.[48] Other key investors include the MacArthur Foundation, the Colorado Housing and Finance Authority, Rose Community Foundation, Mile High Community Loan Fund, Wells Fargo, U.S. Bank, and First Bank. The idea emerged from "a collaborative brainstorming process," says Brad Weinig, who directs the Transit-Oriented Development Program for Enterprise Community Partners.

Enterprise assembled the initial $15 million in capital (including a sizable investment of its own money) that allowed the fund to begin operating in April 2010. The ULC provided $1.5 million in start-up capital as well, but it was the City of Denver's initial investment of $2.5 million that got the effort off the ground—the money was mostly public benefit funds collected through a small charge on the electric bills of utility customers. The city also led the effort to secure a highly competitive $2.25 million grant from the MacArthur Foundation. "The city made the commitment that got everybody else on board," says Aaron Miripol, president and chief executive officer of the ULC. Adds Dace West, director of the Denver Office of Strategic Partnerships: "The idea for the fund came from the community. But we quickly realized we'd need government dollars to take that top loss position—to take the most risk."

Enterprise Community Partners manages the Denver TOD Fund. The ULC is the sole borrower of the high-risk but low-cost funds used to acquire, hold, manage, and sell the sites on which green, energy-efficient affordable housing exists or could be built. Once transactions are complete, dollars are returned to the revolving fund and can be used again. The partners expect to revolve the $15 million fund twice over the ten-year life of the project. That's a $30 million investment that Enterprise estimates will leverage more than $500 million in local economic development activity in many of Denver's lowest-income neighborhoods and create jobs.

Results to Date

The Denver TOD Fund is well on its way toward meeting the goal of preserving or creating 1,000 units of affordable housing, and it has preserved or built almost 500 units in just its first two to three years. In one transaction, the ULC tapped the fund to purchase a 0.86-acre lot known as Mile High Vista near the Knox and Decatur-Federal light-rail station in West Denver. Part was sold to the city for a public library, and the rest went to a local affordable housing developer to build sixty units of workforce housing. The Evans Station Lofts, at the Evans light-rail station in South Denver, was the first to use the fund for new construction—fifty units of workforce housing on 7,000 square feet of commercial and retail space.

But Miripol and others say the biggest impact is that the fund has spurred investor interest in redeveloping communities near transit by showing the way and demonstrating the value. "We've brought other investors to the table—including those who were

Figure 5.7. Evans Station Lofts project, Denver, Colorado
The Urban Land Conservancy purchased this site across the street from a light-rail station using $1.2 million from the Denver Transit-Oriented Development (TOD) Fund, which was created to acquire and preserve land for workforce housing. The Evans Station Lofts will feature fifty units of affordable housing as well as retail and commercial office space. Image courtesy of Parikh Stevens Architects.

Figure 5.8. Design schematic, Irving and Colfax Streets, Denver
Transit-oriented development projects are cropping up along the light-rail corridors under construction in Denver, including Mile High Vista, a one-acre mixed-use project of the Urban Land Conservancy. It will feature eighty units of new affordable housing, 10,000 square feet of commercial office space, and a public library. Image courtesy of Del Norte Neighborhood Development Corp.

very squeamish about these deals before—because they've seen these projects can make money," Miripol says. "It's more competitive and difficult to purchase housing and land in these transit corridors now. For example, there are more and more applications for housing tax credits coming from these areas, which wasn't the case before."

Challenges

The fund was negotiated over a period of three years, with most discussion centering on the risk involved, who should shoulder it, and how to do so. "It's hard to be first," Miripol notes. Adds Weinig, "This was the first fund of its kind—uncharted territory. We had a hunch it would work, but it was a gamble." Growing the program into a fund for the entire region served by FasTracks—and not just the city—proved difficult at first. While the City of Denver was able to invest $2.5 million to help capitalize the fund, "surrounding communities don't have that kind of money sitting around," says Weinig, who is tasked with securing additional investors outside of Denver. "It's been hard to find others who are able and willing, but we are making progress."

The fund's focus on preserving existing units of affordable housing has proven difficult because supply is low and cost is high. Consequently, the fund has focused on acquiring land and building new units—all but 50 of the nearly 500 units financed so far will be new construction. Everyone involved acknowledges that the fund is no panacea—1,000 units of affordable housing meet just 5 percent of the demand. "It isn't the only way to provide affordable and energy-efficient housing around stations," notes West. "But it's an important tool."

Key Factors for Success

Factors contributing to the success of the Denver TOD Fund include the following.

Making roles and responsibilities clear. The key to the Denver TOD Fund's success is its strong, strategic cross-sector partnership. "It's about staying true to the mission, having a clear vision and goals, and being really clear about the role each partner plays," says Dace West. She says the city doesn't get deeply involved in individual transactions, which signals trust to the partners and reduces the bureaucratic process and time needed to get deals done.

Being nimble. West cites "openness and nimbleness" as factors that have enhanced learning—"being able to change course as we learn about realities on the ground and different kinds of needs in our community"—and the partnership's effectiveness. She adds that the city has created a shared sense of ownership and responsibility for the fund—for both the risks and the results—among a wide range of stakeholders and investors. "We are able to leverage each other's strengths financially, but we're also able to leverage each other's expertise and roles."

Trust. Brad Weinig of Enterprise Community Partners says the city has been a great partner. "They've made it clear what they care about. But then they've stepped back and let us do what we do best. They made that critical investment of start-up capital and then trusted us to do the work."

6.
Driving Green Progress
Using Indicators

*"We report the good, the bad, and
the ugly. It becomes a conversation.
It is really important that we talk
about where we are not doing well,
so we can figure out what we need
to bring in to these issues."*

—Gayle Prest,
sustainability director,
City of Minneapolis

In the early 1990s, city greening initiatives were goal oriented but were not driven by concrete and measurable objectives. Of the 1,054 cities that signed the U.S. Conference of Mayors Climate Protection Agreement—which committed them to reduce carbon emissions to below 1990 levels by 2012—maybe 10 percent had developed concrete plans for meeting this goal, and only a few dozen cities actually tracked their progress. Many cities were not willing to take the risk of making their performance targets public and then failing to meet them, while others did not have the staff or data to develop comprehensive measurement systems.

The imperative to measure and communicate goals and results is much stronger today, and there are new tools to support these endeavors. Trends to make government more open and transparent and to crowd-source solutions have boosted interest in data sharing. Moreover, cities are competing for increasingly scarce resources from federal agencies and the private sector, and data help to prove the efficacy of their work and results. Cities also are entering into more public-private partnerships in which ongoing data sharing is needed to help partners see what is working and what is not. Finally, the use of performance indicators has been linked to success in achieving sustainability goals. For example, a 2012 survey of Canadian cities found that cities that used indicators and reported publicly on results had much greater success in achieving their goals.[1] Many green city leaders agree with this finding.

Jenita McGowan, chief of sustainability for the City of Cleveland, Ohio, has a long list of the advantages of adopting sustainability performance indicators. For example, they can help reveal which strategies work and why, they can educate and inspire, they can help diverse stakeholders speak the same language, and they can keep all stakeholders moving in the same direction. McGowan says that in Cleveland perhaps the most important result of using indicators has been that they have helped the city engage and activate stakeholders in the city's ten-year initiative to design and develop a thriving and resilient region—the Sustainable Cleveland 2019 plan.[2]

In order for sustainability performance indicators to spur engagement and drive progress, stakeholders must have a process for sharing, interpreting, and acting on the data. The Boston Green Ribbon Commission laid out the characteristics of a best practice engagement process built around sharing data in a report titled "Benchmarking Boston's Sustainability Performance Management Systems":

- The city has a manageable set of goals with measurable targets that are achievable given available resources.
- Constituents are involved in the development, implementation, and tracking of progress toward the goals.
- The goals are incorporated into strategic plans, processes, systems, capital budgets, and individual performance evaluations.
- Metrics are established for each goal for which data can be collected and accountability assigned.
- Systems are built to collect and analyze data.
- Performance is analyzed and regularly discussed by internal and external stakeholders.
- Adjustments are made to goals, strategies, and budgets as needed.

- There is accountability and recognition for progress, which is communicated to internal and external stakeholders.
- Communication is used to involve and educate constituencies and to drive action and resource allocation.
- Action is regularly taken to ensure continued progress.[3]

It can take years to put all these pieces into place. The City of Minneapolis, Minnesota, created a sustainability performance management program in 2003, which is when the city's conversation about indicators began. In 2005, the city amended its comprehensive plan to include sustainability, adopted a first set of sustainability indicators, and mandated that each department incorporate relevant indicators into their business plans. In 2006, the first sustainability report was released. In 2007, city departments adopted departmental plans using the same indicators. In 2011, the indicators and targets were revised. Throughout this process, Sustainability Director Gayle Prest worked with city departments to continually improve their data sources, to collect and analyze results, and to explore the changes needed to meet their performance goals.

Many green city leaders have felt overwhelmed by the complexity of the process of creating and embedding a sustainability performance management system in city practice, but green city leaders in Minneapolis and Santa Monica, California—both early adopters of these systems—urge other cities to "just do it." In both cities, they quickly picked a few indicators that were meaningful to key stakeholders, set targets, started to track progress, and regularly discussed the implications of the results. Once this process has become routine, it is easier to add indicators or improve the ones used to launch the process. In this way—through trial and error—green city leaders can learn which indicators work best to advance sustainability and drive performance.

Adopt Green Goals First

Green city leaders point out that before a city can start experimenting with performance indicators, goals must be established. "In New York we focused on a key set of goals and initiatives that would have the greatest impact on reducing carbon emissions," says David Bragdon, former director of the New York City Mayor's Office of Long-Term Planning and Sustainability. "Being very explicit about the goals and explaining them to people are the most important first steps." New York City codified its goals in PlaNYC, a broad agenda to address a growing population, aging infrastructure, a changing climate, and an evolving economy. PlaNYC went further than most sustainability plans by including indicators for each goal, the budgets required to achieve these goals, and the responsibilities of each department in achieving these goals. New York City has also produced annual progress reports that share both successes and setbacks. This comprehensive approach has served

New York City well. The city has achieved many of the goals in PlaNYC, which is recognized as a best practice planning process.

The development of the sustainability plan is a crucial step in sustainability performance management not only because it signals agreement on goals and progress indicators but also because it helps build shared responsibility for progress toward those goals. As the Boston Green Ribbon Commission discovered, sustainability planning provides time to "build the buy-in, ownership, and agreement from stakeholders that will be needed to deliver progress."[4] Shannon Parry, Santa Monica's deputy sustainability officer, agrees. "One of the things we've been very successful in doing," she says, "is helping people to see themselves and their programs, policies, and passions reflected in the sustainability plan."[5] Stakeholders who feel this sense of ownership make the best stewards of its achievement.

Prioritize Indicators That Drive Action

Even after a city has codified sustainability goals in a plan, it is common for green city leaders to struggle to develop a manageable set of performance indicators that can drive sustainability performance. "Sustainability" is broad and inclusive, cutting across the functions of most city departments. Sustainability plans can include one hundred or more goals, each goal can have several objectives, and each objective can require more than one action. Even if a city doesn't have a sustainability plan, it is likely to have dozens of "sustainability" goals codified in functional plans in areas ranging from transportation to housing to waste and water management. Green city leaders would have no time for action if they had to track progress indicators for all of these goals, objectives, and actions.

Cities have found ways to establish sustainability performance management systems that make it easier to manage the complexity of sustainability. In 2011, the City of Ann Arbor, Michigan, found references to greening and resource efficiency in twenty city plans and as many city council resolutions, which when taken together set more than 200 goals. If every one of these goals included targets and progress indicators, it would be a tremendous burden to manage Ann Arbor's sustainability performance. Instead, the city's green city leaders seized an opportunity to create a citywide vision for sustainability that improved understanding across city government of how these plans related to one another and that resulted in a manageable set of goals and performance indicators. They did this by working with the city's departments and commissions to organize all 200 goals under sixteen overarching citywide sustainability goals. Then staff began working with the same departments and commissions to create performance indicators for the sixteen goals. Departments and commissions still have their separate goals, but it is now easier for them to understand how each contributes to the overarching sustainability goals as well as how each supports the goals of other departments and commissions.

Green city leaders who have developed successful systems for tracking and acting on performance have taken the time to identify a smaller set of key indicators, and they have helped build tiers of indicators with both short- and long-term targets. They have made sure to celebrate progress toward achieving these targets and to recognize key leaders who contributed. Finally, they have created processes for ensuring that missed targets drive modifications in goals and strategies.

Choose Meaningful Indicators That Champions Can Own

Performance indicators need champions in order to drive action. This is why indicators are most effective if they are aligned with issues that matter to the mayor, city council, and other key stakeholders, including community members. Cori Burbach, sustainable community coordinator for the City of Dubuque, Iowa, initiated a broad engagement process to choose the sustainability indicators that would be most meaningful to local leaders. Over four months, the city hosted focus groups with the Dubuque Performance Metrics Committee, the Dubuque City Council, and the Sustainable Dubuque collaboration—which the chamber of commerce and the Community Foundation of Greater Dubuque formed to engage citizens—as well as other city staff and members of the community. Burbach proposed that three criteria be used in the selection process: an indicator must be (1) meaningful, in that it relates to an important goal or project; (2) measurable, in that it includes a performance target, a time frame, and a data source for measuring progress; and (3) feasible, in that the city has the resources to collect and analyze the data and the authority to act on the results.[6]

What makes a "meaningful" indicator varies, depending on the audience. Progress indicators intended to motivate policy makers could be very different from those intended to spur community engagement and action. City leaders may be very motivated to reduce per capita energy use because it will make many city functions—buildings, transportation, water, and waste—more efficient. On the other hand, it may be more effective to talk to residents about the energy costs of housing and transportation and to measure how easy it is for them to access goods and services or parks.

In order for a performance indicator to be truly meaningful, stakeholders have to understand the implications of adopting it.[7] If lower vehicle miles traveled (VMT) is to be a meaningful indicator of progress, for example, stakeholders must understand that this may require investment in transit, transit-oriented development, making neighborhoods more walkable and bikeable, or a combination of these. Once stakeholders understand that these investments are needed, the use of VMT as an indicator can be a powerful

action. The San Diego Regional Quality of Life Dashboard helps stakehold-
d the backstory for each indicator by describing each one and why it is im-
zing progress and explaining the results, providing options for improving
ind illustrating success with stories called "bright spots."

Create Tiers of Indicators

Developing tiers of indicators can help manage the complexity of advancing sustainability. For example, a city can create a top tier of overarching indicators that are tracked and
shared publicly, followed by a longer list of indicators that are parsed out to the departments and stakeholders responsible for the specific actions required to achieve success.
The City of Berkeley, California, has three tiers: (1) system-level metrics to measure the
overall impact of a combination of strategies, for example, to reduce residential energy
use; (2) program-level metrics to measure the impact of specific activities and programs,
such as an increase in bike parking or in energy retrofits; and (3) milestones and status
updates that elaborate on why specific actions have been taken or why not.[8]

Illustrating how indicators relate to one another provides a valuable context for developing and implementing strategies. For example, linking program-level indicators to
system-level indicators enables program managers to understand how their progress contributes to the city's overall success. The City of Vancouver, British Columbia, lists nine-
teen key indicators in its Greenest City 2020 Action Plan and sixty supporting indicators
that are more specifically linked to the projects and strategies to be implemented. Senior
managers in the City of Surrey, British Columbia, asked sustainability staff for a small set
of overarching indicators that reflected the city's priorities. They agreed on fifteen that
provided a good overview, including per capita water consumption, number of homes
within 400 meters of amenities, percentage of vegetative cover in the city, average cost of
rental housing, number of jobs per worker, and criminal code offenses per 1,000 residents.

One benefit of having overarching indicators—which the City of Berkeley refers to
as system-level metrics—is that measuring the impact of a combination of strategies
helps cities and communities break down silos and promotes collaboration among diverse stakeholders. The Sustainability Plan for the City of St. Louis, Missouri, which was
championed by Sustainability Director Catherine Werner, makes the case for this kind of
integration. The plan defines success as finding the optimal balance of economic health
(affecting prosperity), social equity (affecting people), and environmental stewardship
(affecting the planet). For example, air quality is an environmental indicator and also an
indicator of economic health and social equity. As the plan points out, air quality is a key
determinant of asthma rates in children, especially in lower-income neighborhoods near
heavily traveled transportation corridors, and if poor air quality exacerbates asthma, these

children may have to miss school, their parents may have to miss work to care for them, and the family may incur medical costs—thereby affecting all three areas of concern.[9]

The City of Albany, New York, with leadership from senior planner and green city leader Doug Melnick, sought out metrics for the city's sustainability plan, "Albany 2030: Your City, Your Future," that would measure the intersection between environmental, social, and economic goals too.[10] One example of an enviro-socioeconomic metric is the percentage of people who can take care of all their daily needs by walking or biking because they live within a half mile of health care, employment, education, stores selling fresh and healthy food, and parks and recreation or because they live within a half mile of public transit that can take them to these destinations. Another metric that cuts across disciplines is VMT because a reduction in VMT is also a reduction in traffic, air pollution, energy consumption, and household energy expenditures.[11]

A city needs to work with an array of stakeholders to make progress toward these overarching indicators. For example, measuring the number of "vacant lots occupied or restored" could bring together stakeholders interested in neighborhood redevelopment, open space management, economic development, urban agriculture, and land use planning. These stakeholders would need to work together to determine how to make progress

Figure 6.1. Cyclists, Albany, New York
One enviro-socioeconomic metric is the percentage of people who can walk, bike, or ride transit in order to take care of daily needs—these are healthier and more affordable alternatives to driving.

in each of these areas of interest with an eye toward accomplishing the overarching goal. This is the work of breaking down silos. Progress in meeting short-term targets can build momentum for efforts to achieve longer-term goals. Challenges in meeting short-term targets can inform adjustments to strategies for achieving longer-term goals.

Set Short- and Long-Term Performance Targets

Green city leaders find advantages in adopting both short-term and long-term performance targets. The City of Surrey, British Columbia, created a task force in 2009 to recommend aspirational long-term targets as well as short-term targets. Even though the long-term targets measured an "ideal outcome," the task force still spent time identifying the "change agenda" that would get the city there. In Chicago, soon after Mayor Rahm Emanuel was elected, he championed the launch of the 2015 Sustainable Chicago Action Agenda to add more immediacy to the goals set in the earlier Chicago Climate Action Plan (CCAP)—which include reducing greenhouse gas emissions by 80 percent by 2050— as well as to put more emphasis on economic development. When green city leaders in New York City updated PlaNYC, they kept the 2030 targets while also adopting new short-term goals to drive immediate action.

Plan for How Missing Targets Can Drive Change

To drive change, each performance indicator needs to have targets and deadlines for improvements. The targets should be ambitious but technically, economically, and legally achievable. Targets may not be achieved for many reasons, including changes in funding, leadership, or federal or state policies. While achieving targets is a cause for celebration and recognition, missing them is information that should not be hidden from public view. Political leaders in a growing number of cities are willing to accept the risk of being criticized for not achieving targets and may even view the ensuing dialogue as an opportunity.

Being transparent is an effective way to build public trust and spur action. Minneapolis has done this, as has New York City and Santa Monica, California. The website for the City of Minneapolis states that the city has "made it a priority to show the public areas in which it is making progress and areas that need more attention." The City of Surrey, British Columbia, launched an online Sustainability Dashboard, on which it tracks and shares the city's progress. Data for each metric are available for download.[12] Santa Monica's sustainability progress report includes detailed data analysis and describes program challenges and successes for each indicator. The report card, which is reviewed and approved by an external task force, grades the city both for success and for effort. "We added the second grade [for effort] because some of our goals are aggressive," explains Deputy

Sustainability Officer Shannon Parry. For example, a community may fall short on meeting a goal such as ending homelessness, but because this goal is essential to becoming a sustainable community, the community must keep working at it.

One benefit of sharing disappointing results with the public is that members of the community can help fix problems. As Dean Kubani, director of Santa Monica's Office of Sustainability and the Environment, explains, "There are a lot of challenges, and the reason we're reporting on them is because we want help. This approach has caused problems, but it's also been incredibly useful. Reporting on things that aren't going well prompts us to change what we do." In the city's first progress report, for example, the sustainability staff could not report on the condition of Santa Monica's urban forest because there was no tracking mechanism. This prompted the city council to create a new position for someone who would oversee the urban forest and track performance. The council also provided additional resources and supported changes in policy in order to improve the city's grades.

One way municipalities can limit their responsibility for results that are beyond their control is to flag these goals. Anna Mathewson, sustainability manager for Surrey, British Columbia, recommended that the city organize the indicators thematically in the city's Sustainability Charter Action Framework and then flag those over which it had no control.

Even when government is this transparent, the city may still be blamed when goals

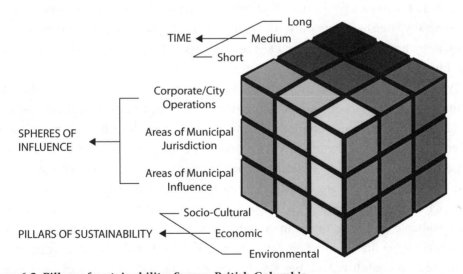

Figure 6.2. Pillars of sustainability, Surrey, British Columbia
The City of Surrey has organized its Sustainability Charter into three pillars of sustainability, three spheres of influence, and three implementation time frames, calling this framework the Sustainability Cube.

are not met. This is less likely to happen, however, if there is community-wide buy-in to the plan and if there has been an inclusive and transparent process enabling the community to help develop both the plan and the performance indicators. Even so, the media and some critics may use failure as an excuse to criticize city staff and leadership, and because of this some politicians may continue to resist releasing data on missed targets.

Making the Best of Poor Access to Data

Brendon Slotterback, sustainability program coordinator for the City of Minneapolis, says the fact that the city's sustainability work is data driven is an important element of the city's success. (He also cites mayoral leadership, champions in many departments, accountability, a willingness to report bad news, using data to make changes, and having strong community support and partnerships.)[13] But even in Minneapolis, green city leaders say they must continually compromise because the available data have so many limitations.

Many cities do not have access to the data they need. A core aspect of sustainability, for example, is increased resource efficiency, but providing cities with the data necessary to measure performance in this arena is outside the scope of work of most electric and natural gas utilities. Utilities track energy consumption by meter and by account for billing purposes but not by geographic boundaries—the data set that cities need in order to assess efficiency. Moreover, utilities are required to protect customer privacy and generally will share data only at a highly aggregated scale, whereas cities need data on usage by housing type, size, and age of residents to target energy actions to areas of high impact.[14]

Typically, cities don't have a centralized data source for VMT, either, and they have to turn to metropolitan planning organizations or state government and ask staff to do special runs of their transportation demand models, even though these models aren't designed to provide the community-scale data that cities need. The National Transit Database, for example, provides information on the energy use of transit but not at the scale of the community, and many transit systems traverse jurisdictional boundaries.[15]

Many cities pause at the fork in the road before choosing either to use the most easily available data or to invest in creating data that are more meaningful. But green city leaders agree that even when data are imperfect, collecting the data helps create a culture of accountability. And they say that decent data, put into context, can be better than perfect data obtained at a high cost. Cori Burbach, sustainable community coordinator in Dubuque, Iowa, decided to use readily available data while keeping on the lookout for better and newer data. "There are a few indicators for which we don't have any data, but we are keeping them because they are important and we'll figure it out later on," she says.

Investing in data can pay off if it advances a critical goal. Green city leaders in New York City decided they couldn't determine the importance of planting trees and creating pedestrian plazas to help the city meet federal air quality standards unless they could measure the effects of these activities in particular neighborhoods. So PlaNYC installed air quality monitors in 150 locations around the city.[16]

One benefit of building a sustainability plan and performance metrics in close collaboration with other stakeholders, and with shared responsibility for executing the plan, is that everyone can help generate the data to measure performance. In Minneapolis, for example, a variety of departments collect data on specific goals and then pool it for reporting purposes.

Many green city leaders hope that data will become more readily available and easily collected via a central database. Utilities, state governments, and national governments could do a lot to achieve this dream. Until then, however, green city leaders will have to continue to standardize data requirements, collect and check the data, and then massage it and present it. In Dubuque, students at the University of Iowa helped create the city's first report card in 2012, and they developed spreadsheets and tools that Sustainability Community Coordinator Cori Burbach and her team could use to update the data going forward. Burbach worries about the quality of data, but like Gayle Prest in Minneapolis, whose efforts were explained at the beginning of this chapter, she's pushing forward.

Embedding Progress Indicators in Everyday Municipal Practice

The Boston Green Ribbon Commission report discussed earlier in this chapter concluded from its scan of best practices that embedding performance indicators in everyday processes required that (1) designated staff have to be held accountable, and (2) the indicators have to be incorporated into strategic plans, processes, systems, capital budgets, and individual performance evaluations.[17]

It is difficult to get to this point without strong mayoral support, however. Green city leaders in Minneapolis have benefited from the strong leadership of Mayor R. T. Ryback, who asks for regular progress reports, incorporates indicators into departmental performance reviews, publicly acknowledges successes, and asks for improvement from those who fall short—and then offers them his support. Vancouver, British Columbia, has also incorporated an evaluation of sustainability performance into individual performance reviews, as has Burlington, Vermont, where there is an annual town meeting to celebrate the progress of the Burlington Legacy Project and to review its goals and metrics. Members of the Legacy Project's steering committee and staff of city departments report on the results, and department heads commit to specific projects or actions for the next year.

Green city leaders play a big role in institutionalizing this work. They help staff surmount barriers and find ways to reward those who make progress—through recognition or by arranging for their departments to share in any savings, for example. Gayle Prest has made it her mission to solve problems for other departments every step along the way in Minneapolis.

Using Indicators for Collective Learning

Perhaps the most critical step in institutionalizing sustainability indicators is creating the space to talk about progress with key stakeholders. Indicators have value only if people understand what they mean, why they are important, and what the strategies are to reach them. Judith Innes and David Booher wrote an article on sustainability indicators in 2000 that concluded:

> History shows that millions of dollars and much time of many talented people has been wasted on preparing national, state and local indicator reports that remain on the shelf gathering dust. . . . While many indicator reports have been little used, a few indicators have had significant impacts on public action. . . . Indeed in many of these cases it was not the indicators themselves that mattered most. Rather it was the learning and change among key players that took place during the course of their development and the new shared meanings and changed discourses that often made the critical difference.[18]

Indeed, indicators are most likely to have an impact when they are created, analyzed, and acted on in regular discussions with decision makers and stakeholders. Santa Monica's Task Force on the Environment, a group of seven outside experts on environmental policy appointed by the city council, creates a forum for understanding the results of performance indicators. Discussions with the task force yield focused solutions to barriers.

Setting time aside for reflection is a lot easier when people can see the high payoff in terms of impact and saved time and resources. In Berkeley, California, it became apparent that more aggressive upgrades than had been planned in the city's 2011 Climate Action Plan update would be necessary to meet the 2020 goal of reducing overall energy use in municipal buildings by 33 percent below 2000 levels. It was because this performance metric made this fact clear that the city could decide to take additional action.[19]

Using Performance Indicators for Broad Engagement in Action

Using indicators to share the progress that's been made can provide occasion to celebrate with the community, highlight the work of green city champions and the issues that are being addressed, and spur further collaboration. The Boston Green Ribbon Commission's report on best practices in sustainability performance management found that cities go public with this information for several reasons:

- To give stakeholders credit for progress, thereby creating incentives for greater participation and performance improvement
- To provide constituent support for initiatives
- To communicate underperformance in order to create pressure for improvement
- To spur action and involvement in the community

Nils Moe, climate change advisor to the mayor of the City of Berkeley, takes advantage of the opportunity to build momentum when sharing results with the community. Headlines such as "Data Show Significant Water Savings in Berkeley over Last Ten Years" and "In Berkeley, More Households Don't Equal More Energy Use" acknowledge the progress that residents have made and celebrate it. The city also uses these public reports to build momentum by suggesting additional steps that could result in even greater success.

Green city leaders in New York City have had a lot to celebrate with the community when it comes to PlaNYC, which commits to "reimagining" 4,000 acres of city-owned land so that all New Yorkers can live within a ten-minute walk of a park, among many other goals. In 2007, New York City had fewer acres of green space per person than most other American cities. In 2012 alone, the program repurposed existing land in a way that brought more than 240,000 additional New Yorkers within ten minutes of a park. The city celebrated this success with residents. Adam Freed, past deputy director of the Mayor's Office of Long-Term Planning and Sustainability, says the city's annual progress reports keep the community engaged and expecting more.

But regular reporting on indicators is a resource-intensive activity, especially for small communities. One way to manage this burden is to report less often. The City of Santa Monica, California, went from annual to biennial reporting a few years ago. "When we reported annually we found that all we were doing was collecting data," says Deputy Sustainability Officer Shannon Parry. "We never had an 'off year' to develop and integrate sustainability into city programs and policies and achieve change on the ground."[20]

Managing When Others Rate You

A dozen or so green city indices have been developed to rank cities in the United States and around the world by organizations and businesses ranging from the Natural Resources Defense Council to *Scientific American* to the *Economist* magazine's Intelligence Unit. While these rankings generate considerable media attention, they have big limitations: the criteria are subjective, the comparisons often don't account for contextual differences among cities, and the different methodologies used for each ranking tend to generate different results. For example, the green media company SustainLane ranked New York City thirtieth for waste reduction, whereas the city ranked third in the *Economist*'s Green City Index for pretty much the same performance indicator. These rankings rely heavily on publicly available data, so a ranking may show greenhouse gas emissions from five years ago, ignoring significant advances that have been achieved, or it may use county data for a city even though the city may be more dense or may have a different building stock, walkability score, or transportation options.

Cities typically provide data to the entities doing the rankings even though they know it may be misinterpreted. But the rating systems are rarely built in consultation with cities—which would help provide a better understanding of the constraints of the data. Having an outside entity point out a city's shortcomings can sometimes be useful, however: if a city does poorly, green city leaders can use the results to advocate for new policies and more resources to improve performance. But if a city does well in the rankings, this provides green city leaders with an opportunity to recognize their partners and ask for more resources in order to do even better.

Frustration with the misrepresentation that sometimes results from these rankings was one factor that prompted more than forty cities and the organizations with which they partner to create their own rating system, the STAR Community Rating System, to provide external validation for the successes cities claim. This rating system was also intended to enable cities to compare performance across cities and to help them set goals, develop performance measures, and interpret the results. The STAR Community Rating System launched a pilot program with thirty-two North American communities in October 2012 and plans to scale up in 2013.

Conclusion

Indicators are only as valuable as the process built around them. They can be effective in driving change if key stakeholders own them, learn from them, and act on them. Dean Kubani, sustainability director for the City of Santa Monica, says, "Initially there was very little interest in our sustainability indicators or in collecting data outside of our own office. But when we transitioned from an environmental focus to a focus on the triple bottom line, and from a focus on internal indicators to community indicators, a lot of departments came on board, we built ownership, and people got used to collecting and sharing data." Today, he says, these indicators are driving sustainability progress in Santa Monica.

The lessons learned by green city leaders that are listed at the end of the introduction to this book all apply to performance management as well, with minor modifications:

Figure 6.3. Living Garden, Santa Monica
Within the City of Santa Monica, California, there wasn't much interest in sustainability indicators and data collection until the focus was shifted from the environment to the triple bottom line. This got the attention of a lot of city departments.

- Since you can't do everything and do it well, focus on the indicators that are aligned with the city's most important goals.
- Find indicators that capture more than one aspect of the triple bottom line because this will help to spur collaboration across silos in city government and the community.
- Encourage data sharing by sharing the city's internal data, and lead by example to achieve a paradigm shift toward collaborative, community-wide performance management.
- Help others help you by distributing responsibility for both championing specific sustainability goals and collecting the data to track progress.
- Build ownership for success by giving others opportunities to report on the city's progress at press events and to take credit for successes.
- Tap into competitive instincts—if other cities are outperforming your city, you can use this to argue for more resources and better policies and programs.
- Don't let the perfect be the enemy of the good; you will need to compromise to get things done.

CASE IN POINT:

Sustainability Performance Management in Minneapolis

Of all the challenges that green city leaders face, creating and sustaining a robust performance management system—establishing strong metrics, collecting and analyzing quality data, regularly reporting on progress, and holding key stakeholders responsible for results—is among the most important and difficult to achieve. Other cities can learn much from Minneapolis, which has in place one of the longest-standing and most effective sustainability performance management programs in North America.

In 2012, the city released its seventh annual sustainability report, titled "Minneapolis Living Well," which shares data on progress against twenty-six indicators of the community's economic, environmental, and social health. Each of the city's eighteen departments, as required by a city council mandate, integrates the relevant indicators and targets into its business plan, and most have assumed—and even embraced—the responsibility of collecting and submitting the necessary data that go into the report.

Minneapolis's systematic and sustained approach to tracking and reporting its progress against indicators and targets has helped to earn it a widespread reputation as one of North America's greenest cities. More important, it's helped to make sustainability part of the community's identity. "It's really part of our DNA now," says Minneapolis Sustainability Director Gayle Prest of the triple bottom line approach that is embedded in the city's sustainability program and indicators. "It's about being a vital and healthy city, and what that looks and feels like."

The Inside Story

The Minneapolis City Council created the Minneapolis Sustainability program in 2003, establishing principles and setting in motion a process for developing indicators and numerical targets. Two years later, the council amended the city's comprehensive plan to include sustainability, adopting an initial set of indicators, mandating an annual reporting process, and requiring all departments to incorporate relevant indicators into their business plans. The first "Minneapolis Living Well" report was released in late 2006, and one has been published annually ever since.

From the beginning, the city's sustainability program and the report that tracks its progress adopted a triple bottom line of economic, environmental, and social health. "From the start our leaders and our community understood that sustainability is about overall livability, not just environmental quality," Gayle Prest says. But the city's initiative to create sustainability metrics was stalled when she took over the reins in early

2006. A lot of draft indicators were under development, and not all of them were well understood by the general public. The lack of focus and clarity was holding the effort back. Moreover, there was relatively little engagement in and ownership of the process outside of the city environmental agency for which Prest worked at the time. So when she became the sustainability director, working out of the City Coordinator's Office, she moved quickly to shore up mayoral and city council support for the project and to more deeply engage the interdepartmental Environmental Coordinating Team (composed of staff and managers from Community Planning and Economic Development, Operations and Regulatory Services, Public Works, Health and Family Support, Parks and Recreation, and other departments) in a process to reduce the number of indicators.

With the goal of continuously improving and adapting to changing data and dynamics, the enabling resolution called for the indicators to be reexamined on a regular basis, and Prest and her team have interpreted that to be every two to three years. In 2007, air quality was added to the list of indicators in response to increasing concerns about air pollution in the city and region and its impact on public health and the economy. In 2009, the city added indicators related to local food production and consumption to capitalize on growing community interest, and measures related to waste reduction and recycling were added because of concerns about stalled recycling rates.

The city council added a number of social and community health indicators to the mix and, in a key move, directed that many indicators be broken down by race and ethnicity. For example, the infant mortality rate is tracked by ethnic group, with the goal of reducing the overall rate as well as the rate within each group. Similarly, an employment and poverty indicator is intended to help the city reduce racial and ethnic disparities in unemployment by 25 percent by 2016. Looking at the data in these different ways helps the city better track progress toward meeting its social equity goals, Prest says, and paints a more nuanced picture of the city's overall health.

"Minneapolis Living Well" now reports on twenty-six indicators in three categories: A Healthy Life, which includes public health metrics such as healthy infants, teen pregnancy, and asthma; Greenprint, which includes environmental health indicators related to air quality, tree canopy, and climate change; and A Vital Community, including social and economic indicators such as employment and poverty, violent crime and homelessness. Because each indicator is associated with more than one target, the city is tracking progress against fifty-five targets. In most cases, these are specific, quantifiable goals, such as "Reduce infant mortality rates overall and within each ethnic subgroup from 7.1 deaths per year to 6.6 deaths per year," "Reduce community-wide greenhouse gas emissions by 15 percent by 2015 and 30 percent by 2025 against a

Figure 6.4. Biking in Minneapolis
The City of Minneapolis, Minnesota, tracks progress against twenty-six sustainability indicators and fifty-five specific targets, including, for example, the number of on-street bike lanes and off-street bike trails and the percentage of bike commuters. Photo courtesy of Meet Minneapolis.

2006 baseline," and "Achieve 30 percent growth in green jobs in Minneapolis by 2015 against a 2010 baseline."

Results to Date

The process of collecting, analyzing, and writing up the data for the city's "Minneapolis Living Well" report has become increasingly efficient and less time-consuming as individual departments have progressively assumed and embraced those responsibilities over the seven years it has been published. The website for the effort is a strong resource, so only an executive summary of the report is actually printed. Ownership of and responsibility for the sustainability indicators have been incorporated into the business plans of each department. "It's really part of our brand as a city now," says Prest. "And so it's much easier! Now I'm not the lead on many of the initiatives. We've got a mayor and thirteen city council members and eighteen department directors—and they all believe in sustainability."

As an example, in 2011 the local convention bureau launched a new branding

Figure 6.5. Fishing in Minneapolis
Minneapolis's convention bureau touts the city's green assets in a new branding campaign. "Sure, some cities scatter trees around buildings," the City by Nature website boasts, "but we have a park every six blocks." Photo courtesy of Meet Minneapolis.

campaign titled "Minneapolis: City by Nature," touting the city's green assets and reputation. "Sure, some cities scatter trees around buildings, but we have a park every six blocks," the City by Nature website boasts. "Rivers, lakes, parks, farmer's markets, we've got them all. We're really a city that is infused with and surrounded by nature. That's why we chose 'City by Nature.' Minneapolis truly is a city sprung forth from nature, as if concrete structures sprouted from the earth."

The fact that the indicators and targets were adopted by the city council *and* are reported on annually is a powerful combination that drives change in a way that even a lengthy sustainability plan may not, Prest says. This effort has bolstered and solidified the city's reputation as a leader, and Minneapolis consistently appears in the top tier of sustainable city rankings. It was ranked the tenth greenest city in North America in the 2012 Green City Index. "Minneapolis was one of the first cities in the U.S. to incorporate environmental sustainability into city planning, which encouraged other similarly sized cities in and outside of the region to follow suit," the report noted. "Often considered 'one to watch' by environmentalists, prospects are good for continued environmental action in Minneapolis."[21]

Challenges

Among the most common and daunting challenges are finding good data; figuring out how to collect, analyze, and report on the data and determining who should take on this task; and making difficult decisions about how much time and effort should be invested in measuring progress, as opposed to actually making progress. "Just get started!" Prest advises. "Don't wait for the perfect set of indicators and perfect information. It doesn't exist. Just get going in the right direction, and be ready to make improvements along the way."

Prest and her team have been vigilant about decentralizing the responsibility for data collection and analysis, both to help manage the workload and to create the shared sense of ownership that is necessary for success. They provide one-on-one consultations to help departments meet data-related challenges, integrate sustainability indicators into their business plans, and develop associated policies and programs.

Another challenge is sharing "less good" news about progress in the highly political environment of municipal government, where media scrutiny can be intense and the jobs and reputations of elected officials can be on the line. Prest's earnest and no-nonsense communication style helps in this regard, as does the fact that she is a civil servant and not a political appointee. "I remember sitting down with the mayor near the beginning and talking this through," recalls Prest. "I told him that not all the news is going to be pretty but that this would allow us to have a dialogue about problems that emerge. I said, 'We aren't going to greenwash it. We're better than that.' And to his credit, he agreed."

Perhaps an even bigger challenge than creating a robust indicators initiative is sustaining it. One key to success is sticking with it long enough that it influences attitudes and behaviors as well as policies, programs, and on-the-ground decisions about resource allocation. Most cities have two- or four-year electoral cycles and one- or two-year budget cycles, which makes it difficult to sustain any initiative that takes longer than a couple of years to come to fruition. Minneapolis has been fortunate to have strong and consistent leadership by a three-term mayor and many city council leaders as well. This gives Prest and other green city leaders confidence that even though Mayor Rybak will depart in 2014, the program is sufficiently mature and embraced, both internally and externally, to endure.

In addition, Prest and her team have worked hard to integrate the sustainability indicators—and the philosophy and practices that they embody—into the fabric of city government and the community by tirelessly engaging both internal and external stakeholders. For example, in addition to the interdepartmental Environmental Coordinating Team described earlier, the Citizens Environmental Advisory Committee—a group of eighteen community representatives appointed by the city council and staffed by Prest and her team—has played a central and critical role, including helping to decide on the indicators and to oversee the process of tracking and reporting on them. Says Prest about the unusual longevity of the Minneapolis program: "You keep it alive, you keep it fresh, you keep it relevant, and you keep the stakeholders engaged every single step of the way."

Key Factors for Success

What decisions and dynamics have allowed green city leaders to create one of the most robust and long-standing sustainability performance management systems in North America? Key success factors include the following.

Using metrics as a silo-busting mechanism. From the beginning, Prest and her partners have seen the triple bottom line sustainability indicators as a silo-busting mechanism that results in integration and collaboration across city agencies and sectors of the community. When Prest took on the job, a lot of environmental efforts were under way in Minneapolis, "but there was no umbrella—just a lot of silos built up in different departments." The indicators have helped change that dynamic, Prest says. "I love the fact that, when we're talking about our 'healthy life' and our 'vital communities' indicators, we've got the health department and the school district and the parks department and the police department all sitting around the table, talking about ways to collaborate to solve problems."

Embedding green metrics into a citywide performance management system. Green or sustainability metrics that exist outside the official or formal processes that a municipality uses to measure performance and hold senior managers accountable are much less likely to make a real difference on the ground. Minneapolis has addressed that challenge by committing to an annual report, integrating sustainability goals and indicators into the comprehensive plan, and requiring all departments to incorporate relevant sustainability indicators into their business plans.

Requiring transparent annual reporting. The city council requires an annual update about the progress in meeting the performance measures. Keeping the data fresh, accurate, and easily accessible ensures that policy makers and the public trust and use the data.

Building a sense of shared ownership and responsibility. Prest and her team work aggressively to share ownership, responsibility, and credit. "I try to not be the one quoted in the paper," Prest says. "When we did a press conference to showcase our efforts to buy greener cleaning products, it wasn't the mayor or me or even the property services director up there talking to the reporters; it was the maintenance guys."

CASE IN POINT:

Ensuring Sustainability Remains a Priority in New York City

Adam Freed, who was deputy director of the New York City Mayor's Office of Long-Term Planning and Sustainability, says he doesn't regret the months of staff time dedicated to the first update of New York City's sustainability plan, PlaNYC. Green city leaders had advocated not only for annual progress reports to the city council but also for quadrennial plan updates. The reason, says Freed, is that "when New York City released PlaNYC in 2007, we knew that not only did we not have all the right answers, but we probably weren't asking all the right questions." He says he believed the plan updates would allow the city to adapt to changes in the environment and to lessons learned about goals and strategies. The requirement to produce these plan updates would also help ensure that sustainability did not fall off the list of the mayor's priorities.

The Inside Story

The 2011 PlaNYC update was built on a strong foundation. In 2007, New York City used PlaNYC to tie together all of its sustainability activities in an overarching plan to create a greener, greater New York. The plan called for the implementation of 127 initiatives that defined the city's approach to land use, housing, water, energy, air quality, transportation, and climate change. It was an exceptional plan that included tactics, time lines, progress indicators, funding sources, and the agencies responsible for leading each initiative.

As expected, a lot changed between 2007, when PlaNYC was launched, and 2010, when work on the update began in earnest. "We knew that a lot was going to be different because the economic climate was so different," says Freed. A proposed traffic congestion fee for vehicles traveling into or within the central business district, which was to have funded new transit projects, never came to a vote in the state assembly, and city leaders were not able to achieve changes in state and federal policy that were necessary to advance some initiatives. The budget constraints of a down economy meant that planned marquee projects, such as the conversion of hundreds of schoolyards into community playgrounds, were going to require more time. The city had to do more with less, and the new imperative was to link any action to economic development and job growth. As a result, whereas the theme of the 2007 plan had been securing the future of New York City, the theme of the 2010 plan was transitioning to a green economy.

Staff consulted an increasingly broad set of stakeholders for the plan update in a process similar to the one used in 2007, except that this time the Mayor's Office of Long-Term Planning and Sustainability, which was created to champion the implementation of

CATEGORY	METRIC	2030 TARGET	FIGURE FOR MOST RECENT YEAR	TREND SINCE BASE YEAR
HOUSING AND NEIGHBORHOODS	**Create homes for almost a million more New Yorkers while making housing and neighborhoods more affordable and sustainable**			
	Increase in new housing units since January, 2007	314,000	122,969[1]	↗
	Total units of housing in NYC	INCREASE	3,352,041[1]	↗
	% of housing affordable to median-income NYC household	INCREASE	60.0%[1]	↘
	Vacancy rate of least expensive rental apartments	INCREASE	1.0%[1]	↗
	% of new units within a 1/2 mile of transit	>70%	85.5%[1]	NEUTRAL
	Residential building energy use per capita (source MMBTU) (3 yr rolling avg)	DECREASE	49.3[2]	NEUTRAL
PARKS AND PUBLIC SPACE	**Ensure all New Yorkers live within a 10-minute walk of a park**			
	% of New Yorkers that live within a 1/4 mile of a park	85%	75.6%[1]	↗
BROWNFIELD	**Clean up all contaminated land in New York City**			
	Number of vacant tax lots presumed to be contaminated	DECREASE	1,500-2,000[1]	NEUTRAL
	Number of tax lots remediated in NYC annually through the Brownfield Cleanup Program	INCREASE	0[1]	NEUTRAL
WATERWAYS	**Improve the quality of our waterways to increase opportunities for recreation and restore coastal ecosystems**			
	Fecal coliform rates in New York Harbor (Cells/100mL) (5 yr rolling avg)	DECREASE	35.3[1]	↗
	Dissolved oxygen rates in New York Harbor (mg/L) (5 yr rolling avg)	INCREASE	6.6[1]	NEUTRAL
WATER SUPPLY	**Ensure the high quality and reliability of our water supply system**			
	Number of drinking water analyses below maximum contaminant level	INCREASE	99.9%[1]	↗
	Water usage per capita (gallons per day) (3 yr rolling avg)	DECREASE	123.6[1]	↘
TRANSPORTATION	**Expand sustainable transportation choices and ensure the reliability and high quality of our transportation network**			
	Sustainable transportation mode share (Manhattan CBD bound commute)	INCREASE	73.6%[2]	NEUTRAL
	Change in transit volume minus change in auto traffic volume since 2007	POSITIVE	0.9%[2]	↗
	Vehicle revenue miles (Miles transit vehicles travel in revenue service)	INCREASE	924,589, 268[2]	↗
	% of bridges meeting a state of good repair (FY)	100%	41%[1]	NEUTRAL
	% of roads meeting a state of good repair (FY)	100%	72%[1]	↗
	% of transit station components meeting a state of good repair	100%	68%[1]	↗
ENERGY	**Reduce energy consumption and make our energy systems cleaner and more reliable**			
	Greenhouse gas emissions per unit of electrical power (lbs CO2e/MWh)	DECREASE	696.9[2]	↘
	System reliability: CAIDI (Customer Average Interruption Duration Index)	DECREASE	2.71[1]	↗
	System reliability: SAIFI (System Average Interruption Frequency Index)	DECREASE	147.0[1]	↘
	Energy use per capita (source MMBTU) (3 yr rolling avg)	DECREASE	146.9[2]	NEUTRAL
AIR QUALITY	**Achieve the cleanest air quality of any big U.S. city**			
	City ranking in average PM 2.5 (3 yr rolling avg)	#1 (LEAST)	6.7[2]	↘
	Change in average PM 2.5 (year-on-year % change in 3 yr rolling avg)	DECREASE	10.3%[2]	↘
SOLID WASTE	**Divert 75% of our solid waste from landfills**			
	Percentage of waste diverted from landfills (includes fill)	75%	56%[2]	↗
CLIMATE CHANGE	**Reduce greenhouse gas emissions by more than 30%**			
	Increase the resilience of our communities, natural systems, and infrastructure to climate risks			
	Greenhouse gas emissions (MTCO2e)	DECREASE 30%	54,348,841[2]	↘
	Greenhouse gas emissions (100% = 2005 GHG emissions)	70%	88%[2]	↘
	Greenhouse gas emissions (MTCO2e) per GCP ($M)	DECREASE	97.4[2]	↘
	Greenhouse gas emissions (MTCO2e) per capita	DECREASE 30%	6.7[2]	↘

1 Results are for FY or CY 2011
2 Results are for FY or CY 2010; data is only available with a lag

Figure 6.6. PlaNYC 2012 progress report

In 2007, New York City used PlaNYC to tie sustainability activities into an overarching plan and lay out 127 initiatives as well as tactics, time lines, indicators, funding sources, and the responsibilities of city agencies.

PlaNYC, was already mobilized. Freed used the 2010 progress report as a launching point for the 2011 update. All policy leads and the departments they worked with were asked to discuss what was working and what was not, as well as any new needs that had come up. Freed's team consulted more than 250 grassroots organizations and held eleven community town hall "conversations."

For every idea that made it into the plan, five others did not. Staff kept large spreadsheets of the ideas that had resonated with stakeholders and looked for opportunities to group them together into bigger and bolder steps. It required discipline to stay focused, but the consultation and prioritization process was easier in 2010 than it had been in 2007 because people knew about PlaNYC and had followed its progress. This made it easier to convince people to come to the table, which made publicity less important. Trust had been built.

The update affirmed most of the 2030 goals included in the 2007 report. Some deadlines were extended, a new chapter and a new goal for reducing solid waste were included, a few initiatives were dropped and new ones were added, and crosscutting issues were highlighted—including public health, natural systems, and food. Transportation goals changed the most because transportation projects that depended on major new revenue sources could not go forward, and the chapter on energy illustrated the value of revisiting the goals: PlaNYC leaders had learned a great deal about the energy use of the building sector over the three years, and they were smarter about what it would take to shift energy demand.

Freed and his team made sure the updated plan included new marquee projects to garner broad attention and support. In 2007, residents had been most enthusiastic about a commitment to plant 1 million trees, and the update needed a similarly bold and meaningful project—and one was found. On the day the plan update was released, the mayor announced the Clean Heat Campaign, designed to address the problem of soot, a powdery black substance consisting mostly of carbon produced by the incomplete burning of organic matter. The press release noted that just 1 percent of all buildings in the city produced 86 percent of the soot from buildings—more than was produced by all the cars and trucks in New York City combined. The centerpiece of the Clean Heat Campaign was a prohibition on use of the heating oil that produced the most soot, which would be phased out over three years, along with a slower phasing out of other heavy heating oils. The city simultaneously provided incentives to help the owners of buildings make the switch to cleaner heating fuels, including financing, streamlined permitting, and educational programs.

Results to Date

PlaNYC codified the requirement that future mayors update the plan at least once every four years, issue an annual report tracking the progress of each initiative, and provide a greenhouse gas inventory. The Mayor's Office of Long-Term Planning and Sustainability has distributed the responsibility for achieving the goals among various city departments and has provided support to sustain momentum and help break down departmental silos. Many sustainability issues cross departments and jurisdictions, and the mayor's office has systematically brought departments together and urged them to collaborate. The plan has helped institutionalize sustainability in New York City, although it is uncertain how it will fare under a new mayor.

New York City has already made great progress toward achieving measurable results with the 2007 plan's 127 initiatives. Greenhouse gas emissions are 16 percent below 2005 levels, and 84 percent of New Yorkers now live within a ten-minute walk of a park—an 8 percent increase since 2007. All new trips into the city have been on mass transit rather than in private cars, and the number of New Yorkers who bike to work has doubled. Per capita electricity use, which had been increasing for years, is in decline. Sharing openly with stakeholders what has succeeded and what has failed has contributed to the plan's success.

Challenges

Even with the annual performance reports and related announcements, stakeholders are less aware of the plan and the progress than green city leaders hoped. The lesson learned is that it's important to continue outreach and engagement efforts throughout the year, not just when it's time for an annual report or update. More resources should be dedicated to expanding the plan's constituency and creating more champions.

PlaNYC focuses on all five boroughs, but the perception is that the plan is mainly about Manhattan. Green city leaders believe that creating maps showing the distribution of the benefits, including new parks and energy retrofits, would help them make a stronger case for citywide benefits.

Initially, it took staff two to three months to complete the annual progress report—a lengthy diversion of staff time from implementation. The report's narrative has been reduced in length, though performance is still measured, saving time without compromising accountability. But it has been difficult for staff to work on both implementing and updating the current plan.

Key Factors for Success

The main drivers of PlaNYC's success to date include the following:

Make it local. The plan meant more to residents when staff could point to a new park, bike path, or other neighborhood improvement, which enabled people to understand the plan's value.

Make it real. In 2010, ICLEI—Local Governments for Sustainability issued a report titled "The Process behind PlaNYC: How the City of New York Developed Its Comprehensive Long-Term Sustainability Plan" and quoted Dan Doctoroff, former deputy mayor for economic development and rebuilding. "We actually looked at the city almost block by block, neighborhood by neighborhood, system by system, out 23 years," said Doctoroff. "We vowed not to make a single proposal that we couldn't identify the source of funds for. . . . We demanded of ourselves that our progress be publicly tracked."

Report often. Annual reporting helped sustain the public's interest and build

Figure 6.7. PlaNYC 2012 progress report cover
Annual reporting helps PlaNYC sustain the public's interest as well as that of the mayor. It provides the mayor with clear wins that he or she can tout. Sharing results between annual reports is important for the same reason.

momentum, even though few residents read the reports, and it helped maintain the buy-in and commitment of the mayor because it provided him with clear wins that he could tout. Sharing the results of initiatives between annual reports is important too, and both the original plan and its update had a press strategy that included weekly announcements of programs that had been launched or completed. Staff lost that discipline as they got deeper into implementation, but they believe that continuing these weekly briefings would pay off.

Create a broad plan, but also focus. Freed and his team focused on one big issue each year while continuing to work with departments to make progress on all the goals. Congestion pricing was the big issue the first year, and the next year it was the Greener, Greater Buildings Plan. The third year, it was air quality and clean heat. These big and highly visible programs, such as MillionTreesNYC and others, garnered the interest and support of the city council and the public, providing opportunities to engage stakeholders and keep them involved.

Find a champion for the plan. The Mayor's Office of Long-Term Planning and Sustainability was the quarterback for PlaNYC and kept its myriad initiatives in the forefront and moving down the field. Not only did the office engage and help other departments; it also fostered partnerships with federal and state government as well as with for-profit and nonprofit organizations, foundations, and community groups.

Conclusion
From Green to Resilient Cities

The green city movement in North America has come a long way. Fifteen years ago, only a handful of cities—mostly larger or more progressive cities such as Chicago, New York, Minneapolis, Seattle, and Portland, Oregon—had environmental or sustainability directors on staff. Today, several hundred cities, including smaller communities in more conservative regions such as Fayetteville, Arkansas, and Charlotte, North Carolina, have hired staff to work on sustainability, and most sit in influential, senior-level positions, reporting directly to mayors, city managers, or directors of key departments. A quiet but robust revolution—led in part by these green city leaders, as we have called them in this book—is very much in progress, and it is transforming the way cities conduct their business and engage with their communities. As a result, cities, once perceived as a menace to the environment, are increasingly seen as perhaps our greatest hope. Even as recently as the turn of the twenty-first century, many of us tended to see cities as the main culprits behind the degradation of natural resources and quality of life. Today, more and more of us see cities as not only part of the solution but the driving force behind it.

Still, it's not *nearly* enough. In this book, we have showcased a small yet inspiring sampling of the innovative work under way, but neither the scale nor the speed of that work is adequate. The need for even more advancements and investments in the long-term vitality of our cities has never been more obvious and urgent. Hurricane Sandy emphatically made that point in October 2012 when it slammed into New York City and other communities along the coast of New York and New Jersey, killing more than 125 people and costing $10–$20 billion in property damage and lost business, with overall economic damage estimated at $30–$50 billion. The whole world took notice, not only the coastal cities but communities everywhere that already find themselves struggling to anticipate and manage all manner of climate-related risks, from heat waves that imperil their most vulnerable residents to droughts that threaten regional supplies of food, water, and energy. Sandy's message to cities everywhere was loud and clear: the race to resilience is on. Can it be won? We see a number of trends that give us considerable hope, as well as some persistent challenges that need more and better attention.

Promising Trends

As we've showcased in these pages, there is a transformation under way in cities across North America. In particular, the following signs of change give us hope that our urban future can be a green and resilient one.

The lines between mitigation and adaptation are blurring. Many cities finally are beginning to reject the false dichotomy between mitigation, the reduction of greenhouse gas emissions, and adaptation, the assessment and management of climate-related risks— which has characterized urban climate action for many years. We see this as a promising and necessary shift in thinking. Reducing emissions and managing climate risk are parts of the same whole, and resilience lies at their intersection. Treating them as separate approaches has hindered holistic solutions and slowed progress. A greener, lower-carbon city is also a more resilient city because it uses finite supplies of energy and water more efficiently and is less dependent on fossil fuels and on highly centralized—and therefore much more vulnerable—energy, water, and food systems. A city that is more aware of, prepared for, and able to adapt to climate impacts will require less expensive and less carbon-intensive investments to bounce back when those impacts occur, as they surely will.

Until relatively recently, with few exceptions, cities focused primarily or even solely on reducing their carbon footprints, not wanting to be perceived as giving up on the fight to address climate disruption at its roots. Chicago's 2008 climate action plan was the first in North America to address both mitigation and adaptation at the same time. One of the plan's five major sections focused on adaptation and featured actions ranging from managing the heat island effect to encouraging businesses to analyze and address their climate-related vulnerabilities. Now other cities are following suit. Seattle's first climate action plan, released in 2005, made only a passing mention of climate-related risks and how to manage them. The draft 2013 update of the plan, in stark contrast, features not only a new set of carbon reduction actions but also a large section on adaptation, including recommendations for enhancing the resilience of the city's energy, water, and transportation systems and evaluating and preparing for sea level rise on city shorelines.

Similarly, in 2012 the city council of Vancouver, British Columbia, unanimously adopted a climate adaptation plan to complement its emissions reduction work, and it is spending nearly $1 million to conduct a coastal risk assessment that will identify and cost out options for dealing with sea level rise.

Cities are tripling their bottom line. Although the concept of sustainable development, since its inception, has been about integrating economic, environmental, and social goals, many have misunderstood it to be simply the latest phase, or phrase, of the environmental movement. But more and more cities finally are moving toward a truly triple bottom line approach, merging their economic development, environmental stewardship, and social welfare strategies and investments. A decade ago, most green city leaders focused primarily, if not exclusively, on environmental goals and solutions, lacking the mandate or skills—or both—to tackle economic and social sustainability challenges as well. Since then, green city leaders have been progressing, slowly but steadily, toward a more systematically integrated approach. Impelled in part by the financial crisis of 2007–2008 and the ensuing economic downturn, more and more environmental practitioners are recognizing that it is difficult, if not impossible, to win support for green solutions that don't make good economic sense. And those practitioners whose work historically has been rooted in and focused on economic growth and development are seeing more clearly that environmental degradation *does* have economic costs—and in the case of climate events such as Hurricane Sandy they are massive costs—*and* that green solutions can be a promising pathway to long-term economic prosperity and resilience.

"One of the biggest drivers for greening our cities is the economy," says Carolyn Bowen, who manages the Office of Sustainability in the City of Calgary, Alberta. "When we looked at the expected growth of our city ten years into the future, we projected an infrastructure budget deficit of about $10 billion, assuming current practices. That's just not affordable." Adds Dennis Murphey, chief environmental officer for Kansas City, Missouri, "Sustainability is becoming part of our corporate culture here in Kansas City and in many other communities. The planners have been involved for quite some time, but we're starting to see that the budget people understand these issues as well. We're starting to see a focus on how to develop urban infrastructure in a more sustainable manner."

The City of El Paso, Texas, has taken an additional and unusual step that will likely become much more common in North American cities: its has merged its environmental sustainability and economic development departments. "Many cities are integrating their environmental and economic development efforts, not only because of the politics but also because they see that this is how we will achieve true sustainability," says Marty Howell, who runs El Paso's newly formed Department of Economic Development and Sustainability.

Social equity has been the last of the three pillars of sustainable development to get its due, but that is beginning to happen now. As described in chapter 3, green city leaders are more focused than ever on solutions that are developed in more inclusive ways and that deliver shared benefits. "A key trend is the increased emphasis on diversity, access, and equity," observes Jennifer Green, sustainability director for Burlington, Vermont. "More and more, greening cities will be about ensuring that all people are part of the dialogue and empowered to make change."

The silos are shrinking. The institutional and political hurdles we face are higher and harder than the technological challenges. Creating resilient cities will require an unprecedented amount of communication, coordination, and collaboration among individuals, agencies, institutions, sectors of communities, and levels of government. Overcoming the historical disconnects within and across these stakeholder groups remains perhaps our biggest challenge. The good news is that we see the silos breaking down. Motivated in part by constrained resources but also by the realization that complex, multidimensional challenges require sophisticated, holistic solutions, people and institutions are coming together in extraordinary and innovative ways to pool ideas and resources and develop integrated solutions at appropriate scales.

We see city agencies working together across historical silos, exemplified by El Paso's merger of its environmental sustainability and economic development functions. We see cities working more effectively than ever before with their suburbs, counties, and regional planning agencies—forming regional food councils and creating regional food hubs, developing and implementing sustainable economic development strategies, and designing, funding, and building regional transit systems. We see cities collecting, sharing, and encouraging the use of data, not only to make government more transparent but also to unleash creative and collaborative solutions that improve the quality of urban life. Examples include Cycle Atlanta, which gathers data from cyclists to help the city identify and prioritize needed infrastructure improvements; the City of San Francisco Recreation and Parks Official Mobile App, a smart phone application that provides information on the San Francisco Recreation and Parks Department's 1,200 facilities and allows users to reserve picnic sites and barbecue pits; and Street Bump, a crowd-sourcing project and mobile app in Boston that allows residents to report road conditions, providing government with the information it needs to improve roads. James Solomon, who directs the Street Bump program out of Boston's Office of New Urban Mechanics, says, "We are all using open data and new technology to explore new ways of improving our cities with and for our residents."

Perhaps most promising, we see city governments and companies working together to advance the fine but difficult art of public-private partnerships, which have resulted in more electric vehicles and charging stations in places such as Raleigh, North Carolina, and Houston, Texas, for example; dramatically more energy-efficient buildings in New York City and Charlotte, North Carolina; and revitalized neighborhood districts in places such as Kansas City, Missouri, and North Charleston, South Carolina. "Budget constraints are driving new and interesting partnerships with companies and nonprofits," observes Celia Vanderloop, director of the City and County of Denver's Division of Environmental Quality. "We will be doing a lot more through public-private ventures, and there will be a lot more integration across functions, roles, and agencies."

Green is going mainstream. In addition, there are positive and promising signs that sustainability is being scaled up and institutionalized in North American cities, especially in cities that have been at it for a while. The focus is shifting from "green" buildings to "net zero" and "living" buildings and from a focus on single buildings—such as a new LEED-certified city building—to the integrated redevelopment of whole neighborhoods or eco-districts. There is also a shift from reliance on big, centralized systems to smaller-scale, decentralized solutions, such as local food systems and the on-site management of storm water by residences and businesses.

In many places, sustainability is being sewn into the fabric of the community. "Sustainability is being incorporated into the DNA of our city," says Gayle Prest, sustainability director for the City of Minneapolis. "I am no longer driving it. As younger people come to work for the city, it's going to happen more and more. Every job will be the sustainability director's job."

In some cities, the push for sustainability is at least as much from the bottom up as it is from the top down. "City greening and sustainability will be talked about by every city and every mayor," predicts Laura Spanjian, Houston's sustainability director. "Every city will embrace it because they need to and because they want to. People are clamoring for more livable cities. In Houston, for example, for the first time in thirty years an annual survey of attitudes of residents found that more people want to live in an urban environment than in a suburban environment. Our mayor sees those numbers changing."

"We've got changing demographics and desires on our side," adds David Bragdon, former director of the New York City Mayor's Office of Long-Term Planning and Sustainability. "People like living in walkable neighborhoods, and they put a high premium on green spaces and parks. There is growing awareness of the costs of business as usual—traditional ways of managing storm water and the true costs of the automobile—and growing concern about the rising cost of energy. All these trends are moving in our favor."

Help is not just on the way—it's already here. Chapter 2 mentions two frameworks that cities can use to do triple bottom line sustainable development at the district or neighborhood scale—the US Green Building Council's LEED-ND (Leadership in Energy and

Environmental Design for Neighborhood Development) rating system and the Portland Sustainability Institute's Eco-Districts Framework. Similarly, the Institute for Sustainable Infrastructure offers a rating system called Envision to help cities and others evaluate the economic, environmental, and community benefits of infrastructure projects.[1] And the STAR Community Rating System, launched in the fall of 2012, is "the nation's first voluntary, self-reporting framework for evaluating, quantifying, and improving the livability and sustainability of U.S. communities."[2]

These are just a few of the new tools available to support the green city movement. In addition, active networks of green city leaders, such as the Urban Sustainability Directors Network (USDN) in North America and the global C40 Cities Climate Leadership Group, help cities support and learn from one another. And innovative training and technical assistance programs such as the Sustainable Communities Leadership Academy[3] have been developed to build the capacity of cities to advance, accelerate, and scale up green solutions.

Persistent Challenges

Cities are demonstrating that they can reduce their carbon pollution and other waste even while continuing to accommodate more people. A range of challenges remain, however. Paramount among them are the following.

Changing our hearts and minds. At the end of the day, the race to resilience will be won not through the invention of some new technology that will save us from ourselves but by the decisions and actions that we ourselves take—as individuals and institutions, acting alone and together—to use resources wisely and efficiently, break our dependence on fossil fuels, and understand, prepare for, and adapt to the impacts of climate disruption in our households, neighborhoods, communities, jobs, and lifestyles. As Nils Moe, climate change advisor to the mayor of Berkeley, California, puts it, "We can come up with wonderful technologies, but if we can't get people to change their behavior at the very local level, we're sunk." Green city leaders such as Moe have begun to integrate the latest research and methodologies emerging from the behavioral sciences, but they recognize that this work needs to be expanded, accelerated, and scaled up. Local governments need more help from the social science and social marketing fields—more and better tools and approaches, for example—in order to help people make green choices.

Investing in strong social infrastructure too. Resilience, like sustainability, has an important social side. Cities that are serious about making themselves safer and stronger in the face of climate disruption—or any type of disruption, for that matter—need to make strategic investments to shore up not only their roads, bridges, energy and water infrastructure, and telecommunications systems but also their neighborhood-based groups, local businesses, and programs that engage, prepare, and connect their communities. Eric Klinenberg, a sociologist and author who has closely studied climate-related disasters such as the 1995 heat wave in Chicago and Hurricane Sandy, puts it this way: "Increasingly, governments and disaster planners are recognizing the importance of social infrastructure: the people, places, and institutions that foster cohesion and support."[4]

Building stronger partnerships across levels of government. We will win the race to resilience only if local, state, and federal government agencies come together and align their policies, programs, and investments much more closely than they have in the past. Too often, city leaders feel as though they are swimming upstream when it comes to making their cities greener and more resilient, struggling against a powerful current of fluctuating, confusing, conflicting, or downright undermining signals or actions from their counterparts in state and federal government. Cities need more and better support. They need stronger and more consistent public policy; better coordination across agencies, policies, and programs; and more direct support with technical and financial assistance.

- *Stronger policy.* Perhaps the most obvious examples of policy impediments are in the transportation and energy arenas. As long as state and federal policies heavily favor car-related investments in new or expanded roads and highways over infrastructure that promotes public transportation, biking, and walking, there will be a limit to what cities can do to make their transportation systems both more sustainable and resilient. Similarly, it's difficult for cities to green the energy supplies that they produce or purchase if state and federal governments aren't doing the same. "The most challenging thing about my job is that energy is so underpriced relative to its true cost," says David Bragdon, former director of the New York City Mayor's Office of Long-Term Planning and Sustainability. "It would help us to have a price on carbon at the national scale. That would drive real change throughout the transportation, energy, and building sectors. It would help us with everything from community design to energy independence to public health."

- *More and better coordination.* State and federal government agencies have at least as much trouble coordinating with one another as city departments do. At best, this results in confusion, frustration, and lost opportunities. At worst, it is a tragic waste of limited resources and constrains local innovation. In the United States, the Partnership for Sustainable Communities represents a big step in a better direction. Through this innovative partnership, three major US government agencies—the US Department of Transportation (DOT), the US Department of Housing and Urban Development (HUD), and the US Environmental Protection Agency (EPA)—are working to align their policies and investments with a cohesive vision of sustainable community and regional development. We need much more of that type of collaboration and integration.

- *More direct support.* Cities are not a narrow and myopic interest group, hanging out near state and federal funding troughs begging for handouts—they are the engines of innovation and economic growth. In the United States, metropolitan areas accounted for 98 percent of job growth and 86 percent of economic growth in 2011, according to a report prepared for the U.S. Conference of Mayors. "This report demonstrates clearly the vital role of America's cities in our national economy," says Boston mayor Thomas Menino. Simply put, cities need more direct support from their counterparts in federal, provincial, and state government if they are to compete in the race to resilience. They need financial as well as technical assistance to improve, accelerate, and scale up local energy, climate, transportation, and sustainable development solutions. Several funding programs launched by the federal government in the past few years provide a solid foundation on which to build—most notably the US Department of Energy's Energy Efficiency and Conservation Block Grants, HUD's Sustainable Communities Regional Planning Grants, the DOT's Transportation Investment Generating Economic Recovery (TIGER) grants, and the EPA's Climate Showcase Communities Program.

Pooling our limited resources. Of course, the answer isn't just federal government funding and investments. Given the enormity of the challenge and the size of the collective investment that is needed to meet the challenge, it's becoming obvious to more and more people that no single entity or sector has sufficient human and financial resources to create resilient cities. If we're to win the race to resilience, we're going to have to do it together. We're going to have to do some things we haven't done well in the past: pooling our ideas and our money across agencies and institutions and accelerating and scaling up the development of innovative mechanisms for aligning resilience-building investments by governments at all levels, as well as companies and philanthropic organizations.

Our willingness and our ability to do this are improving, but not fast enough. Many local government officials remain wary of partnering with the private sector, in part out of fear that they will be "taken for a ride" or criticized by constituents for lining the pockets of already wealthy developers and business leaders. At the same time, many business leaders still fail to fully appreciate or share the costs of building the critical public infrastructure that is the backbone of economic prosperity, including streets, bridges, parks, and mass transit systems. "The number one thing that needs to change is figuring out how to pay for new ideas," says Brendan Shane, policy and sustainability director for the Department of the Environment in Washington, DC. "We need to align private capital and institutional investors to the scale of the change needed. We need investors to participate in the conversation and understand the benefits."

Building a positive and broadly supported vision of the future. As we hope this book makes clear, the green city movement *is* indeed a movement. But it's far from a fait accompli.

There is tremendous momentum, but we haven't yet arrived at the tipping point. Not everybody feels a part of it, and not everybody is on board. There are pockets of passive indifference and even concerted opposition. The backlash against local sustainability planning that began in the late 2000s is one prominent example. Some have described this as nothing more than oil industry–backed bluster.[5] And that is part of it, in our view. But there is a lot more to it than that. Underlying this vocal, if not widespread, opposition is a very real and perfectly human fear of change and a growing distrust of government that cannot be ignored or dismissed out of hand. Behind the rants lurks something real: an abiding belief by some that the world that green city leaders are envisioning and working to create is worse, not better, than the one we live in now—with more government control and less individual freedom, more hardship and less prosperity, more sacrifice and less joy.

It falls on us to build a positive and broadly owned and supported vision of *better* cities, *better* lives, and a *better* world for *everybody*—one characterized by more choices, more prosperity, and more joy, not less. And we need to do it in honest, open, and respectful ways that assuage fears rather than stoke them and that build trust rather than continuing to erode it—engaging people early and often in envisioning the community they want, listening rather than advocating, and using language that resonates with local values.

An Obligation and Opportunity for North American Cities

It's essential that cities sustain and accelerate the promising trends outlined above while at the same time rising to meet these persistent challenges. The stakes are high. As mentioned in the introduction to this book, the world's urban population is growing almost exponentially. By 2050 world populations are estimated to be 9.3 billion, and the vast majority of that growth will occur in urban areas in Asia, Africa, and Latin America. Urban populations will increase by about 2.6 billion people, the equivalent of plopping another 315 cities the size of New York City onto the planet in just the next forty years. Among other things, this will require a doubling of annual capital investments in physical infrastructure—from $10 trillion to $20 trillion—according to a June 2012 report by the McKinsey Global Institute. "Cities have been the world's economic dynamos for centuries," the report states. "But what is different about today's wave of mass urbanization is its unprecedented speed and scale. It is not hyperbole to say that we are observing the most significant shift in the earth's economic center of gravity in history."[6]

North Americans have both an opportunity and an obligation to lead the way. American and Canadian cities are among the wealthiest in the world, and their prosperity was built in large part on a carbon-intensive development model that we now know lies at the root of the climate crisis and the economic and human suffering it causes, especially in poorer places. It's up to us to build and share a better mousetrap. The rapidly growing cities of Asia, Africa, and Latin America are looking to their counterparts in North America and Europe for inspiration. We must give them something healthier and more hopeful to emulate.

It's a big responsibility but a big opportunity as well. The payoff would be nothing short of improving the lives of more than 6 billion urban dwellers around the globe, including the nearly 3 billion people who will be born in or migrate to urban areas between now and 2050. The green city movement and the race to resilience aren't about planting a bunch of trees, restoring a few wetlands, weather-stripping some houses, and checking the box of "gone green." They are about creating next-generation cities—vibrant and beautiful urban communities in which people enjoy clean air and water, healthy food, access to affordable shelter and meaningful work, and a sense of belonging and worth. Our goal, and our hope, in putting forward this snapshot of the green city movement in North America to date is to inspire more and more cities to take up this critical task and to help them on their journey.

Notes

Introduction: The New Urban Imperative

1. Richard Florida, "Which Cities Tend to Be the Greenest? The Answer May Surprise You," *The Atlantic Cities*, April 17, 2012, http://www.theatlanticcities.com/jobs-and-economy/2012/04/which-us-cities-tend-be-greenest/860/.

2. Alan Berube and Carey Anne Nadeau, "Metropolitan Areas and the Next Economy: A 50-State Analysis," Brookings Institution, Metropolitan Policy Program, February 24, 2011, http://www.brookings.edu/research/papers/2011/02/24-states-berube-nadeau.

3. "Much of Today's Environmental Impacts Originate in Cities," fact sheet, Down to Earth: Science and Environment Online, March 15, 2008, http://www.downtoearth.org.in/node/4295.

4. World Resources Institute, "Population and Human Well-Being: Urban Growth," in *World Resources 1998–99: Environmental Change and Human Health* (Washington, DC: World Resources Institute, United Nations Development Programme, and World Bank, May 1998), http://www.wri.org/publication/content/8479.

5. United Nations Educational, Scientific and Cultural Organization (UNESCO), World Water Assessment Programme, *The United Nations World Water Development Report 3: Water in a Changing World* (Paris: UNESCO, 2009), http://www.unesco.org/new/fileadmin/MULTI MEDIA/HQ/SC/pdf/WWDR3_Facts_and_Figures.pdf.

6. Florida, "Which Cities Tend to Be Greenest?"

7. UNESCO, *Water in a Changing World*.

8. United Nations Educational, Scientific and Cultural Organization (UNESCO), World Water Assessment Programme, "Facts and Figures: The Urban Population Is Expected to Double between 2000 and 2030 in Africa and Asia," http://www.unesco.org/new/en/natural-sciences/environment/water/wwap/facts-and-figures/all-facts-wwdr3/fact-30-urban-expansion/.

9. Down to Earth, "Impacts Originate in Cities."

10. Edward L. Glaeser, "The Lorax Was Wrong: Skyscrapers Are Green," *New York Times*, March 10,

2009, http://economix.blogs.nytimes.com/2009/03/10/the-lorax-was-wrong-skyscrapers-are-green/.

11. Ibid.

12. Peter Calthorpe, *Urbanism in the Age of Climate Change* (Washington, DC: Island Press, 2011), 4.

13. Rex Burkholder, Metro councilor, District 5, Portland, Oregon (speech given at Bogotá Summit: Cities and Climate Change, Bogotá, Colombia, November 20, 2012).

14. Gilles Brücker, "Vulnerable Populations: Lessons Learnt from the Summer 2003 Heat Waves in Europe," editorial, *Eurosurveillance* 10, no. 7 (July 1, 2005), http://www.eurosurveillance.org/ViewArticle.aspx?ArticleId=551.

15. United Nations Human Settlements Programme (UN-HABITAT), "State of the World's Cities 2006/7," feature/backgrounder, http://www.unhabitat.org/documents/media_centre/sowcr2006/SOWCR%2013.pdf.

16. See William Harless and Liz Robbins, "River Begins to Recede in Tennessee," *New York Times*, May 4, 2010, http://www.nytimes.com/2010/05/05/us/05flood.html?_r=0.

17. United Nations Educational, Scientific and Cultural Organization (UNESCO), World Water Assessment Programme (WWAP), "Facts and Figures: Adapting to Climate Change Could Cost 100 Billion Dollars a Year Several Decades from Now," http://www.unesco.org/new/en/natural-sciences/environment/water/wwap/facts-and-figures/all-facts-wwdr3/fact-12-cost-of-adaptation/.

18. United Nations General Assembly, *Report of the World Commission on Environment and Development: Our Common Future*, 1987, transmitted to the General Assembly as an annex to document A/42/427, *Development and International Co-operation: Environment*, http://www.un-documents.net/wced-ocf.htm, accessed February 15, 2009.

19. Walker Wells, "What Is Green Urbanism?," Planetizen, October 1, 2010, http://www.planetizen.com/node/46245.

20. Timothy Beatley, *Green Urbanism: Learning from European Cities* (Washington, DC: Island Press, 2000), 6–8.

Chapter 2. Leading from the Inside Out: Greening City Buildings and Operations

1. Lucia Athens, *Building an Emerald City: A Guide to Creating Green Building Policies and Programs* (Washington, DC: Island Press, 2010), xvii.

2. See ibid. for a much more extensive description and exploration of Seattle's Green Building Program.

3. McGraw-Hill Construction, "Green Outlook 2011: Green Trends Driving Growth" (Bedford, MA: McGraw-Hill Construction, 2010).

4. US Energy Information Administration, "Assumptions to the *Annual Energy Outlook 2008*," Report No. DOE/EIA-0554(2008) (Washington, DC: US Department of Energy, 2008).

5. US General Services Administration, Public Buildings Service, Office of Applied Science, "Assessing Green Building Performance: A Post-Occupancy Evaluation of 12 GSA Buildings" (Washington, DC: US General Services Administration, June 2008).

6. Booz Allen Hamilton, "U.S. Green Building Council Green Jobs Study" (McLean, VA: Booz Allen Hamilton, 2009).

7. For more information, see https://ilbi.org/lbc.

8. Clinton Climate Initiative, "City of Houston Building Retrofit Case Study," http://c40.org/c40cities/houston/city_case_studies/city-of-houston-building-retrofit-case-study.

9. See http://www.livingcityblock.org/.

10. John Robert Meyer and José A. Gómez-Ibáñez, *Autos, Transit, and Cities* (Cambridge, MA: Harvard University Press, 1981).

11. Smart Growth America, National Complete Streets Coalition, "Complete Streets Policy Analysis 2011," August 2012, http://www.smartgrowthamerica.org/documents/cs/resources/cs-policyanalysis.pdf.

12. City of Los Angeles, Department of Public Works, Bureau of Street Lighting.

13. See http://www.seattle.gov/util/MyServices/DrainageSewer/Projects/GreenStormwater Infrastructure/CompletedGSIProjects/index.htm.

14. Elisa Durand, "Five Key Questions of Green Fleet Management," *Government Fleet*, October 2011, http://www.government-fleet.com/channel/green-fleet/article/story/2011/10/five-key -questions-of-green-fleet-management.aspx.

15. Institute for Sustainable Communities, "Creating Connected Communities: A Resource Guide for Local Leaders," October 2012, http://sustainablecommunitiesleadershipacademy.org /resource_files/documents/ISC%20Resource%20Guide%20-%20Creating%20Connected %20Communities.pdf.

16. Melanie Nutter, personal communication.

17. RenewableEnergyWorld.com, "Taber Wind Farm Opens in Alberta," October 25, 2007, http ://www.renewableenergyworld.com/rea/news/article/2007/10/taber-wind-farm-opens-in -alberta-50384.

18. "Boulder Votes for Municipal Utility," *Wall Street Journal*, November 3, 2011, http://online .wsj.com/article/SB10001424052970204621904577014231689288216.html.

19. US Environmental Protection Agency, Green Power Partnership, "Top 20 Local Government," http://www.epa.gov/greenpower/toplists/top20localgov.htm.

20. See http://city.milwaukee.gov/milwaukeeshines.

21. City of Philadelphia, Mayor's Office of Sustainability, "Greenworks Philadelphia: Update and 2012 Progress Report," http://www.phila.gov/green/PDFs/GW2012Report.pdf.

22. See http://www.bostonbuyingpower.com/.

23. See http://www.epa.gov/greenpower/communities/index.htm.

24. Eileen V. Quigley and Elizabeth Willmott, "Powering the New Energy Future from the Ground Up: Profiles in City-Led Energy Innovation," Climate Solutions, New Energy Cities, July 2012, http://newenergycities.org/files/powering-the-new-energy-future-from-the -ground-up.pdf.

25. For more information, see http://www.seattle.gov/environment/.

26. See http://www.denvergov.org/.

27. See http://www.cnt.org/.

Chapter 3. Leading in the Community: Using City Assets, Policy, Partnerships, and Persuasion

1. Institute for Sustainable Communities, "Sustainable Communities Leadership Academy: A Resource Guide for Local Leaders," October 2012, http://sustainablecommunitiesleader shipacademy.org/resource_files/documents/Resource-Guide-HUD-SCLA-2.pdf.

2. Ibid.

3. City of Seattle, Office of Economic Development, "Public and Private Investments in South Lake Union," July 2012, http://www.seattle.gov/mayor/media/PDF/120709PR-SLU-Public -PrivateReport.pdf.

4. See http://www.nyc.gov/html/digital/html/opengov/reinventgreen.shtml.

5. See http://www.slcgov.com/slcgreen/coderevisionproject.

6. ICLEI—Local Governments for Sustainability and Institute for Market Transformation, "Case Study: New York City's Greener, Greater Buildings Plan," November 2011, http://www.icleiusa.org/action-center/learn-from-others/ICLEI_NYC_GGBP_Case_Study_final2.pdf.

7. New York City Global Partners, "Best Practice: NYC Greener, Greater Buildings Plan," July 28, 2010 (updated December 21, 2009), http://www.nyc.gov/html/unccp/gprb/downloads/pdf/NYC_GreenBuildings.pdf.

8. Mohammed Al-Shawaf and Chris Guenther, SustainAbility, "Citystates: How Cities Are Vital to the Future of Sustainability," March 13, 2012, http://www.sustainability.com/library/citystates#.UaJvRRzGpJk.

9. Bob Young, "Nickels' Plan for Lake Union Area Questioned," *Seattle Times*, July 9, 2004, http://community.seattletimes.nwsource.com/archive/?date=20040709&slug=development09m.

10. For more about Envision Charlotte, see http://www.envisioncharlotte.com/.

11. See http://www.metrocouncil.org/Communities/Projects/Corridors-of-Opportunity.aspx.

12. For more information, see http://southeastfloridaclimatecompact.org/.

13. See http://www.advantagegreen.org/.

14. City of Santa Monica, California, "Santa Monica Green Business Certification Program," http://www.smgbc.org/faq.htm.

15. Doug McKenzie-Mohr et al., *Social Marketing to Protect the Environment: What Works* (Los Angeles: Sage Publications, 2012).

16. Jennifer Tabanico, Action Research, "Employee Behavior Change Initiatives in the Public Sector" (presentation to the Urban Sustainability Directors Network Sustainable Behavior User Group, May 16, 2012).

17. Clean Energy Works Portland, "Community Workforce Agreement on Standards and Community Benefits in the Clean Energy Works Portland Pilot Project," September 24, 2009, http://www.portlandoregon.gov/bps/article/265161.

18. Institute for Sustainable Communities, "Opportunity Mapping in Mississippi's Gulf Coast: Elevating Social Equity in Sustainability Planning," in "Creating Prosperous and Sustainable Rural Communities: A Resource Guide for Local Leaders," 2012, http://sustainablecommunitiesleadershipacademy.org/resource_files/documents/Opportunity-Mapping-in-Mississippis-Gulf-Coast.pdf.

19. Corridors of Opportunity, "Vision and Principles: Our Vision," http://corridorsofopportunity.org/about/vision-and-principles.

20. Puget Sound Regional Council, "Connecting Farms and Neighborhoods: Regional Food Policy Council," http://www.psrc.org/about/advisory/regional-food-policy-council/.

21. "Plan El Paso: A Policy Guide for El Paso for the Next 25 Years and Beyond," vol. 1, "City Patterns: City Form and Community Character," http://planelpaso.org/comprehensive-plan-elements/, Preface and Introduction, i.2.

22. Chris Crockett, City of Philadelphia Water Department (presentation to the Efficiency Cities Network, May 22, 2012).

Chapter 4. The Green City Leader

1. VOX Global, Weinreb Group Sustainability Recruiting, and Net Impact, Berkeley, "Making the Pitch: Selling Sustainability from *Inside* Corporate America; 2012 Report of Sustainability Leaders," http://voxglobal.com/2012-sustainability-survey/.

2. Matt Stark, director of legislative and policy affairs, City of Providence, Rhode Island, interview, March 12, 2012.

3. Adam Freed, interview, November 5, 2012.

4. Joel Makower, GreenBiz.com, "Why Sustainability Execs Should Shun the S-Word," July 24, 2012, http://www.greenbiz.com/blog/2012/07/24/should-sustainability-execs-shun-s-word.

5. Roy Brooke, director of sustainability, City of Victoria, British Columbia (webinar presentation to the Urban Sustainability Directors Network, June 12, 2012).

6. Institute for Sustainable Communities, "Creating, Leading, and Managing Change: A Resource Guide for Local Sustainability Leaders, Version 2.1," 2012, 27, http://sustainable communitiesleadershipacademy.org/resource_files/documents/Resource-Guide-USLA-2.1 -Web.pdf.

7. Philadelphia Water Department, "Green City, Clean Waters: The City of Philadelphia's Program for Combined Sewer Overflow Control; A Long Term Control Plan Update, Summary Report," September 1, 2009, http://www.city.pittsburgh.pa.us/council/assets/10_LTCPU_Sum mary_LoRes.pdf.

8. Paul Krutko, president and chief executive officer, Ann Arbor SPARK, and former chief development officer, City of San Jose, California (presentation, "Planning for Sustainable Economic Development Across the Americas," Curitiba, Brazil, June 7, 8, 2011).

9. Institute for Sustainable Communities, "Creating, Leading, and Managing Change," 10.

10. John Coleman, sustainability director, City of Fayetteville, Arkansas, correspondence, May 4, 2010.

11. Larry Falkin, director, Cincinnati Office of Environmental Quality, and Lea Eriksen, Cincinnati budget director (presentation to the Urban Sustainability Directors Network, April 10, 2012).

12. Institute for Sustainable Communities, "Creating, Leading, and Managing Change," 11.

13. Sadhu Johnston, interview, July 28, 2012.

14. Urban Sustainability Directors Network, Member Professional Development Survey, February 2011.

15. XiaoHu Wang et al., "Capacity to Sustain Sustainability: A Study of U.S. Cities," *Public Administration Review* 72, no. 6 (November/December 2012): 841–853, 842.

16. Stark, interview.

17. Urban Sustainability Directors Network, "Making the Case for Sustainability," Member Survey, February 2012.

18. Ibid.

19. Andrew Watterson (remarks to the Institute for Sustainable Communities, Urban Sustainability Leadership Academy, 2011).

20. Johnston, interview.

21. Jennifer Tabanico, Urban Sustainability Directors Network, Small Group Discussion, May 16, 2012.

22. John Coleman, Urban Sustainability Directors Network, Small Group Discussion, June 23, 2010.

23. Melanie Nutter, director, San Francisco Department of the Environment, conversation, August 8, 2012.

24. Stark, interview.

25. Matt Naud, environmental coordinator, City of Ann Arbor, Michigan, e-mail, December 16, 2010.

26. See http://nyc.changeby.us/.

27. Urban Sustainability Directors Network, "Making the Case for Sustainability."

28. Roy Brooke, "Canada Should Tap Massive Global Demand for Green Goods and Services," iPolitics Insight, July 4, 2012, http://www.ipolitics.ca/2012/07/04/roy-brooke-canada -should-tap-massive-global-demand-for-green-goods-and-services/.

29. Pete Plastrik (presentation, "Sustaining Sustainability Offices," Urban Sustainability Directors Network Annual Meeting, September 2010).

30. Institute for Sustainable Communities, "Creating, Leading, and Managing Change," 24.

31. John Cleveland, "Asheville, North Carolina, LED Street Light Energy Efficiency Case Study," prepared for Urban Sustainability Directors Network Innovation Working Group, September 3, 2011.

32. Janet Attarian, director of Complete Streets, Chicago Department of Transportation, interview, March 1, 2013.

33. Richard M. Daley and Thomas G. Byrne, "The Chicago Green Alley Handbook: An Action Guide to Create a Greener, Environmentally Sustainable Chicago," http://www.cityof chicago.org/dam/city/depts/cdot/Green_Alley_Handbook_2010.pdf.

Chapter 5. Getting Down to Business: Budgeting, Financing, and Green Economic Development

1. Maggie Ullman, sustainability program manager, City of Asheville, North Carolina (presentation to the Urban Sustainability Directors Network, April 10, 2012).

2. Larry Falkin, director, Office of Environmental Quality, City of Cincinnati, Ohio (presentation to the Urban Sustainability Directors Network, April 10, 2012).

3. Ullman, presentation.

4. Institute for Sustainable Communities, "Creating, Leading, and Managing Change: A Resource Guide for Local Sustainability Leaders, Version 2.1," 2012, 90, http://sustainable communitiesleadershipacademy.org/resource_files/documents/Resource-Guide-USLA-2.1 -Web.pdf.

5. James Hunt, former head of environmental and energy services, City of Boston (presentation to the Urban Sustainability Directors Network, April 10, 2012).

6. See Puget Sound Energy, "Resource Conservation Manager Program," http://www.pse.com /savingsandenergycenter/ForBusinesses/Pages/Resource-Conservation-Manager.aspx.

7. ICLEI—Local Governments for Sustainability, "Fact Sheet: How 38 Local Governments Fund Sustainability Staff and Operations," March 2011, http://www.icleiusa.org/library /documents/ICLEI_Sustainability_Funding_Fact_Sheet.pdf.

8. Sadhu Johnston, interview, July 29, 2012.

9. Garrett Fitzgerald, sustainability coordinator, City of Oakland, California, conversation, May 27, 2011.

10. Urban Sustainability Directors Network webinar, "Building Alliances with Foundations," October 18, 2011.

11. Matt Naud, City of Ann Arbor, Urban Sustainability Directors Network conference call, February 17, 2010.

12. John Cleveland, "Asheville, North Carolina, LED Street Light Energy Efficiency Case Study," prepared for Urban Sustainability Directors Innovation Working Group, September 3, 2011.

13. Larry Falkin, Cincinnati, and Lea Eriksen, budget director, City of Cincinnati (presentation to the Urban Sustainability Directors Network, April 10, 2012).

14. Eric Lantz, "State Clean Energy Policies Analysis: State, Utility, and Municipal Loan Programs," National Renewable Energy Laboratory Technical Report NREL/TP-6A2-47376, May 2010, http://www.nrel.gov/docs/fy10osti/47376.pdf.

15. US Department of Energy, Technical Assistance Program, "CDFIs: Opportunities for Partnerships with Energy Efficiency Programs," PowerPoint presentation, March 17, 2011, http ://www1.eere.energy.gov/wip/solutioncenter/media/CDFI%2520Webinar%2520Slides.pptx.

16. Ibid.

17. Laura Snider, "Boulder County's New Energy-Efficiency Loan Program Kicks Off Wednesday," *Boulder Daily Camera*, August 7, 2012, http://www.dailycamera.com/boulder-county-news /ci_21258366.

18. Lawrence Berkeley National Laboratory, Energy Analysis and Environmental Impacts Department, "Scaling Energy Efficiency in the Heart of the Residential Market: Increasing Middle America's Access to Capital for Energy Improvements," Clean Energy Financing Policy Brief, March 6, 2012, http://emp.lbl.gov/publications/scaling-energy-efficiency -heart-residential-market-increasing-middle-americas-access-ca.

19. Derek Supple and Olivia Nix, Institute for Building Efficiency, "Unlocking the Building Retrofit Market: Commercial PACE Financing; A Guide for Policymakers," December 2010, http://greenpropertyfunds.com/wp-content/uploads/2012/08/Unlocking-the-Building -Retrofit-Market-PACE-Financing.pdf.

20. Casey J. Bell, Steven Nadel, and Sara Hayes, "On-Bill Financing for Energy Efficiency Improvements: A Review of Current Program Challenges, Opportunities, and Best Practices," American Council for an Energy-Efficient Economy Research Report E118, December 2011, http://www.aceee.org/research-report/e118.

21. Ibid.

22. Lawrence Berkeley National Laboratory, Environmental Energy Technologies Division, "Alternative Underwriting Criteria: Using Utility Bill Payment History as a Proxy for Credit; Case Study on Clean Energy Works Oregon," Clean Energy Financing Policy Brief, April 4, 2012, http://eetd.lbl.gov/ea/EMP/reports/mi-policybrief-4-4-2012c.pdf.

23. Jonathan Naimon, Light Green Advisors, "Increasing Equity Investment in Building Energy Efficiency" (presentation to the Efficiency Cities Network, June 9, 2009).

24. Ibid.

25. Bruce Plenk and Leslie Ethen, City of Tucson, Arizona, November 14, 2012.

26. See http://www.metro.net/projects/30-10/.

27. Atlanta BeltLine Project, "The Atlanta BeltLine: The 5 Ws and Then Some," http://beltline .org/about/the-atlanta-beltline-project/atlanta-beltline-overview/.

28. Alisa Valderrama and Larry Levine, Natural Resources Defense Council, "Financing Stormwater Retrofits in Philadelphia and Beyond," February 2012, http://www.nrdc.org/water /files/StormwaterFinancing-report.pdf.

29. "Christopher B. Leinberger and Mariela Alfonzo, "Walk This Way: The Economic Promise of Walkable Places in Metropolitan Washington, D.C.," Brookings Institution, Metropolitan Policy Program, May 2012, http://www.brookings.edu/~/media/research/files /papers/2012/5/25%20walkable%20places%20leinberger/25%20walkable%20places%20 leinberger.pdf.

30. Ibid.

31. Jeffery J. Smith and Thomas A. Gihring, "Financing Transit Systems through Value Capture: An Annotated Bibliography," *American Journal of Economics and Sociology* 65, no. 3 (July 2006): 751.

32. Shishir Mathur and Christopher E. Ferrell, "Effect of Suburban Transit Oriented Developments

on Residential Property Values," Mineta Transportation Institute Report 08-07, June 2009, http://transweb.sjsu.edu/MTIportal/research/publications/documents/Effects%20of %20Sub-Urban%20Transit%20(with%20Cover).pdf.

33. Jay Walljasper, "Bicycling for Better Business," October 31, 2012, http://citiwire.net/columns /bicycling-for-better-business/.

34. Mark Muro, Jonathan Rothwell, and Devashree Saha, with Battelle Technology Partnership Practice, "Sizing the Clean Economy: A National and Regional Green Jobs Assessment," Brookings Institution, Metropolitan Policy Program, 2011, http://www.brookings.edu/~/media /research/files/reports/2011/7/13%20clean%20economy/0713_clean_economy.

35. Collaborative Economics for Next 10, "2012 California Green Innovation Index," April 19, 2012, http://www.next10.org/2012-cgii.

36. City of San Jose, California, "San Jose Green Vision Named Best Sustainable Development Program in U.S. for a Big City by the International Economic Development Council," press release, October 13, 2009.

37. Karen G. Mills, Andrew Reamer, and Elisabeth B. Reynolds, "Clusters and Competitiveness: A New Federal Role for Stimulating Regional Economies," Brookings Institution, Metropolitan Policy Program, April 2008, http://www.brookings.edu/research/reports/2008/04 /competitiveness-mills.

38. Institute for Sustainable Communities, Climate Leadership Academy, "Case Study: Cleveland, Ohio: The Cleveland Evergreen Cooperatives," in "Sustainable Economic Development: A Resource Guide for Local Leaders, Version 2.0," 2011, http://www.iscvt.org/who _we_are/publications/Resource-Guide-Sustainable-Economic-Development.pdf.

39. Jennifer H. Allen and Thomas Potiowsky, "Portland's Green Building Cluster: Economic Trends and Impacts," *Economic Development Quarterly* 22, no. 4 (November 2008): 303–15.

40. James Nixon, Sustainable Systems, Inc., "Sustainable Economic Development: Initiatives, Programs, and Strategies for Cities and Regions," Urban Sustainability Associates, July 2009, http://www.sednetwork.net/wp-content/uploads/2011/08/Sustainable-Economic-Devel opment-Paper.pdf.

41. John Cleveland, Innovation Network for Communities, "Creating a Dialog with Economic Development Peers" (presentation to the Urban Sustainability Directors Network, 2010).

42. Economic & Planning Systems, Inc., "City of San Antonio Sustainable Urban Economics Tool," prepared for City of San Antonio Office of Environmental Policy, September 9, 2011.

43. Cori Burbach, sustainability director, City of Dubuque, Iowa, Urban Sustainability Directors Network webinar, "Building Alliances with Foundations," October 18, 2011.

44. Beth Strommen, sustainability director, City of Baltimore, Maryland, Urban Sustainability Directors Network webinar, "Building Alliances with Foundations," October 18, 2011.

45. City of San Antonio, Texas, Office of Mayor Phil Hardberger, "Mission Verde: Building a 21st Century Economy," January 28, 2009, 3, http://www.sanantonio.gov/Portals/0/Files /Sustainability/MissionVerde/MissionVerdeSustainabilityPlan.pdf.

46. See http://www.enterprisecommunity.com/financing-and-development/community-devel opment-financing/denver-tod-fund.

47. See http://www.urbanlandc.org/denver-transit-oriented-development-fund/.

48. See http://www.denvergov.org/DenverOfficeofStrategicPartnerships/Partnerships/Denver TransitOrientedDevelopmentFund/tabid/436574/Default.aspx.

Chapter 6. Driving Green Progress Using Indicators

1. Don Grant, "The Influence of Sustainability Plans on Implementation" (master's thesis, Royal Roads University, Victoria, British Columbia, July 2012).

2. Jenita McGowan, sustainability manager, City of Cleveland, Ohio, "Tracking Progress," PowerPoint presentation, Sustainable Cleveland 2019 All-Work Group Meeting, March 15, 2012.

3. Boston Green Ribbon Commission, "Benchmarking Boston's Sustainability Performance Management Systems," Discussion Document, June 4, 2012.

4. Ibid.

5. Shannon Parry, City of Santa Monica, interview with Steve Nicholas, July 23, 2012.

6. Cori Burbach, "Sustainable Dubuque Indicators" presentation, 2012.

7. Judith E. Innes and David E. Booher, "Indicators for Sustainable Communities: A Strategy for Building Complexity Theory and Distributed Intelligence," *Planning Theory and Practice* 1, no. 2 (2000): 173–86.

8. Timothy Burroughs, Office of Energy and Sustainable Development, City of Berkeley, California, "Berkeley's Climate Action Plan: Using Data to Prioritize and Track Action" (presentation to the Urban Sustainability Directors Network, September 10, 2012).

9. Planning and Urban Design Agency, City of St. Louis, Missouri, "City of St. Louis Sustainability Plan: Draft for Public Review, 10/1/12," http://stlouis-mo.gov/government/depart ments/planning/documents/city-of-st-louis-sustainability-plan-draft-for-public-review .cfm.

10. Kizzy Charles-Guzman et al., "Metrics and Targets for the Albany 2030 Comprehensive Plan" (Masters of Science in Sustainability Management project, Columbia University, December 2011).

11. Ibid.

12. City of Surrey, British Columbia, "City Launches Sustainability Dashboard to Demonstrate Openness and Accountability," April 23, 2012, http://www.surrey.ca/city-government/11150 .aspx.

13. Brendon Slotterback, "Minneapolis Sustainability Indicators" (PowerPoint presentation, September 12, 2012).

14. Center for Neighborhood Technology, Community Data Project, "The State of Tracking Greenhouse Gases in Communities," White Paper 1, February 1, 2012.

15. Center for Neighborhood Technology, Community Data Project, "Transportation Data for Community Sustainability," White Paper 2, February 1, 2012.

16. Boston Green Ribbon Commission, "Benchmarking Boston's Sustainability Performance Management Systems," Discussion Document, June 4, 2012.

17. Ibid.

18. Judith E. Innes and David E. Booher, "Indicators for Sustainable Communities: A Strategy for Building Complexity Theory and Distributed Intelligence," *Planning Theory and Practice* 1, no. 2 (2000): 173–86.

19. Burroughs, "Berkeley's Climate Action Plan."

20. Parry, interview.

21. Siemens and Economist Intelligence Unit, "US and Canada Green City Index: Minneapolis" (Munich: Siemens Corporate Communications and Government Affairs, 2011), 81, http://www.siemens.com/entry/cc/features/greencityindex_international/all/en/pdf/min neapolis.pdf.

Conclusion: From Green to Resilient Cities

1. For more information, see http://www.sustainableinfrastructure.org/index.cfm.

2. STAR Communities, "The Rating System," http://www.starcommunities.org/.

3. See http://sustainablecommunitiesleadershipacademy.org.

4. Eric Klinenberg, "Adaptation: How Can Cities Be 'Climate-Proofed'?" *New Yorker*, January 7, 2013.

5. For example, see Lloyd Alter, "Exposing the Influence behind the Anti–Agenda 21 Anti-Sustainability Agenda," June 29, 2012, http://www.treehugger.com/environmental-policy/who-behind-agenda-21-paranoia-how-can-we-fight-back.html.

6. Richard Dobbs et al., McKinsey Global Institute, "Urban World: Cities and the Rise of the Consuming Class," June 2012, http://www.mckinsey.com/insights/urbanization/urban_world_cities_and_the_rise_of_the_consuming_class.

About the Authors

Sadhu Aufochs Johnston currently serves as deputy city manager for the City of Vancouver, British Columbia, Canada. He cofounded the Urban Sustainability Directors Network with Julia Parzen, and he led Chicago's green initiatives under Mayor Richard Daley as commissioner of the Department of Environment and in the Office of the Mayor as chief environmental officer.

Steven S. Nicholas is vice president for US programs at the Institute for Sustainable Communities in Vermont, former sustainability director for the City of Seattle, and cofounder of Sustainable Seattle.

Julia Parzen is the coordinator of the Urban Sustainability Directors Network and has led sustainability initiatives in local, state, and federal government, including the development of the Chicago Climate Action Plan.

Index